THE ALLNIGHTER ™

CREATED BY CHIP ZDARSKY AND JASON LOO

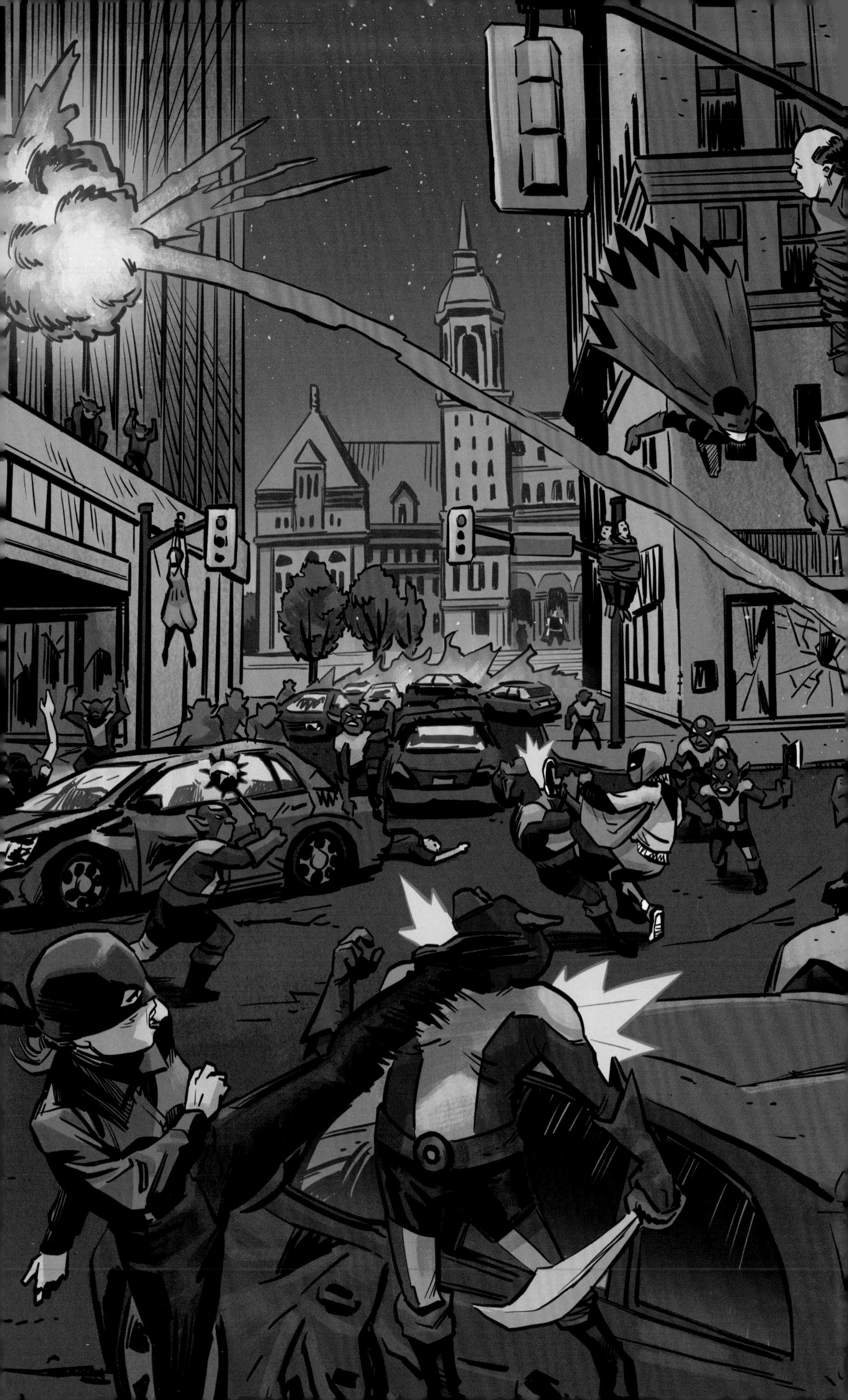

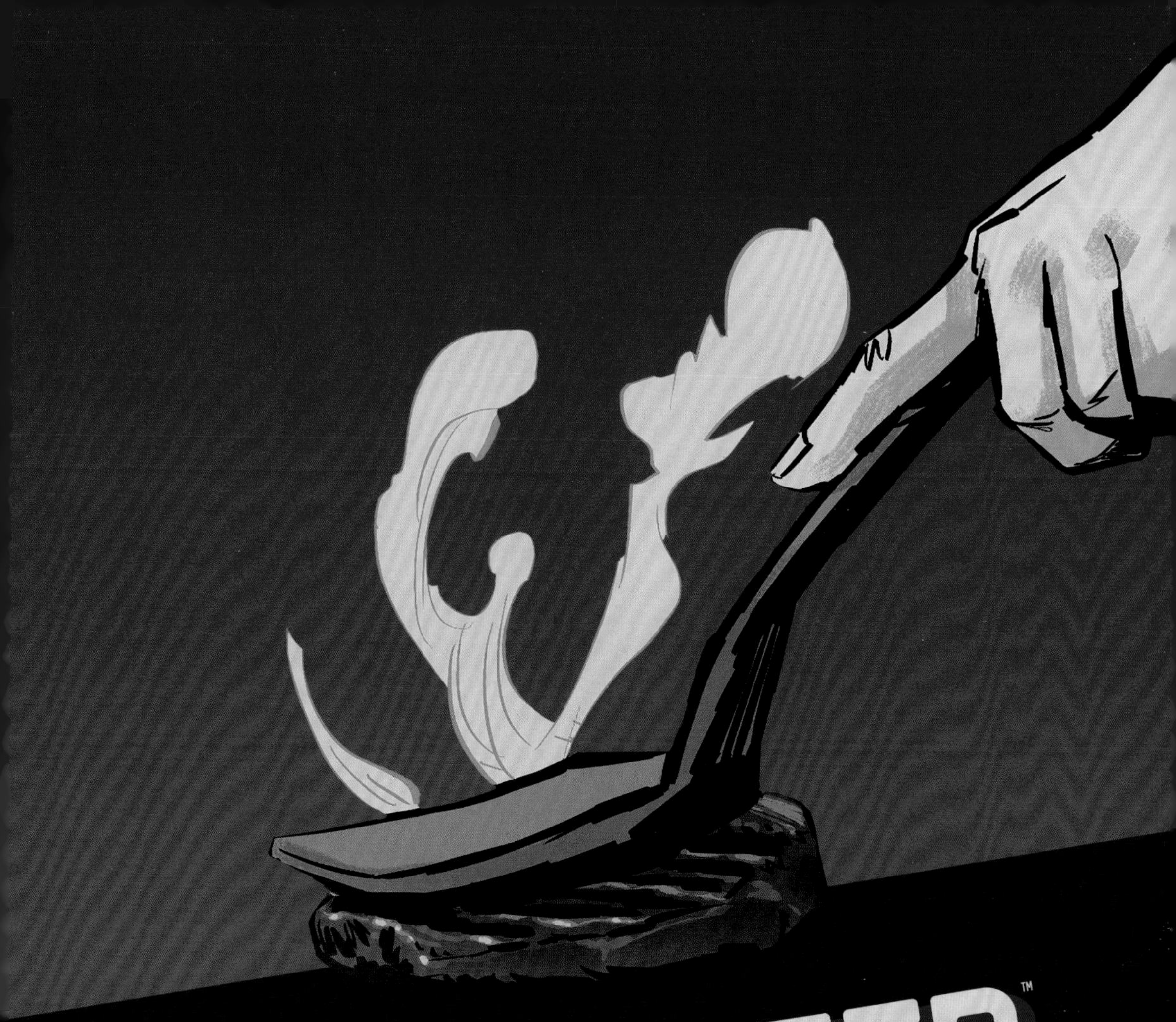

THE ALLNIGHTER™

CHIP ZDARSKY WRITER
JASON LOO ARTIST
PARIS ALLEYNE COLORIST
ADITYA BIDIKAR LETTERER
ALLISON O'TOOLE EDITOR

DARK HORSE BOOKS

DARK HORSE TEAM

MIKE RICHARDSON   PRESIDENT AND PUBLISHER

DANIEL CHABON   EDITOR

CHUCK HOWITT AND KONNER KNUDSEN   ASSISTANT EDITORS

KATHLEEN BARNETT   DESIGNER

JASON RICKERD   DIGITAL ART TECHNICIAN

NEIL HANKERSON EXECUTIVE VICE PRESIDENT / TOM WEDDLE CHIEF FINANCIAL OFFICER / DALE LaFOUNTAIN CHIEF INFORMATION OFFICER / TIM WIESCH VICE PRESIDENT OF LICENSING / MATT PARKINSON VICE PRESIDENT OF MARKETING / VANESSA TODD-HOLMES VICE PRESIDENT OF PRODUCTION AND SCHEDULING / MARK BERNARDI VICE PRESIDENT OF BOOK TRADE AND DIGITAL SALES / RANDY LAHRMAN VICE PRESIDENT OF PRODUCT DEVELOPMENT / KEN LIZZI GENERAL COUNSEL / DAVE MARSHALL EDITOR IN CHIEF / DAVEY ESTRADA EDITORIAL DIRECTOR / CHRIS WARNER SENIOR BOOKS EDITOR / CARY GRAZZINI DIRECTOR OF SPECIALTY PROJECTS / LIA RIBACCHI ART DIRECTOR / MATT DRYER DIRECTOR OF DIGITAL ART AND PREPRESS / MICHAEL GOMBOS SENIOR DIRECTOR OF LICENSED PUBLICATIONS / KARI YADRO DIRECTOR OF CUSTOM PROGRAMS / KARI TORSON DIRECTOR OF INTERNATIONAL LICENSING

SPECIAL THANKS

DAVID STEINBERGER / CHIP MOSHER / BRYCE GOLD

DARK HORSE COMICS LLC / 10956 SE MAIN STREET / MILWAUKIE, OR 97222

PUBLISHED BY DARK HORSE BOOKS / A DIVISION OF DARK HORSE COMICS LLC

FIRST EDITION: FEBRUARY 2022
TRADE PAPERBACK ISBN: 978-1-50672-804-9

1 3 5 7 9 10 8 6 4 2

PRINTED IN CHINA

COMIC SHOP LOCATOR SERVICE: COMICSHOPLOCATOR.COM

THE ALLNIGHTER™

Library of Congress Cataloging-in-Publication Data

Names: Zdarsky, Chip, writer. | Loo, Jason, artist. | Alleyne, Paris,
   colourist. | Bidikar, Aditya, letterer.
Title: The all-nighter / Chip Zdarsky, writer ; Jason Loo, artist ; Paris
   Alleyne, colorist ; Aditya Bidikar, letterer.
Other titles: Allnighter
Description: First edition. | Milwaukie, OR : Dark Horse Books, 2022. |
   "Collects issues #1-5 of The All-Nighter" | Summary: "Welcome to the
   All-Nighter, the only diner in town where you can get coffee and a meal
   from sunset to sunrise! The staff are friendly (kind of) and happy to
   serve you (sometimes), and it would never cross their minds to drink
   their customers' blood ... Alex and his fellow vampires, Joy, Cynthia,
   and Ian, have agreed to blend into human society. Inspired by superhero
   movies, one of few passions in his unlife, Alex decides to don a cape
   and start fighting bad guys."-- Provided by publisher.
Identifiers: LCCN 2021040561 | ISBN 9781506728049 (trade paperback)
Subjects: LCGFT: Vampire comics. | Superhero comics.
Classification: LCC PN6728.A387 Z33 2022 | DDC 741.5/973--dc23
LC record available at https://lccn.loc.gov/2021040561

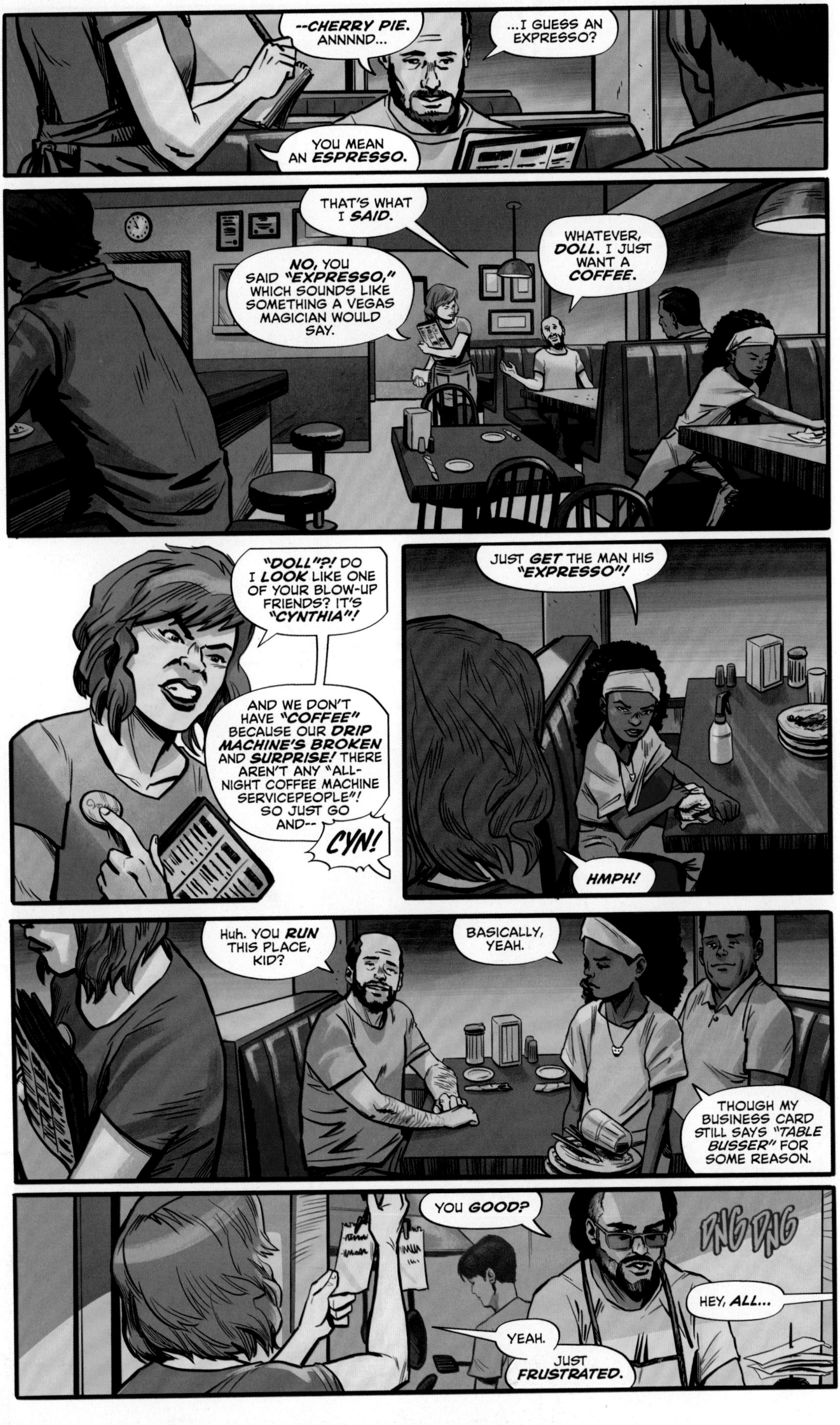
--CHERRY PIE. ANNNND...
...I GUESS AN EXPRESSO?
YOU MEAN AN ESPRESSO.
THAT'S WHAT I SAID.
NO, YOU SAID "EXPRESSO," WHICH SOUNDS LIKE SOMETHING A VEGAS MAGICIAN WOULD SAY.
WHATEVER, DOLL. I JUST WANT A COFFEE.
"DOLL"?! DO I LOOK LIKE ONE OF YOUR BLOW-UP FRIENDS? IT'S "CYNTHIA"!
AND WE DON'T HAVE "COFFEE" BECAUSE OUR DRIP MACHINE'S BROKEN AND SURPRISE! THERE AREN'T ANY "ALL-NIGHT COFFEE MACHINE SERVICEPEOPLE"! SO JUST GO AND--
CYN!
JUST GET THE MAN HIS "EXPRESSO"!
HMPH!
Huh. YOU RUN THIS PLACE, KID?
BASICALLY, YEAH.
THOUGH MY BUSINESS CARD STILL SAYS "TABLE BUSSER" FOR SOME REASON.
YOU GOOD?
DNG DNG
HEY, ALL...
YEAH.
JUST FRUSTRATED.

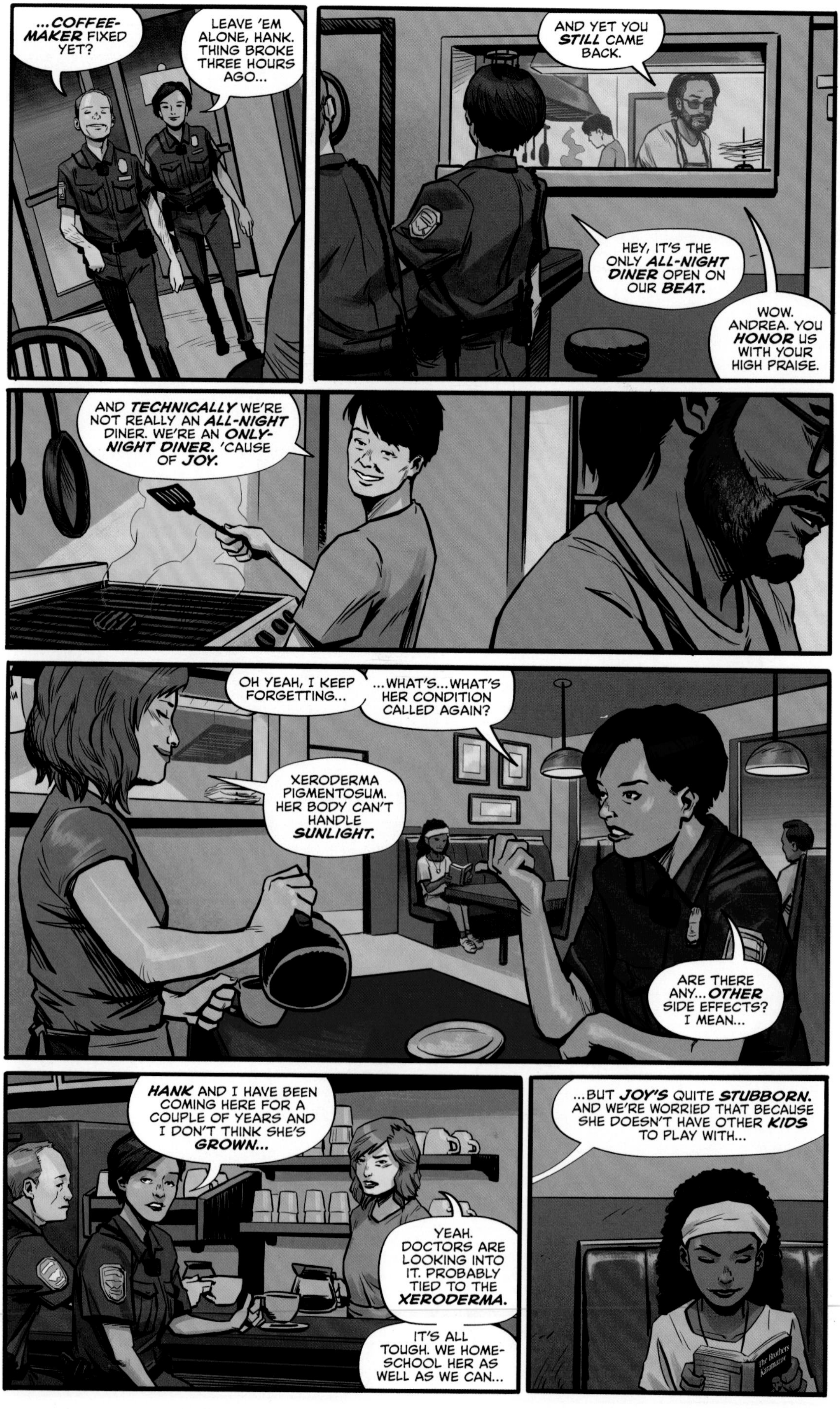
...COFFEE-MAKER FIXED YET?
LEAVE 'EM ALONE, HANK. THING BROKE THREE HOURS AGO...
AND YET YOU STILL CAME BACK.
HEY, IT'S THE ONLY ALL-NIGHT DINER OPEN ON OUR BEAT.
WOW. ANDREA. YOU HONOR US WITH YOUR HIGH PRAISE.
AND TECHNICALLY WE'RE NOT REALLY AN ALL-NIGHT DINER. WE'RE AN ONLY-NIGHT DINER. 'CAUSE OF JOY.
OH YEAH, I KEEP FORGETTING...
...WHAT'S...WHAT'S HER CONDITION CALLED AGAIN?
XERODERMA PIGMENTOSUM. HER BODY CAN'T HANDLE SUNLIGHT.
ARE THERE ANY...OTHER SIDE EFFECTS? I MEAN...
HANK AND I HAVE BEEN COMING HERE FOR A COUPLE OF YEARS AND I DON'T THINK SHE'S GROWN...
YEAH. DOCTORS ARE LOOKING INTO IT. PROBABLY TIED TO THE XERODERMA.
IT'S ALL TOUGH. WE HOME-SCHOOL HER AS WELL AS WE CAN...
...BUT JOY'S QUITE STUBBORN. AND WE'RE WORRIED THAT BECAUSE SHE DOESN'T HAVE OTHER KIDS TO PLAY WITH...
The Brothers Karamazov

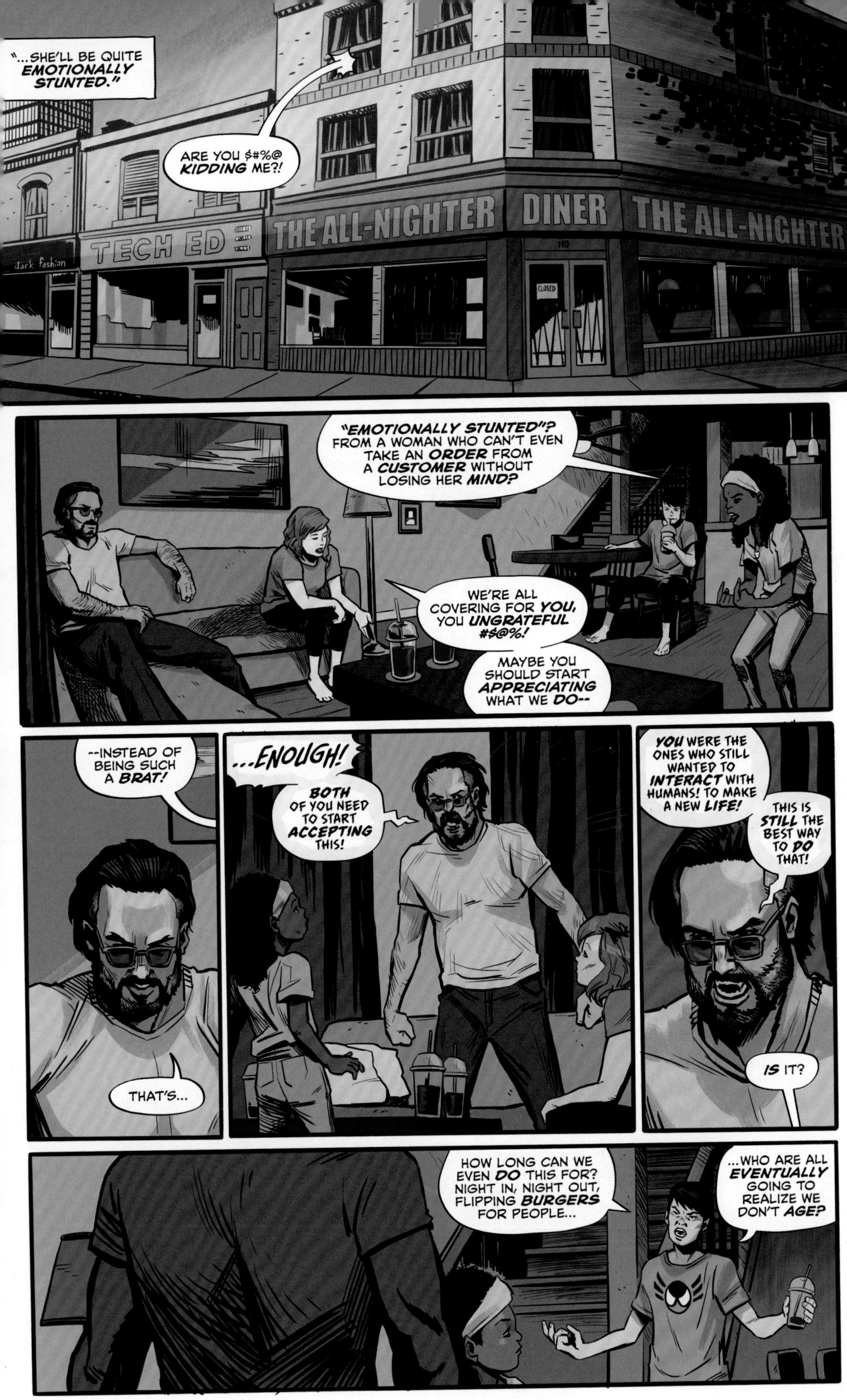
"...SHE'LL BE QUITE EMOTIONALLY STUNTED."
ARE YOU $#%@ KIDDING ME?!
dark fashion
TECH ED
THE ALL-NIGHTER DINER THE ALL-NIGHTER
CLOSED
"EMOTIONALLY STUNTED"? FROM A WOMAN WHO CAN'T EVEN TAKE AN ORDER FROM A CUSTOMER WITHOUT LOSING HER MIND?
WE'RE ALL COVERING FOR YOU, YOU UNGRATEFUL #$@%!
MAYBE YOU SHOULD START APPRECIATING WHAT WE DO--
--INSTEAD OF BEING SUCH A BRAT!
THAT'S...
...ENOUGH!
BOTH OF YOU NEED TO START ACCEPTING THIS!
YOU WERE THE ONES WHO STILL WANTED TO INTERACT WITH HUMANS! TO MAKE A NEW LIFE!
THIS IS STILL THE BEST WAY TO DO THAT!
IS IT?
HOW LONG CAN WE EVEN DO THIS FOR? NIGHT IN, NIGHT OUT, FLIPPING BURGERS FOR PEOPLE...
...WHO ARE ALL EVENTUALLY GOING TO REALIZE WE DON'T AGE?

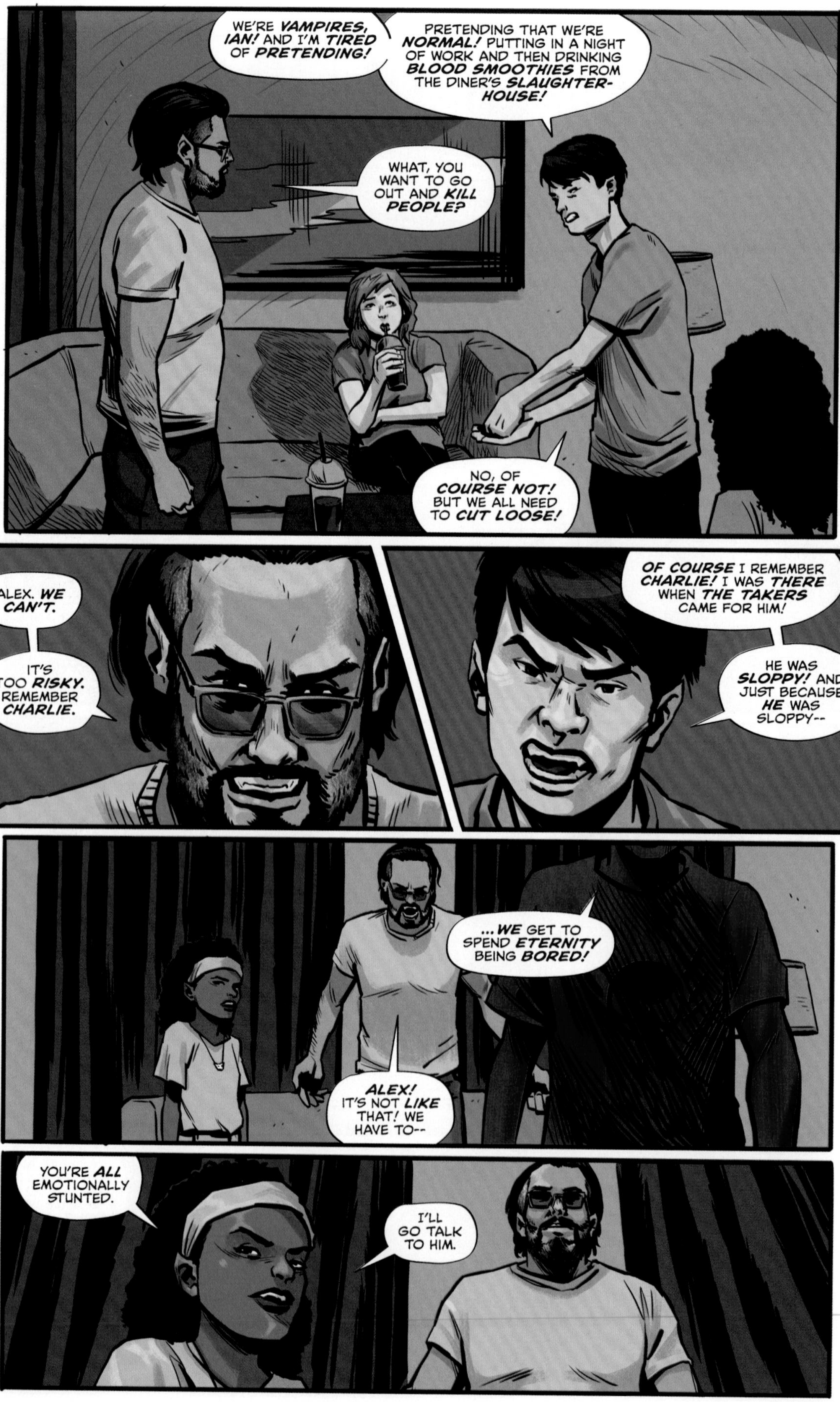
WE'RE VAMPIRES, IAN! AND I'M TIRED OF PRETENDING!
PRETENDING THAT WE'RE NORMAL! PUTTING IN A NIGHT OF WORK AND THEN DRINKING BLOOD SMOOTHIES FROM THE DINER'S SLAUGHTER-HOUSE!
WHAT, YOU WANT TO GO OUT AND KILL PEOPLE?
NO, OF COURSE NOT! BUT WE ALL NEED TO CUT LOOSE!
ALEX. WE CAN'T.
IT'S TOO RISKY. REMEMBER CHARLIE.
OF COURSE I REMEMBER CHARLIE! I WAS THERE WHEN THE TAKERS CAME FOR HIM!
HE WAS SLOPPY! AND JUST BECAUSE HE WAS SLOPPY--
...WE GET TO SPEND ETERNITY BEING BORED!
ALEX! IT'S NOT LIKE THAT! WE HAVE TO--
YOU'RE ALL EMOTIONALLY STUNTED.
I'LL GO TALK TO HIM.

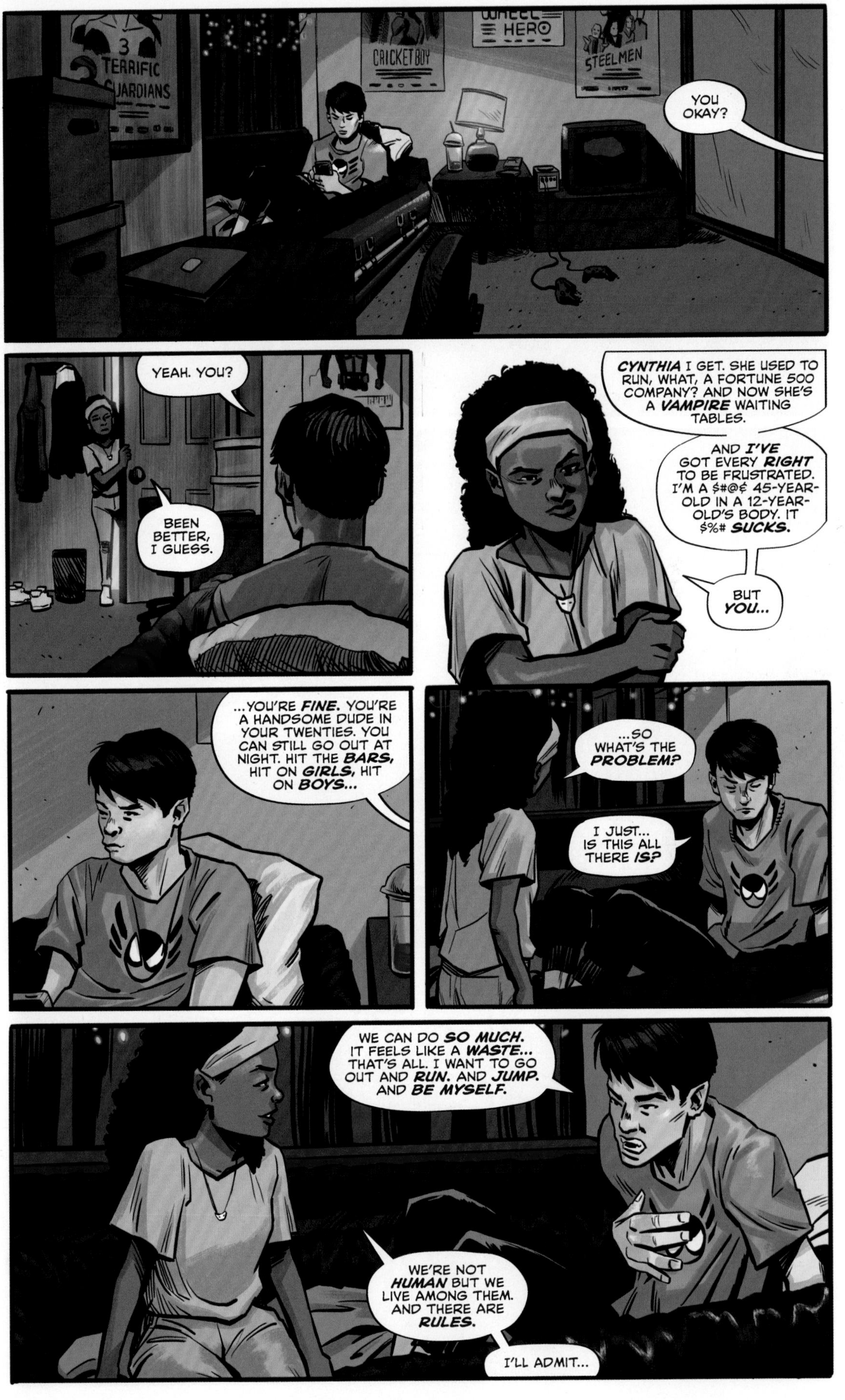
3 TERRIFIC GUARDIANS
HERO
CRICKETBOY
STEELMEN
YOU OKAY?
YEAH. YOU?
BEEN BETTER, I GUESS.
CYNTHIA I GET. SHE USED TO RUN, WHAT, A FORTUNE 500 COMPANY? AND NOW SHE'S A VAMPIRE WAITING TABLES.
AND I'VE GOT EVERY RIGHT TO BE FRUSTRATED. I'M A $#@¢ 45-YEAR-OLD IN A 12-YEAR-OLD'S BODY. IT $%# SUCKS.
BUT YOU...
...YOU'RE FINE. YOU'RE A HANDSOME DUDE IN YOUR TWENTIES. YOU CAN STILL GO OUT AT NIGHT. HIT THE BARS, HIT ON GIRLS, HIT ON BOYS...
...SO WHAT'S THE PROBLEM?
I JUST... IS THIS ALL THERE IS?
WE CAN DO SO MUCH. IT FEELS LIKE A WASTE... THAT'S ALL. I WANT TO GO OUT AND RUN. AND JUMP. AND BE MYSELF.
WE'RE NOT HUMAN BUT WE LIVE AMONG THEM. AND THERE ARE RULES.
I'LL ADMIT...

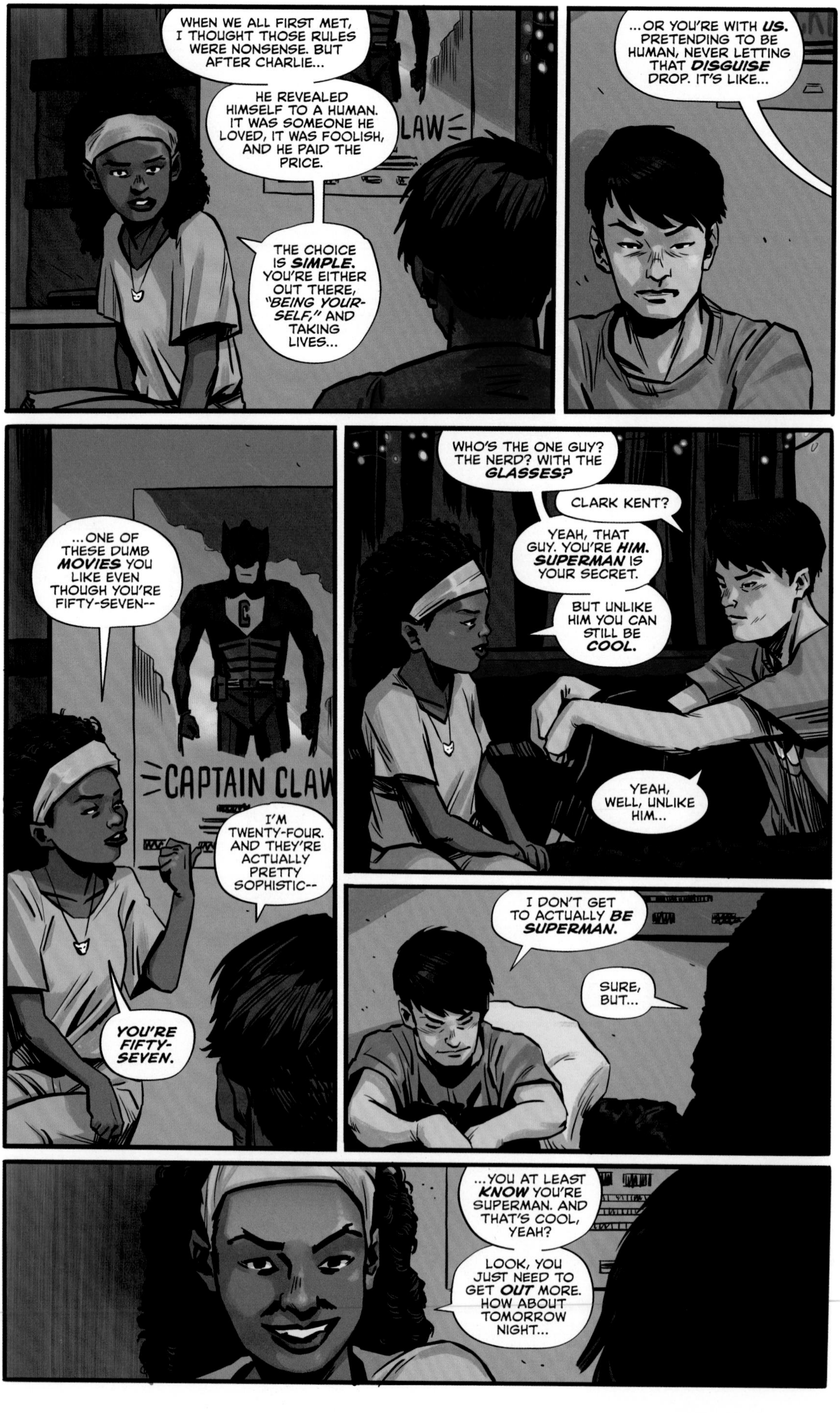
WHEN WE ALL FIRST MET, I THOUGHT THOSE RULES WERE NONSENSE. BUT AFTER CHARLIE...
HE REVEALED HIMSELF TO A HUMAN. IT WAS SOMEONE HE LOVED, IT WAS FOOLISH, AND HE PAID THE PRICE.
CLAW
THE CHOICE IS SIMPLE. YOU'RE EITHER OUT THERE, "BEING YOUR-SELF," AND TAKING LIVES...
...OR YOU'RE WITH US. PRETENDING TO BE HUMAN, NEVER LETTING THAT DISGUISE DROP. IT'S LIKE...
...ONE OF THESE DUMB MOVIES YOU LIKE EVEN THOUGH YOU'RE FIFTY-SEVEN--
CAPTAIN CLAW
I'M TWENTY-FOUR. AND THEY'RE ACTUALLY PRETTY SOPHISTIC--
YOU'RE FIFTY-SEVEN.
WHO'S THE ONE GUY? THE NERD? WITH THE GLASSES?
CLARK KENT?
YEAH, THAT GUY. YOU'RE HIM. SUPERMAN IS YOUR SECRET.
BUT UNLIKE HIM YOU CAN STILL BE COOL.
YEAH, WELL, UNLIKE HIM...
I DON'T GET TO ACTUALLY BE SUPERMAN.
SURE, BUT...
...YOU AT LEAST KNOW YOU'RE SUPERMAN. AND THAT'S COOL, YEAH?
LOOK, YOU JUST NEED TO GET OUT MORE. HOW ABOUT TOMORROW NIGHT...

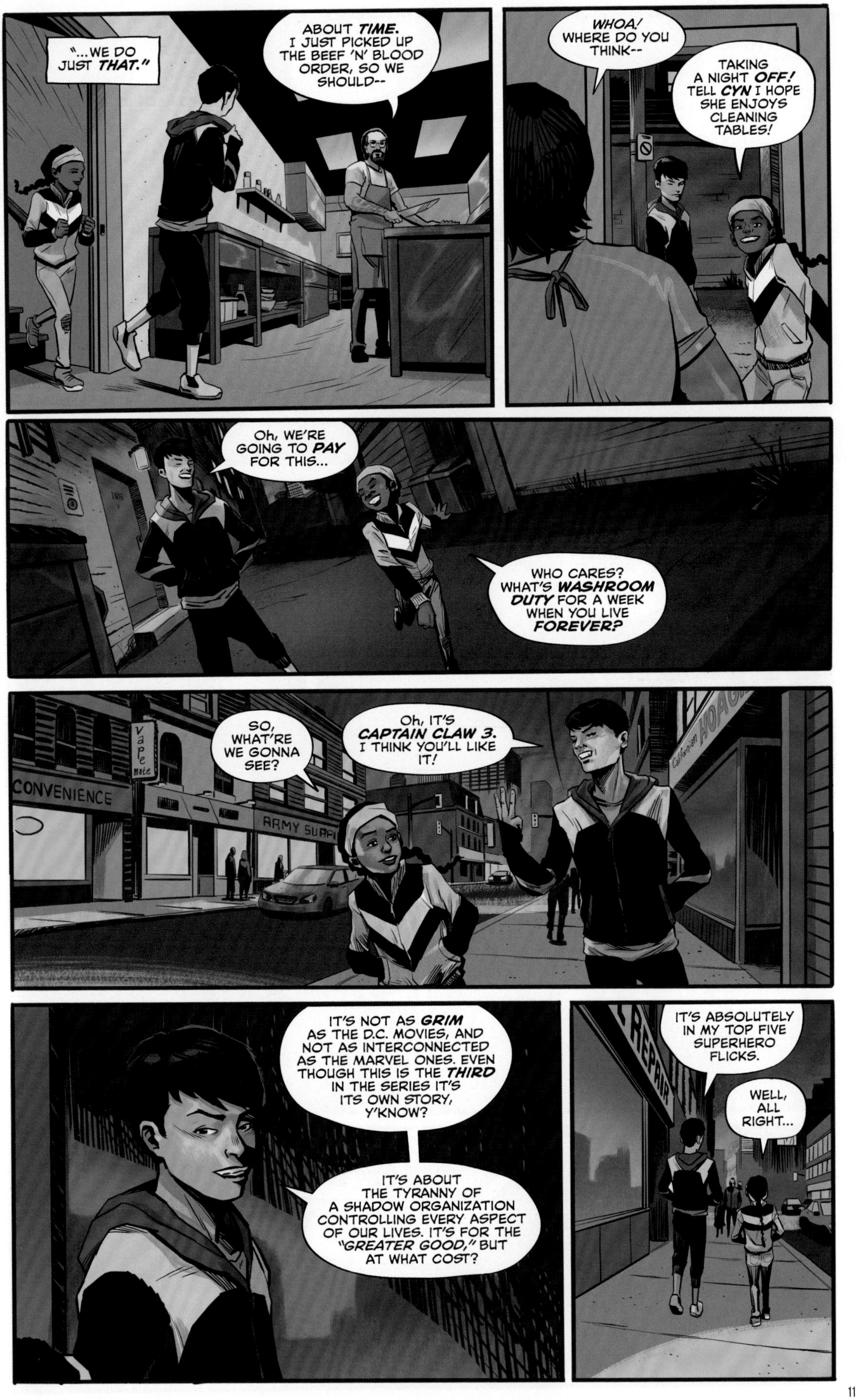
"...WE DO JUST *THAT.*"
ABOUT *TIME.* I JUST PICKED UP THE BEEF 'N' BLOOD ORDER, SO WE SHOULD--
WHOA! WHERE DO YOU THINK--
TAKING A NIGHT *OFF!* TELL *CYN* I HOPE SHE ENJOYS CLEANING TABLES!
Oh, WE'RE GOING TO *PAY* FOR THIS...
WHO CARES? WHAT'S *WASHROOM DUTY* FOR A WEEK WHEN YOU LIVE *FOREVER?*
CONVENIENCE
Vape mate
SO, WHAT'RE WE GONNA SEE?
Oh, IT'S *CAPTAIN CLAW 3.* I THINK YOU'LL LIKE IT!
IT'S NOT AS *GRIM* AS THE D.C. MOVIES, AND NOT AS INTERCONNECTED AS THE MARVEL ONES. EVEN THOUGH THIS IS THE *THIRD* IN THE SERIES IT'S ITS OWN STORY, Y'KNOW?
IT'S ABOUT THE TYRANNY OF A SHADOW ORGANIZATION CONTROLLING EVERY ASPECT OF OUR LIVES. IT'S FOR THE *"GREATER GOOD,"* BUT AT WHAT COST?
IT'S ABSOLUTELY IN MY TOP FIVE SUPERHERO FLICKS.
WELL, ALL RIGHT...

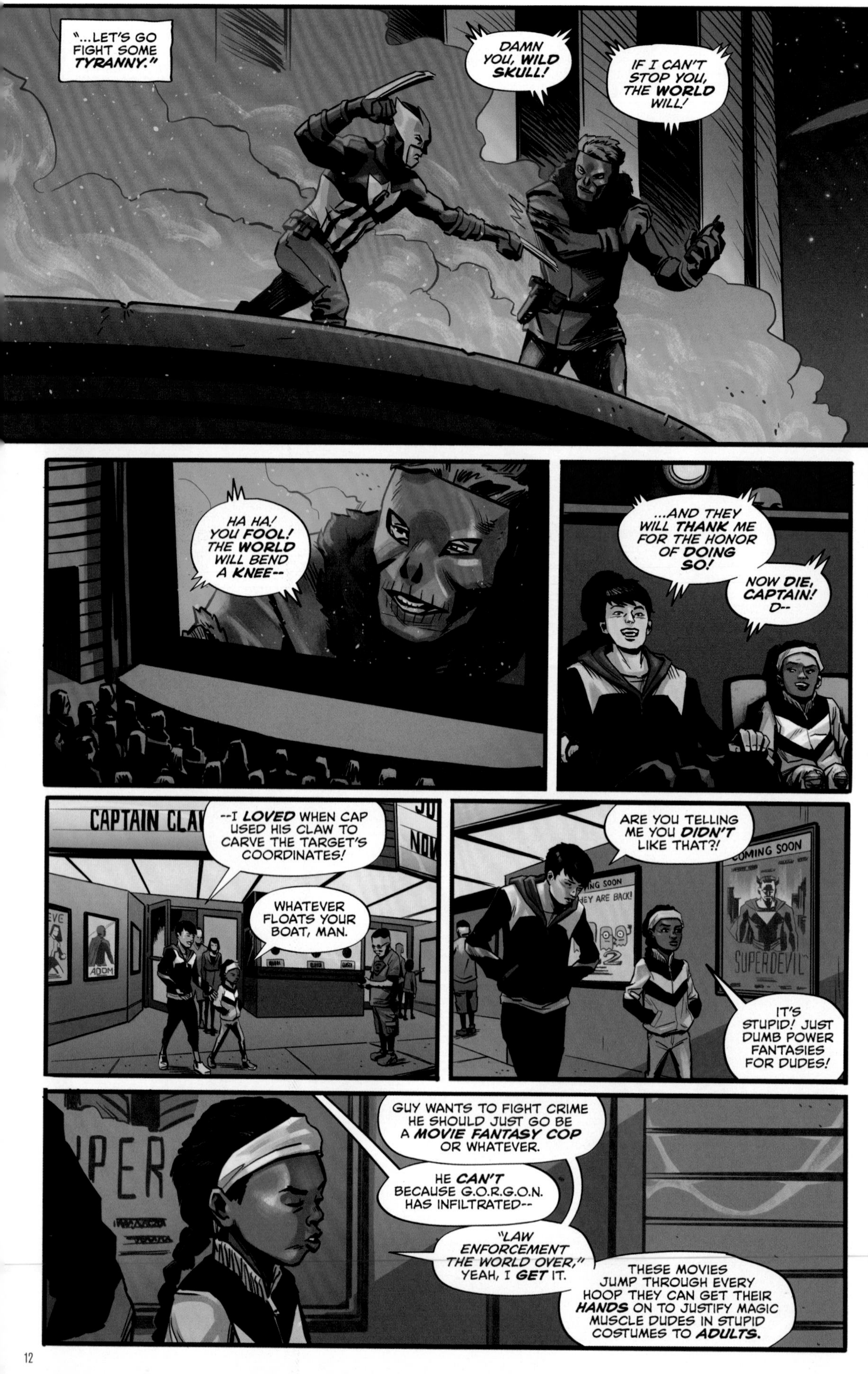

"...LET'S GO FIGHT SOME *TYRANNY.*"
DAMN YOU, **WILD SKULL!**
IF I CAN'T STOP YOU, THE **WORLD** WILL!
HA HA! YOU **FOOL!** THE **WORLD** WILL BEND A **KNEE**--
...AND THEY WILL **THANK** ME FOR THE HONOR OF **DOING SO!**
NOW **DIE, CAPTAIN!** D--
--I ***LOVED*** WHEN CAP USED HIS CLAW TO CARVE THE TARGET'S COORDINATES!
WHATEVER FLOATS YOUR BOAT, MAN.
ARE YOU TELLING ME YOU ***DIDN'T*** LIKE THAT?!
COMING SOON
SUPERDEVIL
IT'S STUPID! JUST DUMB POWER FANTASIES FOR DUDES!
GUY WANTS TO FIGHT CRIME HE SHOULD JUST GO BE A ***MOVIE FANTASY COP*** OR WHATEVER.
HE ***CAN'T*** BECAUSE G.O.R.G.O.N. HAS INFILTRATED--
"LAW ENFORCEMENT THE WORLD OVER," YEAH, I ***GET*** IT.
THESE MOVIES JUMP THROUGH EVERY HOOP THEY CAN GET THEIR ***HANDS*** ON TO JUSTIFY MAGIC MUSCLE DUDES IN STUPID COSTUMES TO ***ADULTS.***

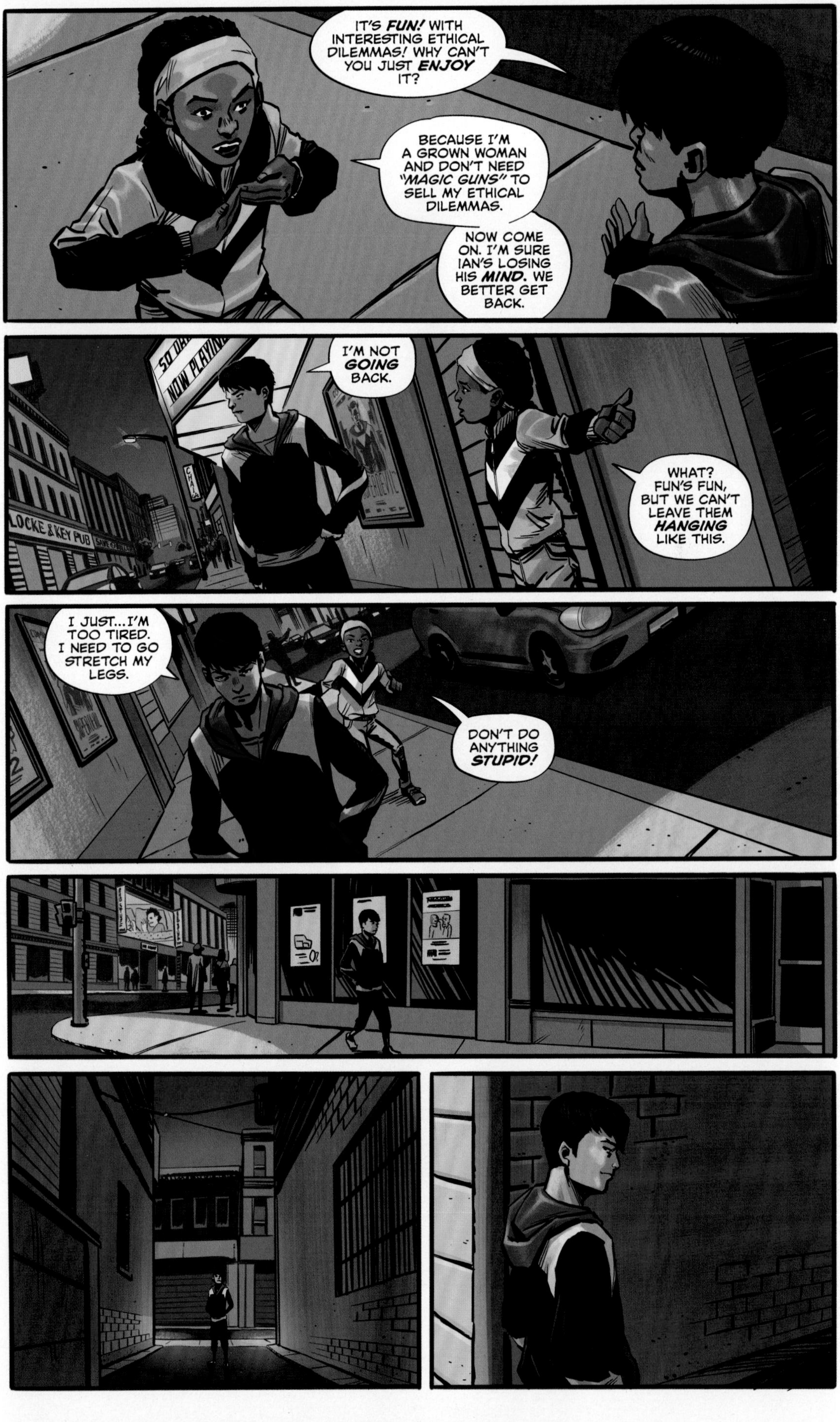
IT'S FUN! WITH INTERESTING ETHICAL DILEMMAS! WHY CAN'T YOU JUST ENJOY IT?
BECAUSE I'M A GROWN WOMAN AND DON'T NEED "MAGIC GUNS" TO SELL MY ETHICAL DILEMMAS.
NOW COME ON. I'M SURE IAN'S LOSING HIS MIND. WE BETTER GET BACK.
NOW PLAYING
I'M NOT GOING BACK.
WHAT? FUN'S FUN, BUT WE CAN'T LEAVE THEM HANGING LIKE THIS.
LOCKE & KEY PUB
I JUST...I'M TOO TIRED. I NEED TO GO STRETCH MY LEGS.
DON'T DO ANYTHING STUPID!

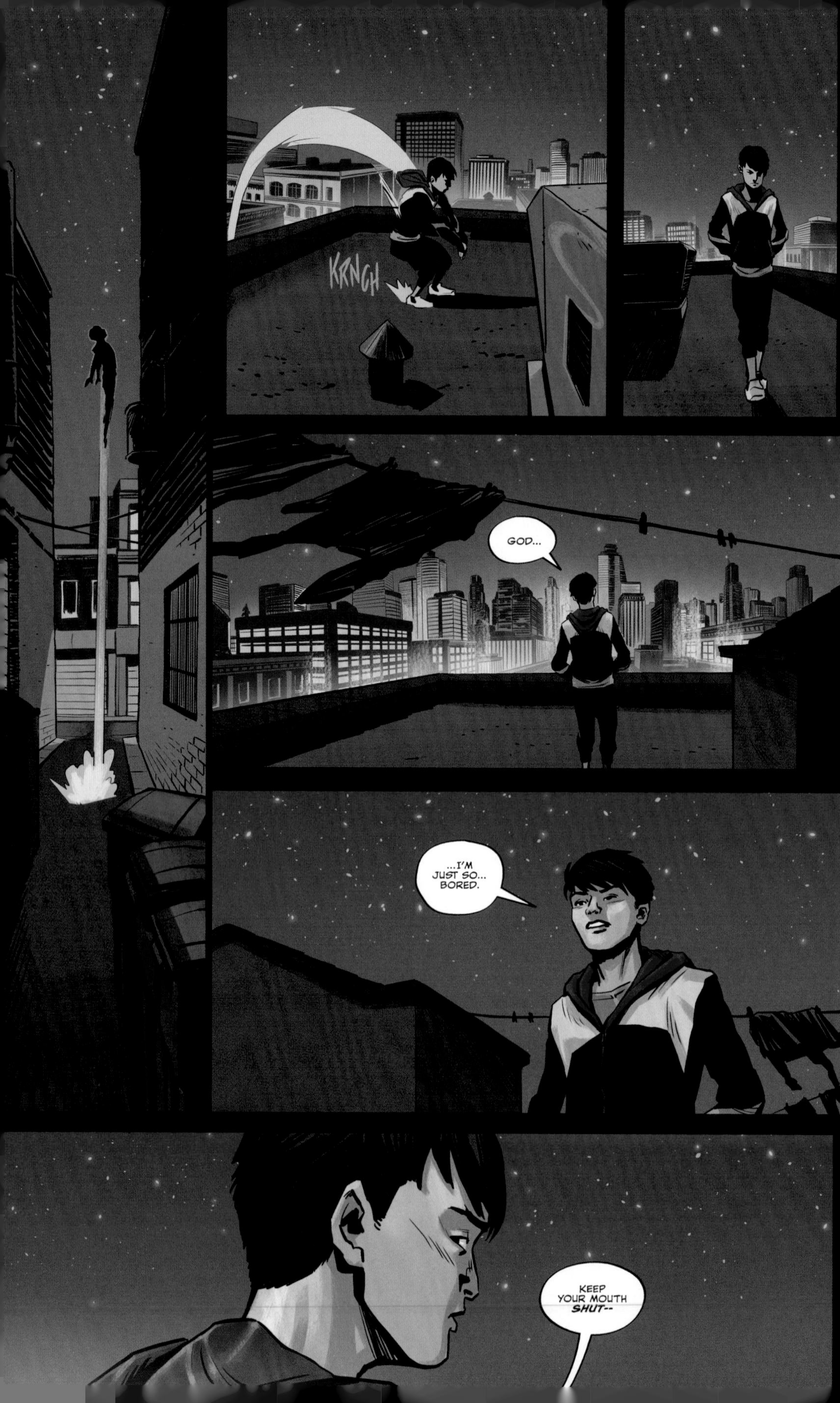
KRNGH
GOD...
...I'M JUST SO... BORED.
KEEP YOUR MOUTH SHUT--

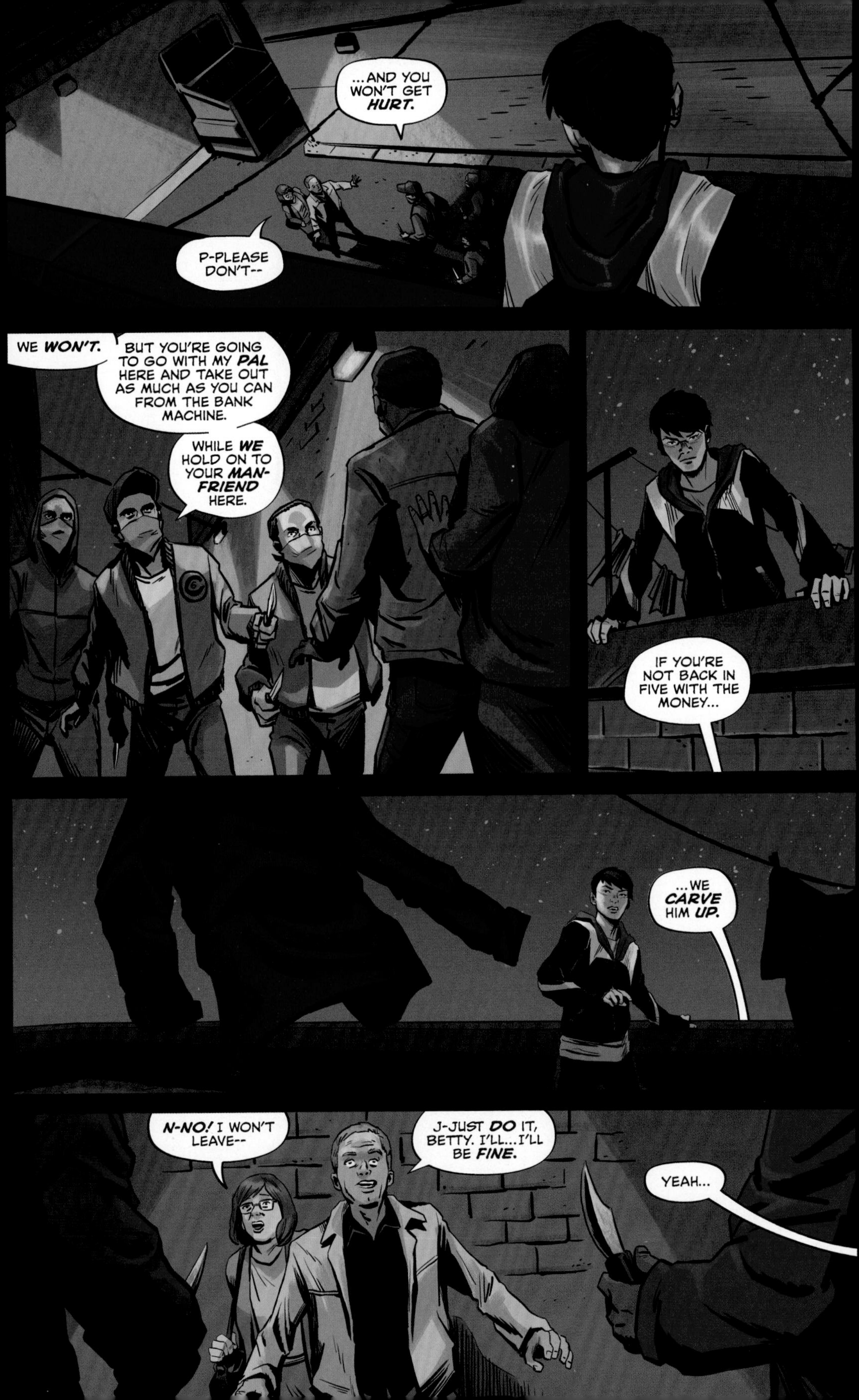
...AND YOU WON'T GET HURT.
P-PLEASE DON'T--
WE WON'T.
BUT YOU'RE GOING TO GO WITH MY PAL HERE AND TAKE OUT AS MUCH AS YOU CAN FROM THE BANK MACHINE.
WHILE WE HOLD ON TO YOUR MAN-FRIEND HERE.
IF YOU'RE NOT BACK IN FIVE WITH THE MONEY...
...WE CARVE HIM UP.
N-NO! I WON'T LEAVE--
J-JUST DO IT, BETTY. I'LL...I'LL BE FINE.
YEAH...

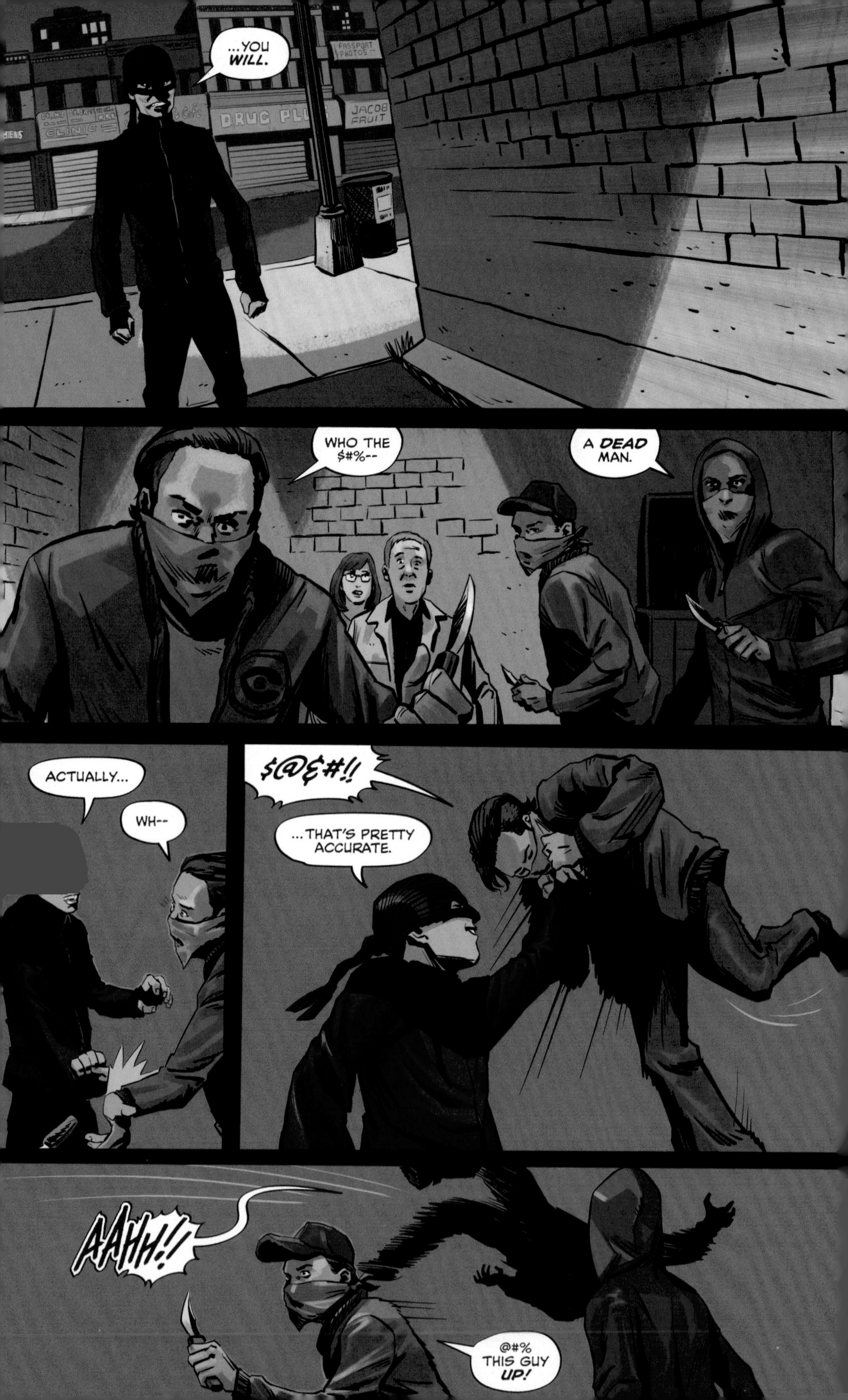
...YOU
WILL.
PASSPORT
PHOTOS
DRUG PLU
JACOB
FRUIT
CLINIC
WHO THE
$#%--
A DEAD
MAN.
ACTUALLY...
WH--
$@&#!!
...THAT'S PRETTY
ACCURATE.
AAHH!!
@#%
THIS GUY
UP!

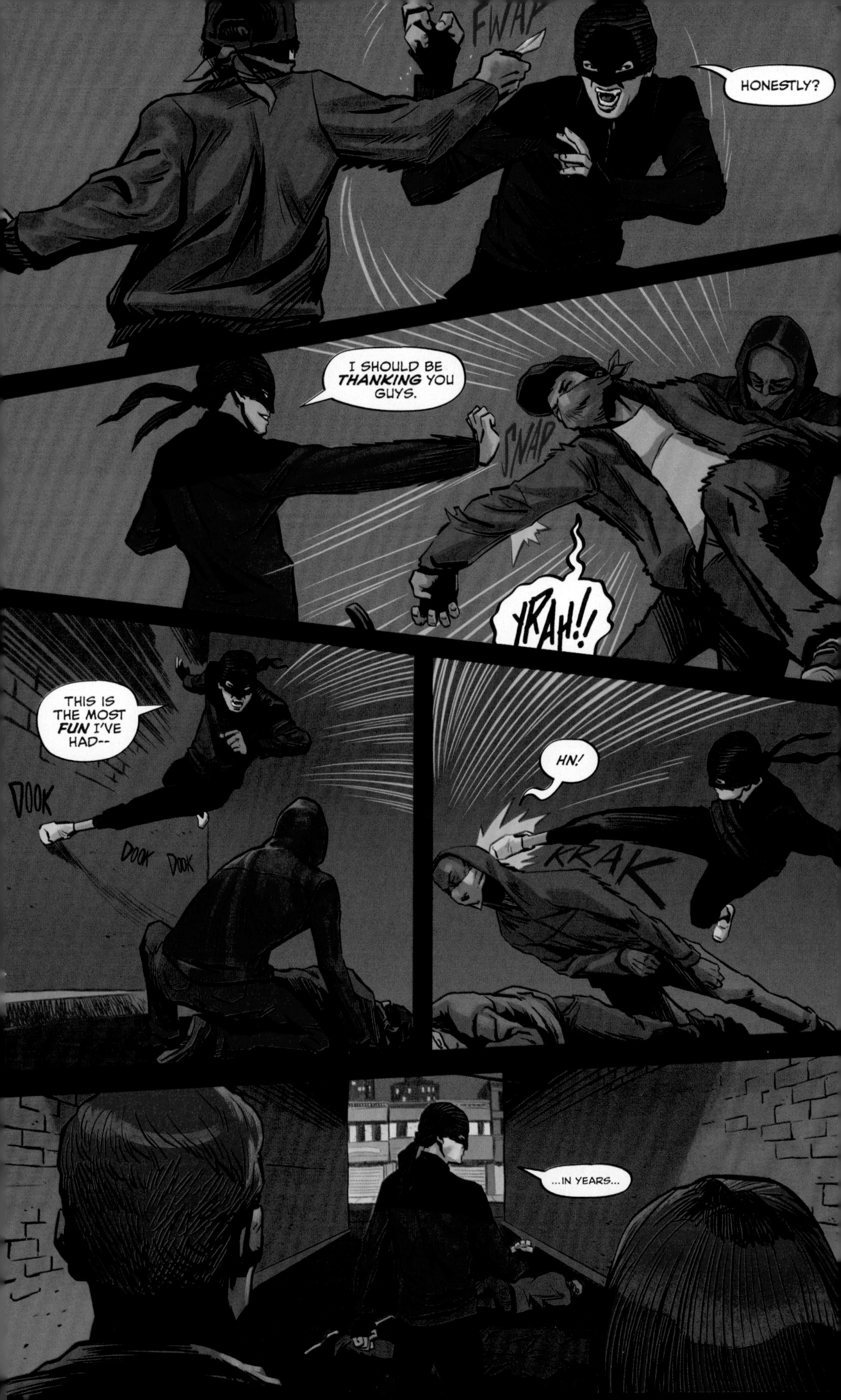

FWAP
HONESTLY?
I SHOULD BE THANKING YOU GUYS.
SNAP
YRAH!!
THIS IS THE MOST FUN I'VE HAD--
DOOK
DOOK
DOOK
HN!
KRAK
...IN YEARS...

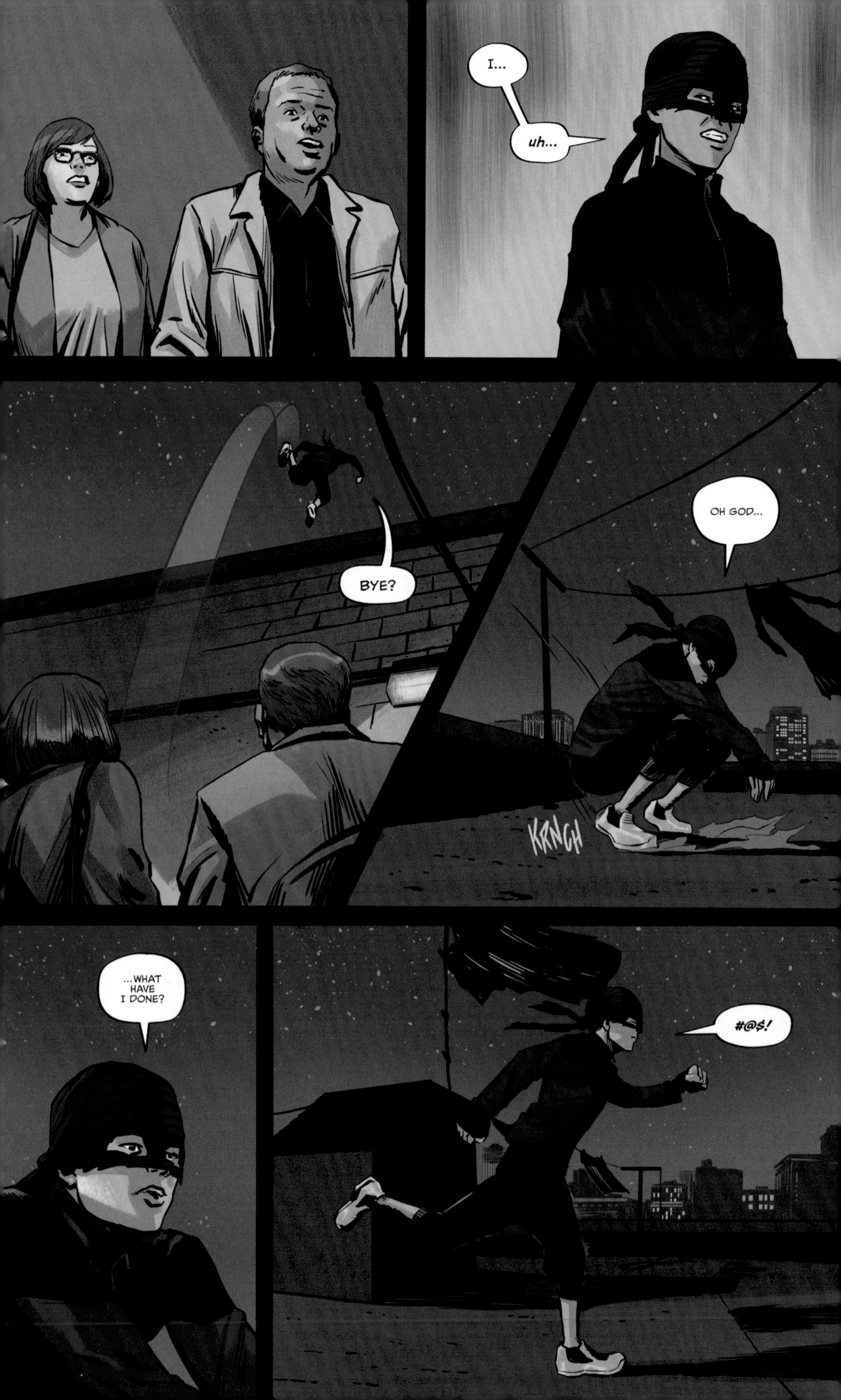
I...
uh...
BYE?
OH GOD...
KRNCH
...WHAT HAVE I DONE?
#@$!

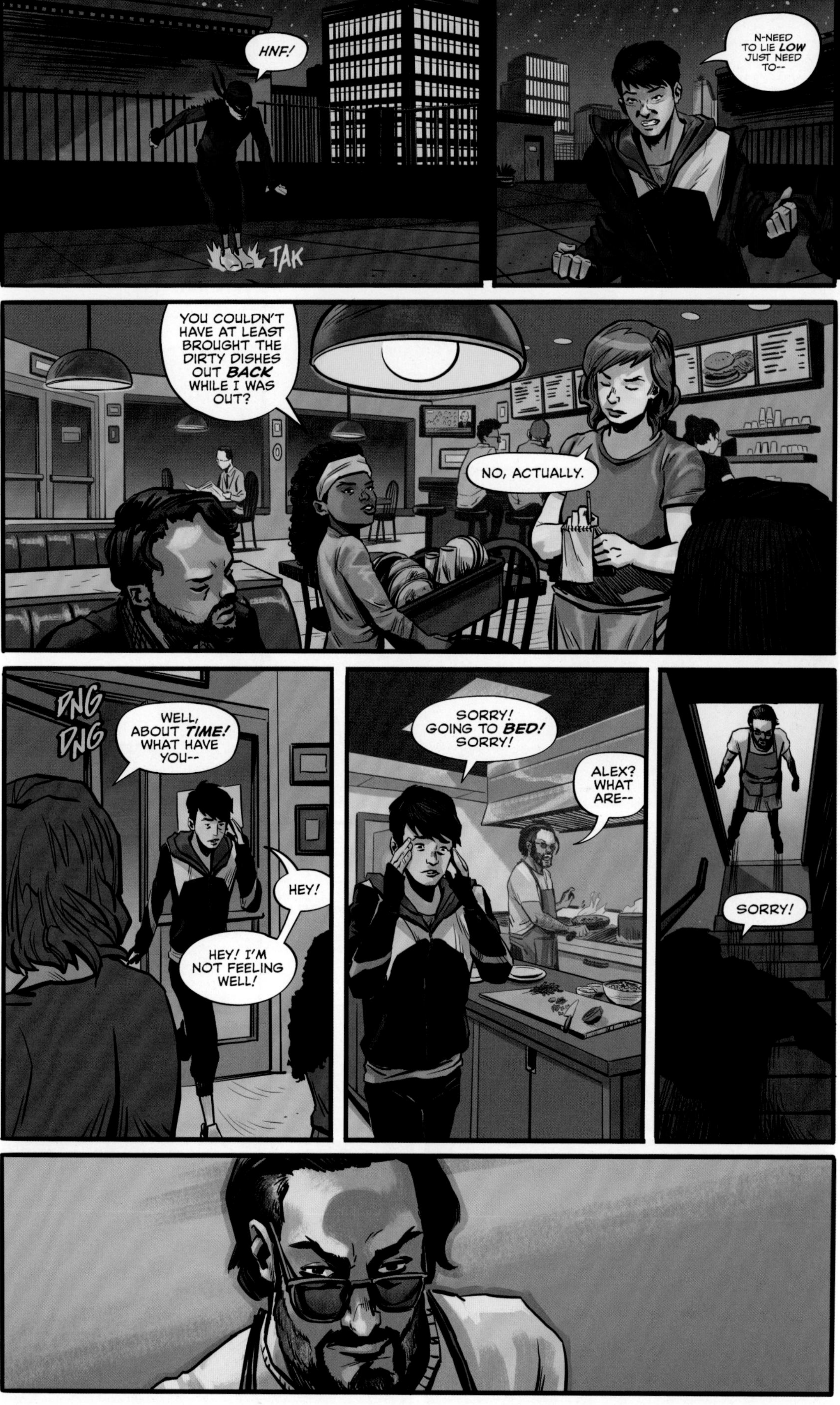
HNF!
TAK
N-NEED TO LIE LOW JUST NEED TO--
YOU COULDN'T HAVE AT LEAST BROUGHT THE DIRTY DISHES OUT BACK WHILE I WAS OUT?
NO, ACTUALLY.
DNG DNG
WELL, ABOUT TIME! WHAT HAVE YOU--
HEY!
HEY! I'M NOT FEELING WELL!
SORRY! GOING TO BED! SORRY!
ALEX? WHAT ARE--
SORRY!

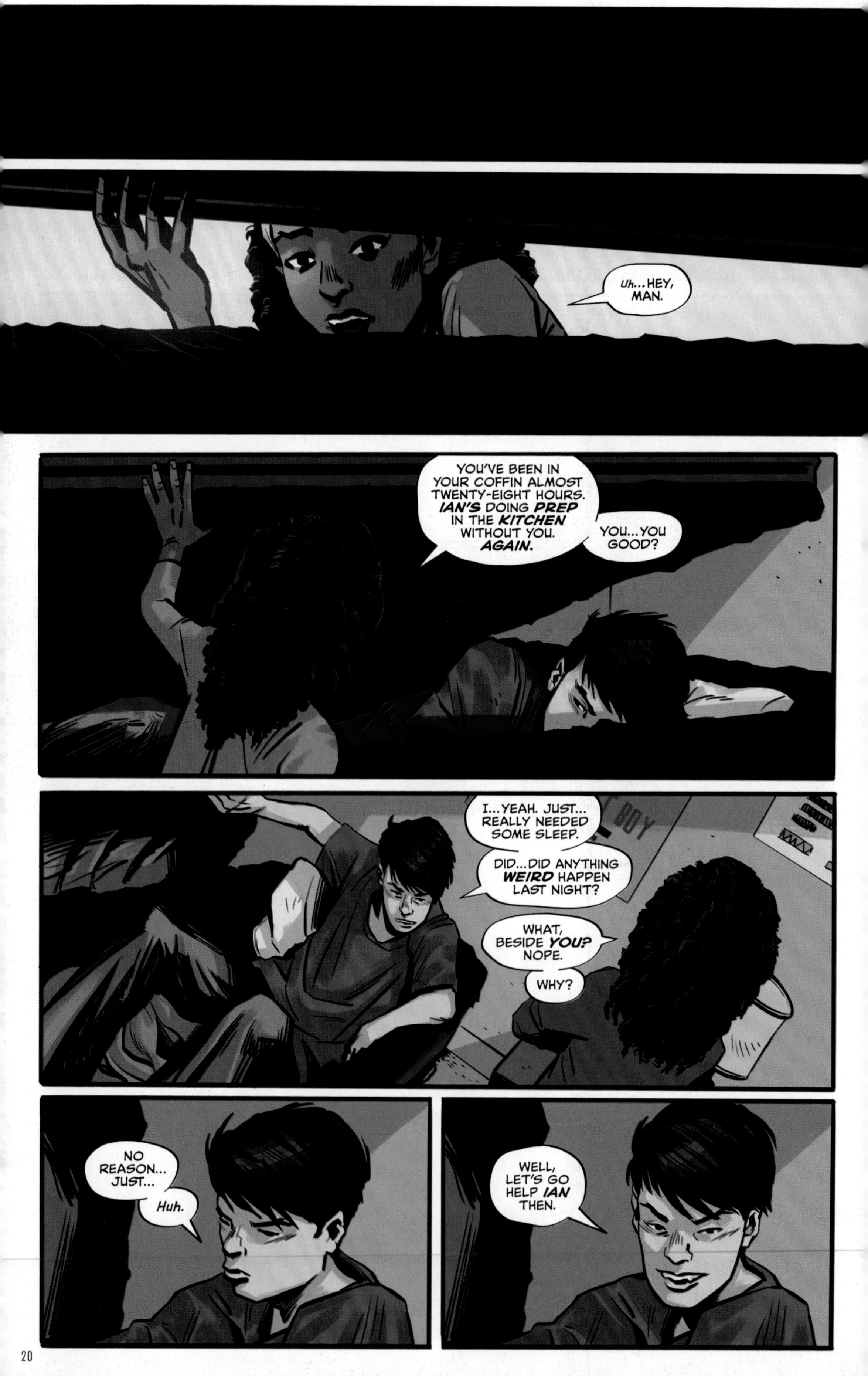

Uh...HEY, MAN.
YOU'VE BEEN IN YOUR COFFIN ALMOST TWENTY-EIGHT HOURS. IAN'S DOING PREP IN THE KITCHEN WITHOUT YOU. AGAIN.
YOU...YOU GOOD?
I...YEAH. JUST... REALLY NEEDED SOME SLEEP.
DID...DID ANYTHING WEIRD HAPPEN LAST NIGHT?
WHAT, BESIDE YOU? NOPE.
WHY?
NO REASON... JUST...
Huh.
WELL, LET'S GO HELP IAN THEN.

TWO WEEKS LATER:

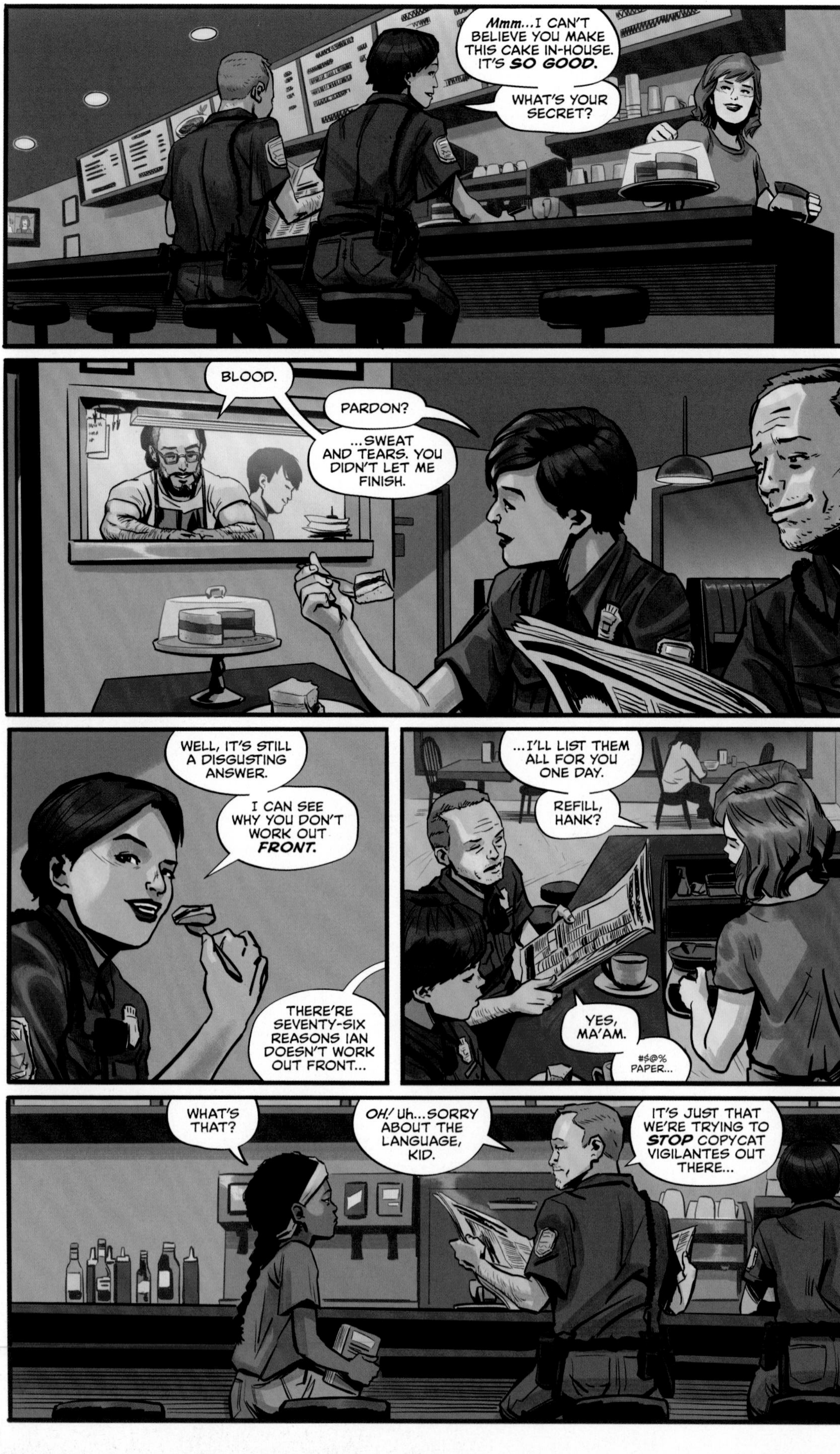

Mmm...I CAN'T BELIEVE YOU MAKE THIS CAKE IN-HOUSE. IT'S ***SO GOOD.***
WHAT'S YOUR SECRET?
BLOOD.
PARDON?
...SWEAT AND TEARS. YOU DIDN'T LET ME FINISH.
WELL, IT'S STILL A DISGUSTING ANSWER.
I CAN SEE WHY YOU DON'T WORK OUT ***FRONT.***
THERE'RE SEVENTY-SIX REASONS IAN DOESN'T WORK OUT FRONT...
...I'LL LIST THEM ALL FOR YOU ONE DAY.
REFILL, HANK?
YES, MA'AM.
#$@% PAPER...
WHAT'S THAT?
OH! Uh...SORRY ABOUT THE LANGUAGE, KID.
IT'S JUST THAT WE'RE TRYING TO ***STOP*** COPYCAT VIGILANTES OUT THERE...

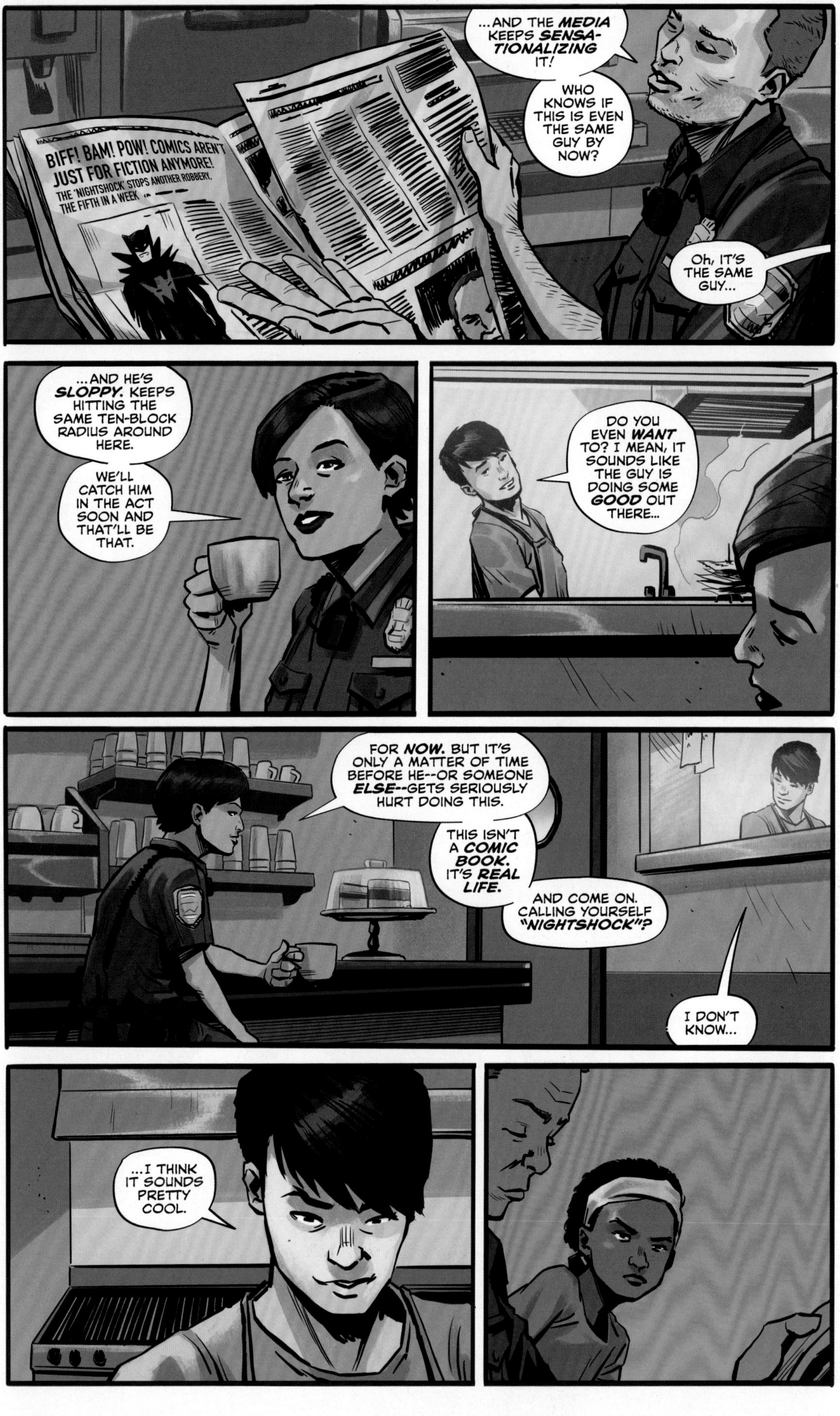
BIFF! BAM! POW! COMICS AREN'T JUST FOR FICTION ANYMORE!
THE 'NIGHTSHOCK' STOPS ANOTHER ROBBERY. THE FIFTH IN A WEEK
...AND THE MEDIA KEEPS SENSATIONALIZING IT!
WHO KNOWS IF THIS IS EVEN THE SAME GUY BY NOW?
Oh, IT'S THE SAME GUY...
...AND HE'S SLOPPY. KEEPS HITTING THE SAME TEN-BLOCK RADIUS AROUND HERE.
WE'LL CATCH HIM IN THE ACT SOON AND THAT'LL BE THAT.
DO YOU EVEN WANT TO? I MEAN, IT SOUNDS LIKE THE GUY IS DOING SOME GOOD OUT THERE...
FOR NOW. BUT IT'S ONLY A MATTER OF TIME BEFORE HE--OR SOMEONE ELSE--GETS SERIOUSLY HURT DOING THIS.
THIS ISN'T A COMIC BOOK. IT'S REAL LIFE.
AND COME ON. CALLING YOURSELF "NIGHTSHOCK"?
I DON'T KNOW...
...I THINK IT SOUNDS PRETTY COOL.

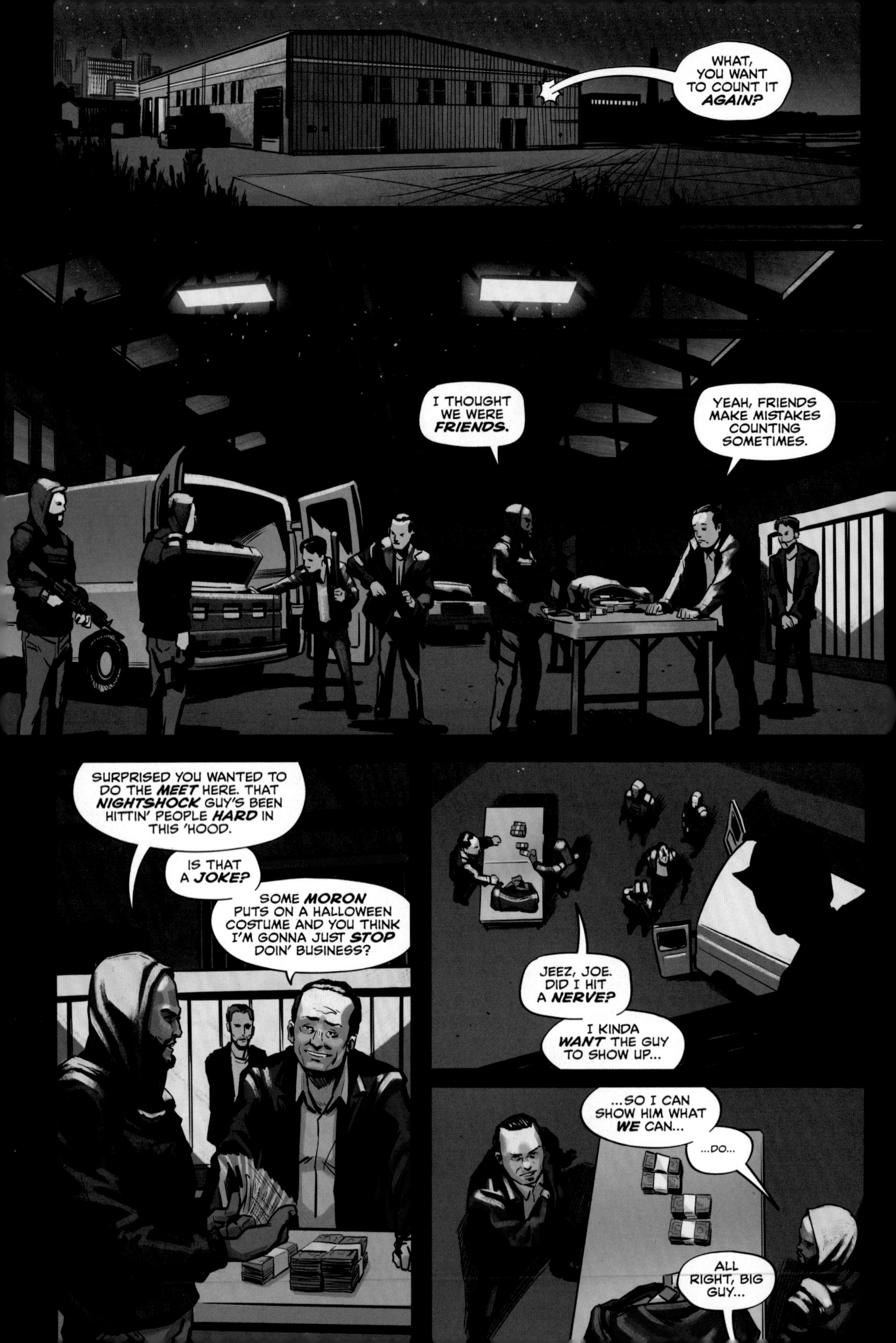
WHAT, YOU WANT TO COUNT IT AGAIN?
I THOUGHT WE WERE FRIENDS.
YEAH, FRIENDS MAKE MISTAKES COUNTING SOMETIMES.
SURPRISED YOU WANTED TO DO THE MEET HERE. THAT NIGHTSHOCK GUY'S BEEN HITTIN' PEOPLE HARD IN THIS 'HOOD.
IS THAT A JOKE?
SOME MORON PUTS ON A HALLOWEEN COSTUME AND YOU THINK I'M GONNA JUST STOP DOIN' BUSINESS?
JEEZ, JOE. DID I HIT A NERVE?
I KINDA WANT THE GUY TO SHOW UP...
...SO I CAN SHOW HIM WHAT WE CAN...
...DO...
ALL RIGHT, BIG GUY...

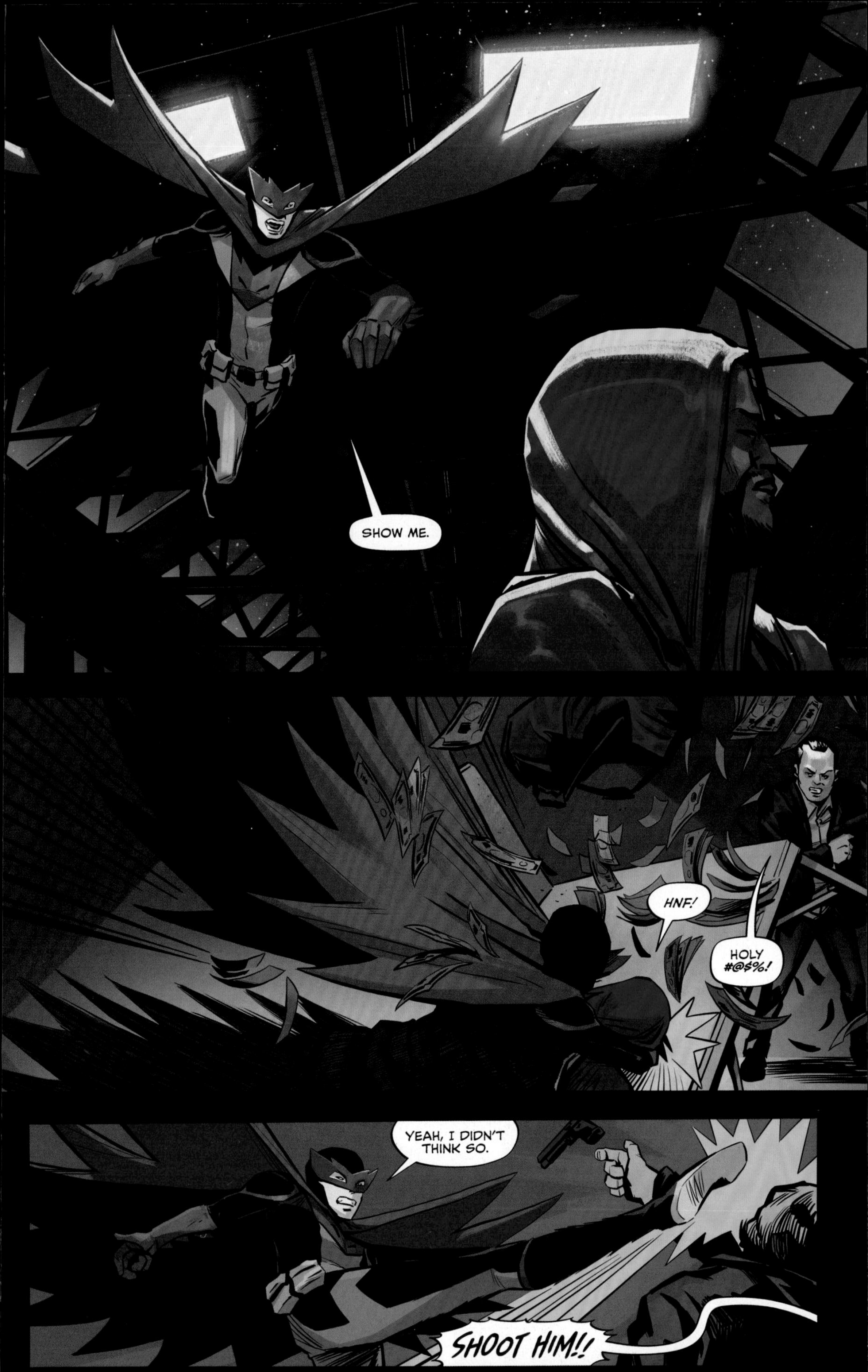
SHOW ME.
HNF!
HOLY #@$%!
YEAH, I DIDN'T THINK SO.
SHOOT HIM!!

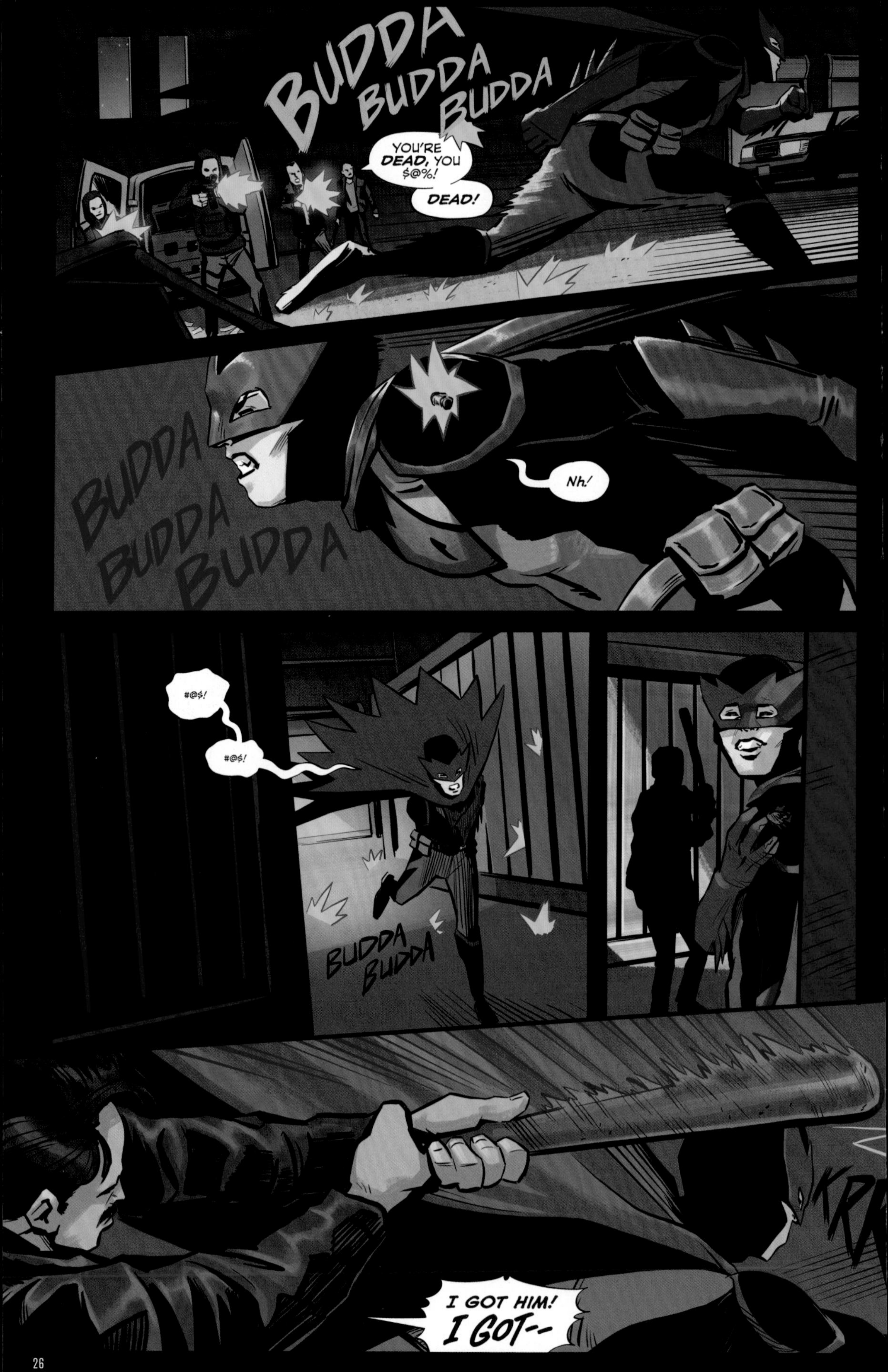
BUDDA
BUDDA
BUDDA
YOU'RE DEAD, YOU $@%!
DEAD!
BUDDA
BUDDA
BUDDA
Nh!
#@$!
#@$!
BUDDA
BUDDA
I GOT HIM! I GOT--

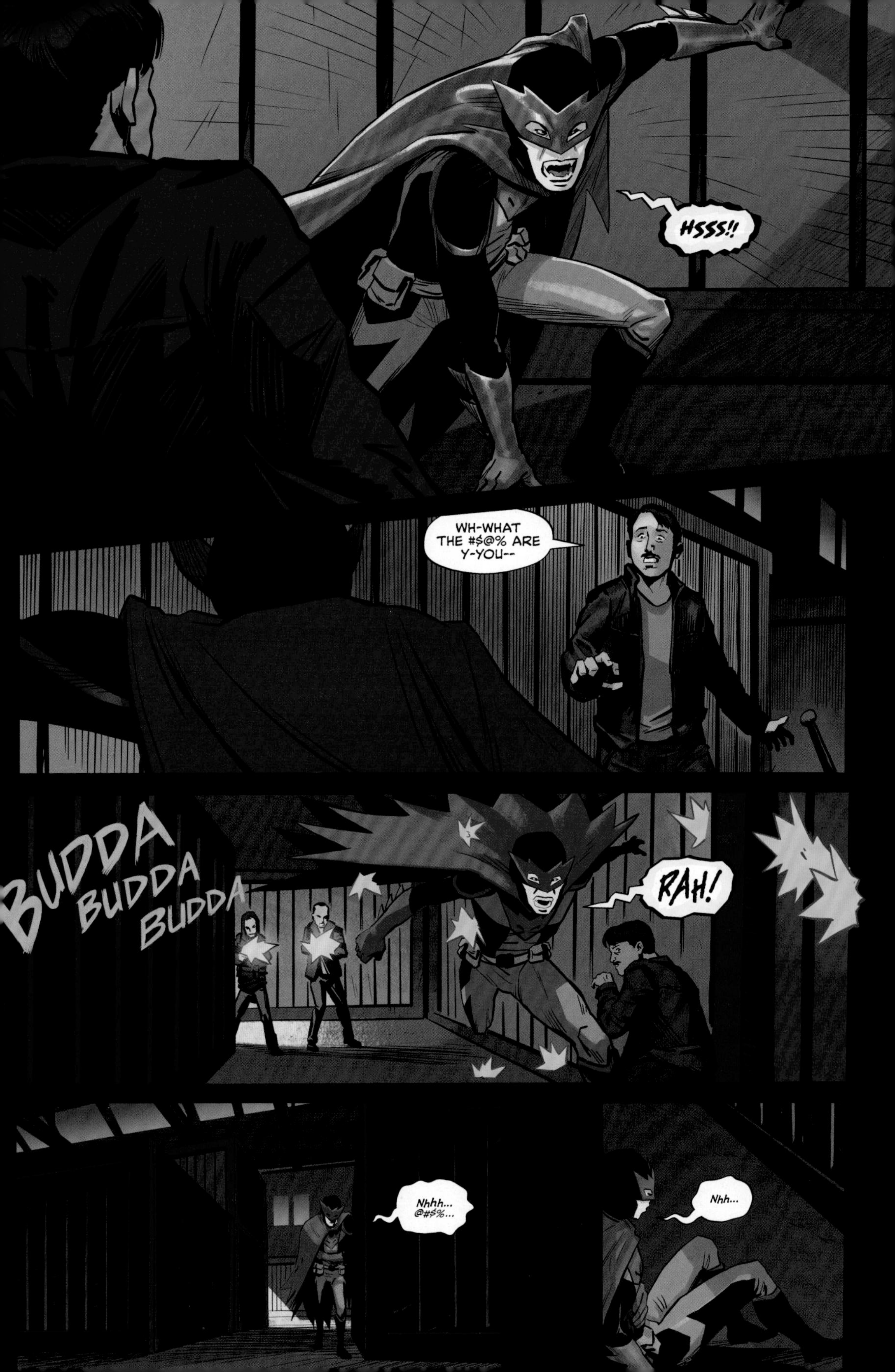
HSSS!!
WH-WHAT THE #$@% ARE Y-YOU--
BUDDA BUDDA BUDDA
RAH!
Nhhh... @#$%...
Nhh...

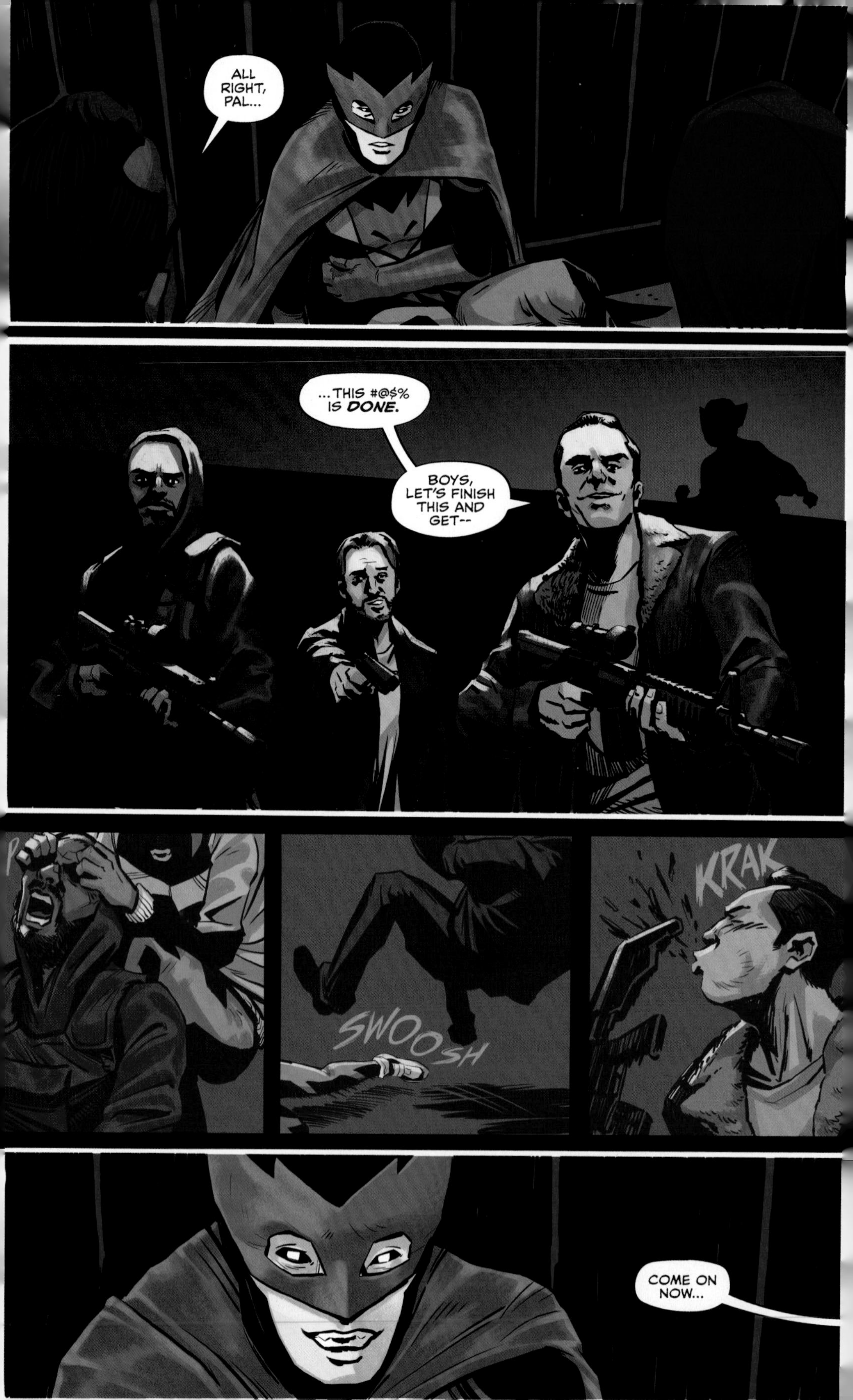
ALL RIGHT, PAL...
...THIS #@$% IS DONE.
BOYS, LET'S FINISH THIS AND GET--
SWOOSH
KRAK
COME ON NOW...

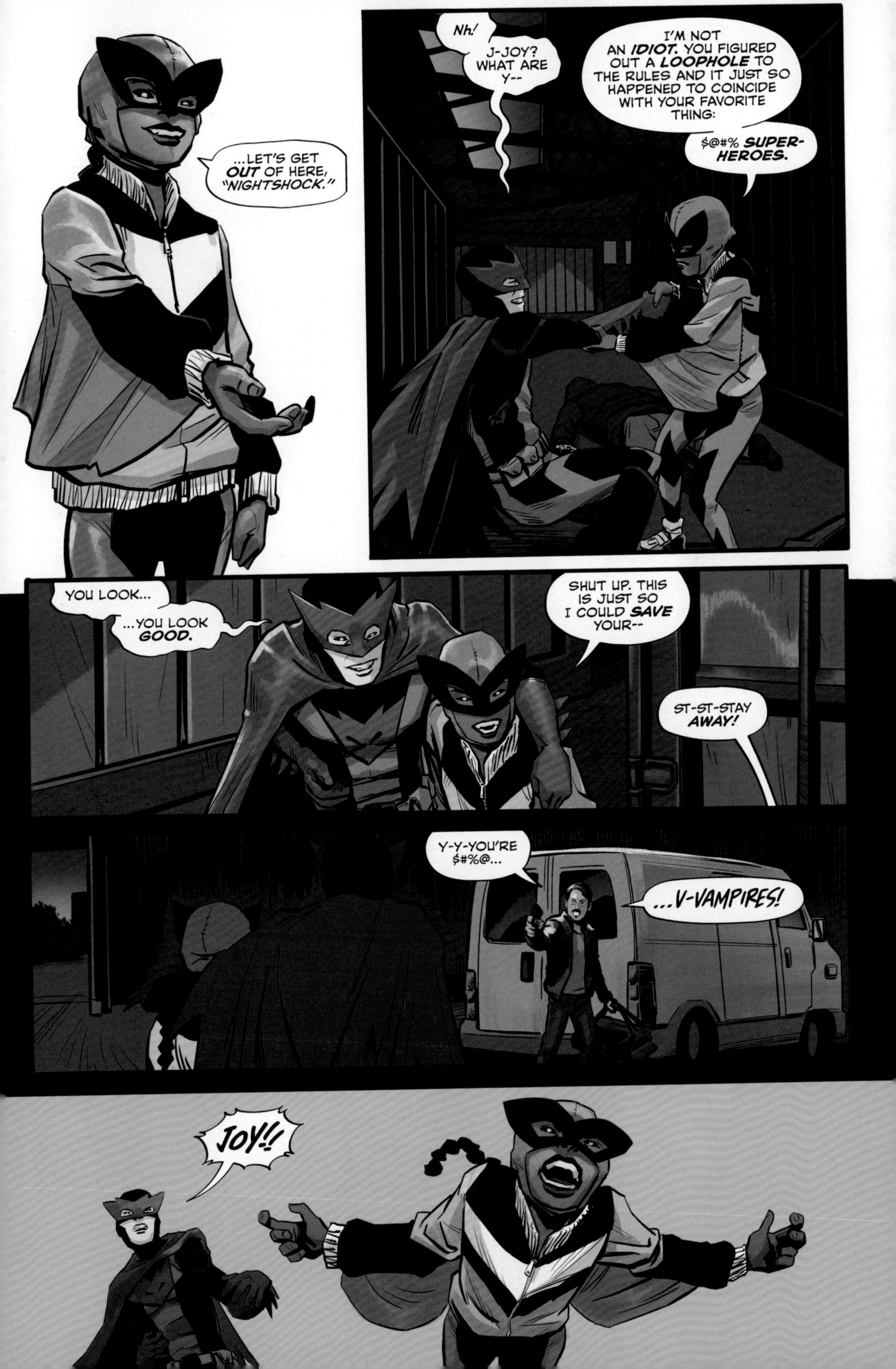
...LET'S GET OUT OF HERE, "NIGHTSHOCK."
Nh!
J-JOY? WHAT ARE Y--
I'M NOT AN IDIOT. YOU FIGURED OUT A LOOPHOLE TO THE RULES AND IT JUST SO HAPPENED TO COINCIDE WITH YOUR FAVORITE THING:
$@#% SUPER-HEROES.
YOU LOOK...
...YOU LOOK GOOD.
SHUT UP. THIS IS JUST SO I COULD SAVE YOUR--
ST-ST-STAY AWAY!
Y-Y-YOU'RE $#%@...
...V-VAMPIRES!
JOY!!

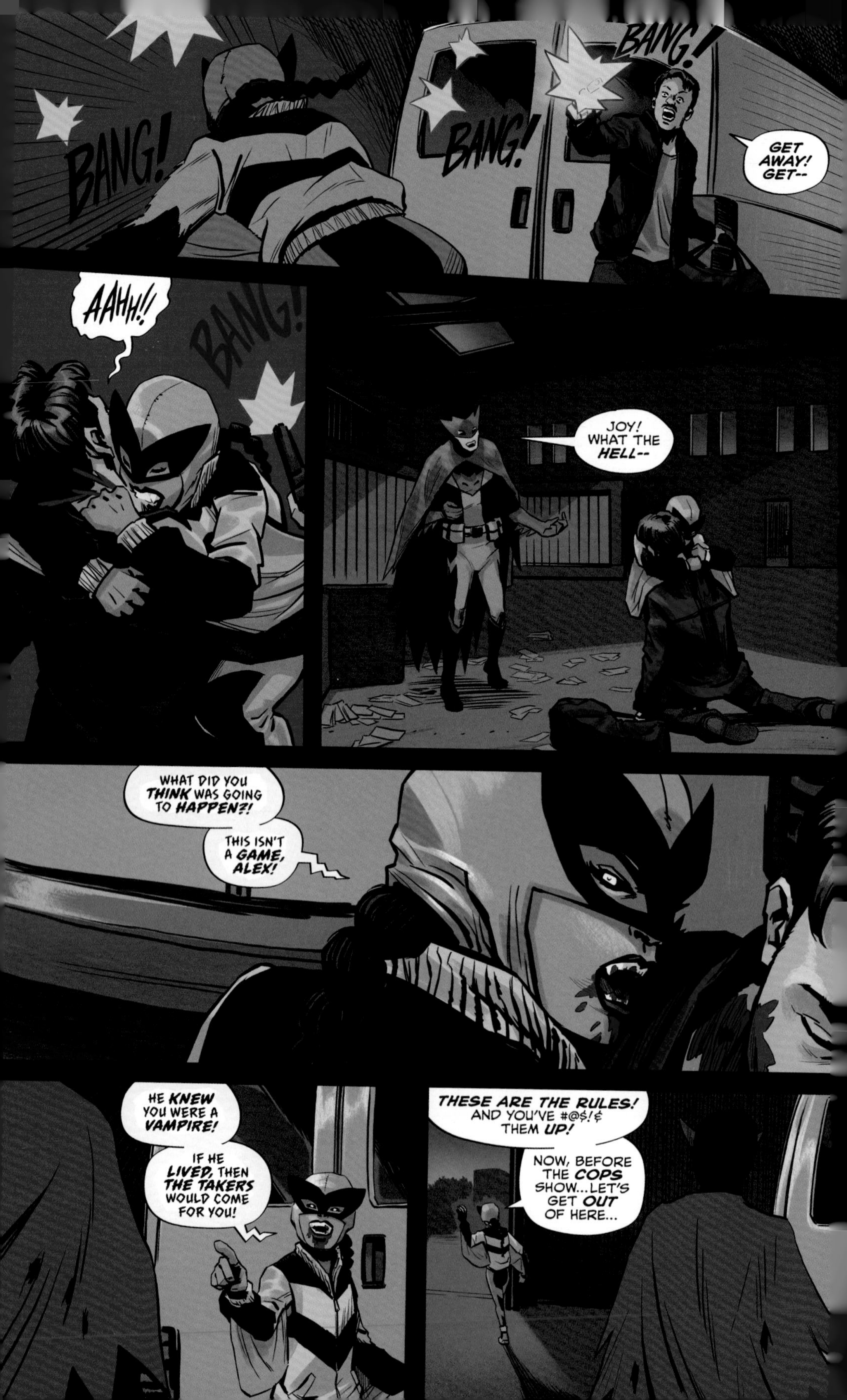
BANG!
BANG!
BANG!
GET AWAY! GET--
AAHH!!
BANG!
JOY! WHAT THE HELL--
WHAT DID YOU THINK WAS GOING TO HAPPEN?!
THIS ISN'T A GAME, ALEX!
HE KNEW YOU WERE A VAMPIRE!
IF HE LIVED, THEN THE TAKERS WOULD COME FOR YOU!
THESE ARE THE RULES! AND YOU'VE #@$!¢ THEM UP!
NOW, BEFORE THE COPS SHOW...LET'S GET OUT OF HERE...

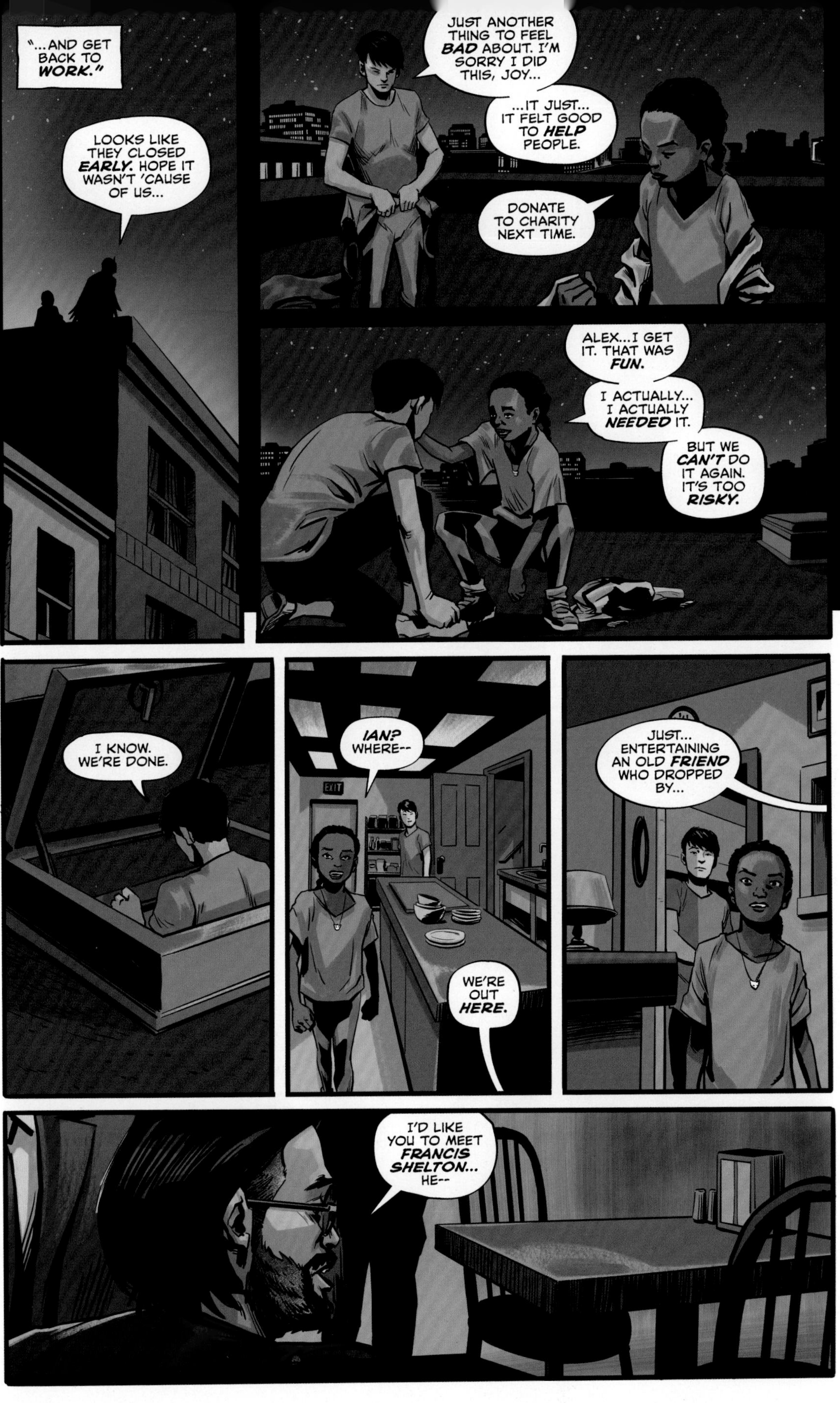
"...AND GET BACK TO WORK."
LOOKS LIKE THEY CLOSED EARLY. HOPE IT WASN'T 'CAUSE OF US...
JUST ANOTHER THING TO FEEL BAD ABOUT. I'M SORRY I DID THIS, JOY...
...IT JUST... IT FELT GOOD TO HELP PEOPLE.
DONATE TO CHARITY NEXT TIME.
ALEX...I GET IT. THAT WAS FUN.
I ACTUALLY... I ACTUALLY NEEDED IT.
BUT WE CAN'T DO IT AGAIN. IT'S TOO RISKY.
I KNOW. WE'RE DONE.
IAN? WHERE--
EXIT
WE'RE OUT HERE.
JUST... ENTERTAINING AN OLD FRIEND WHO DROPPED BY...
I'D LIKE YOU TO MEET FRANCIS SHELTON... HE--

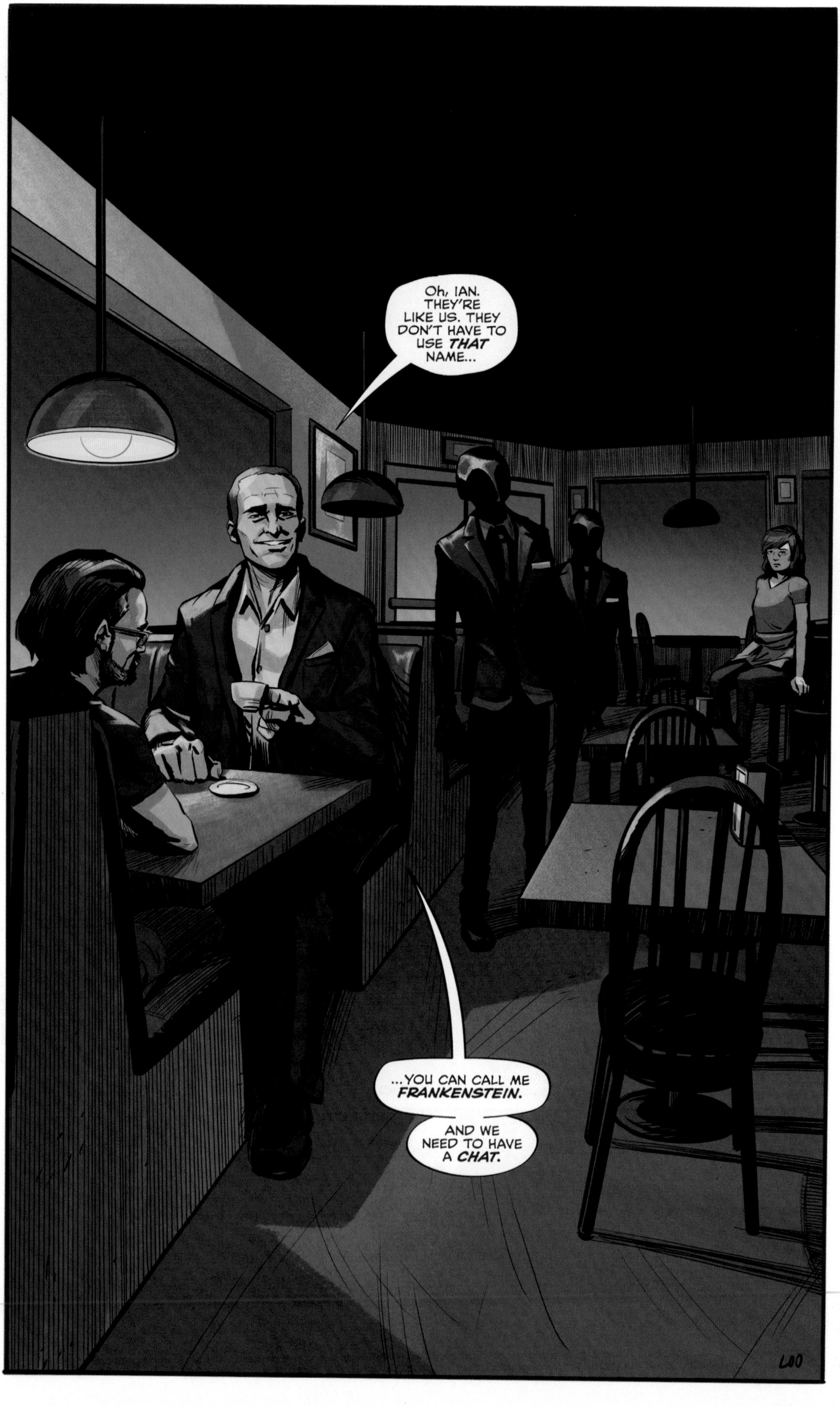
Oh, IAN. THEY'RE LIKE US. THEY DON'T HAVE TO USE *THAT* NAME...
...YOU CAN CALL ME *FRANKENSTEIN.*
AND WE NEED TO HAVE A *CHAT.*
LOO

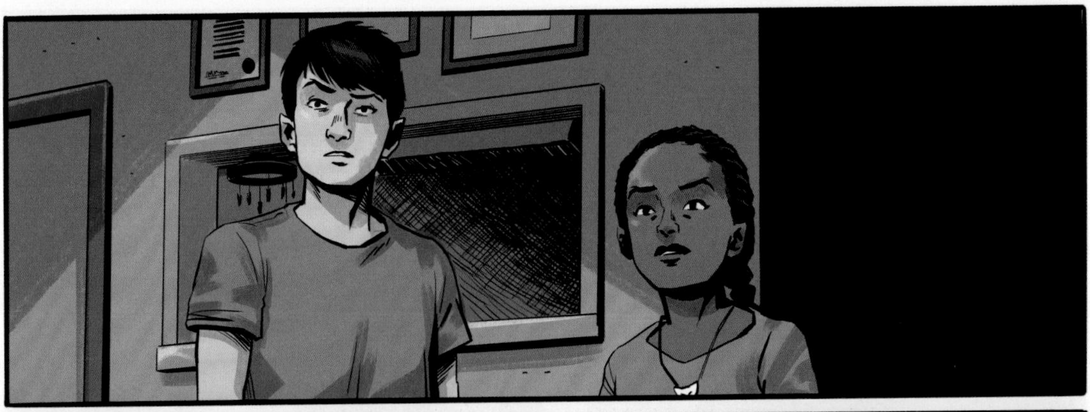
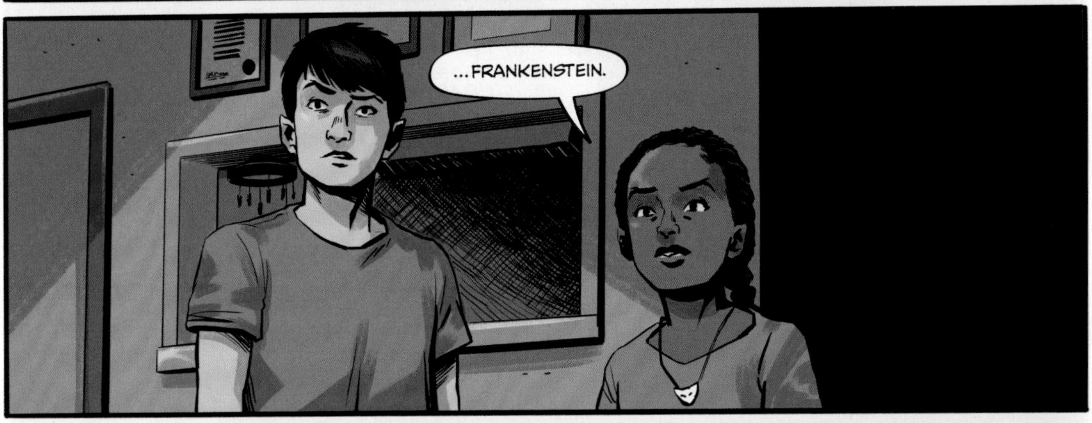
...FRANKENSTEIN.
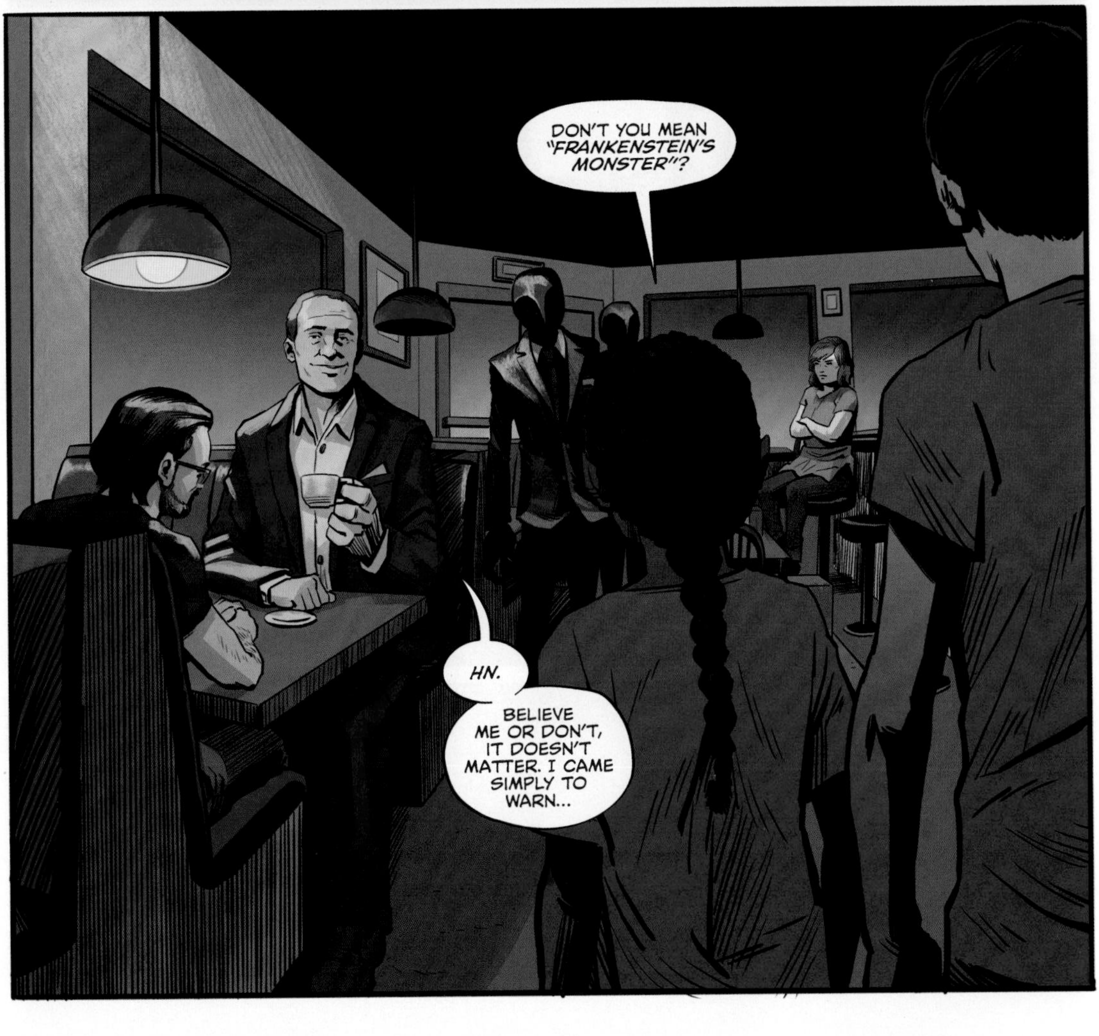
DON'T YOU MEAN "FRANKENSTEIN'S MONSTER"?
HN.
BELIEVE ME OR DON'T, IT DOESN'T MATTER. I CAME SIMPLY TO WARN...

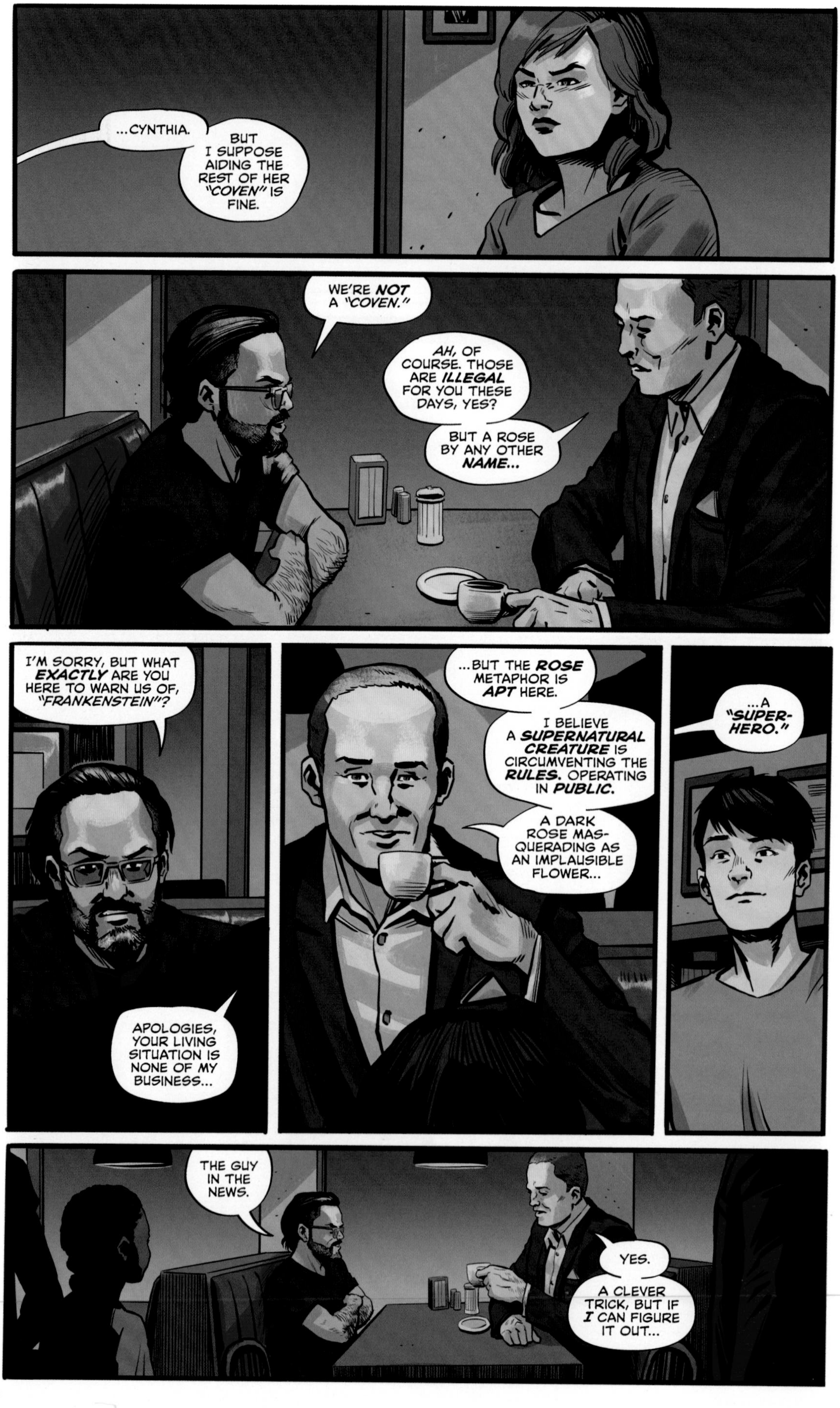
...CYNTHIA.
BUT I SUPPOSE AIDING THE REST OF HER "COVEN" IS FINE.
WE'RE NOT A "COVEN."
AH, OF COURSE. THOSE ARE ILLEGAL FOR YOU THESE DAYS, YES?
BUT A ROSE BY ANY OTHER NAME...
I'M SORRY, BUT WHAT EXACTLY ARE YOU HERE TO WARN US OF, "FRANKENSTEIN"?
APOLOGIES, YOUR LIVING SITUATION IS NONE OF MY BUSINESS...
...BUT THE ROSE METAPHOR IS APT HERE.
I BELIEVE A SUPERNATURAL CREATURE IS CIRCUMVENTING THE RULES. OPERATING IN PUBLIC.
A DARK ROSE MASQUERADING AS AN IMPLAUSIBLE FLOWER...
...A "SUPERHERO."
THE GUY IN THE NEWS.
YES.
A CLEVER TRICK, BUT IF I CAN FIGURE IT OUT...

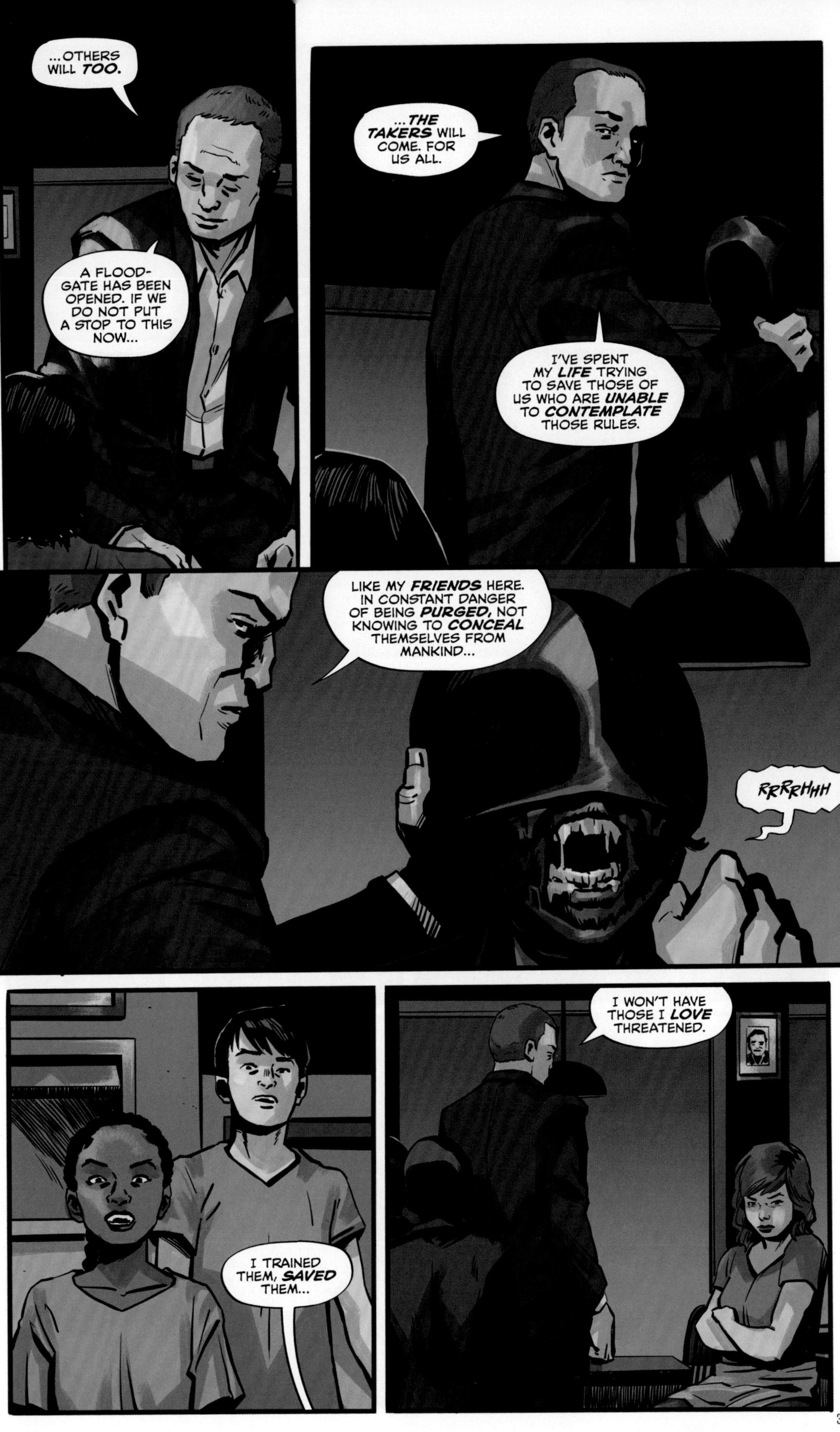
...OTHERS WILL TOO.
A FLOOD-GATE HAS BEEN OPENED. IF WE DO NOT PUT A STOP TO THIS NOW...
...THE TAKERS WILL COME. FOR US ALL.
I'VE SPENT MY LIFE TRYING TO SAVE THOSE OF US WHO ARE UNABLE TO CONTEMPLATE THOSE RULES.
LIKE MY FRIENDS HERE. IN CONSTANT DANGER OF BEING PURGED, NOT KNOWING TO CONCEAL THEMSELVES FROM MANKIND...
RRRRHHH
I TRAINED THEM, SAVED THEM...
I WON'T HAVE THOSE I LOVE THREATENED.

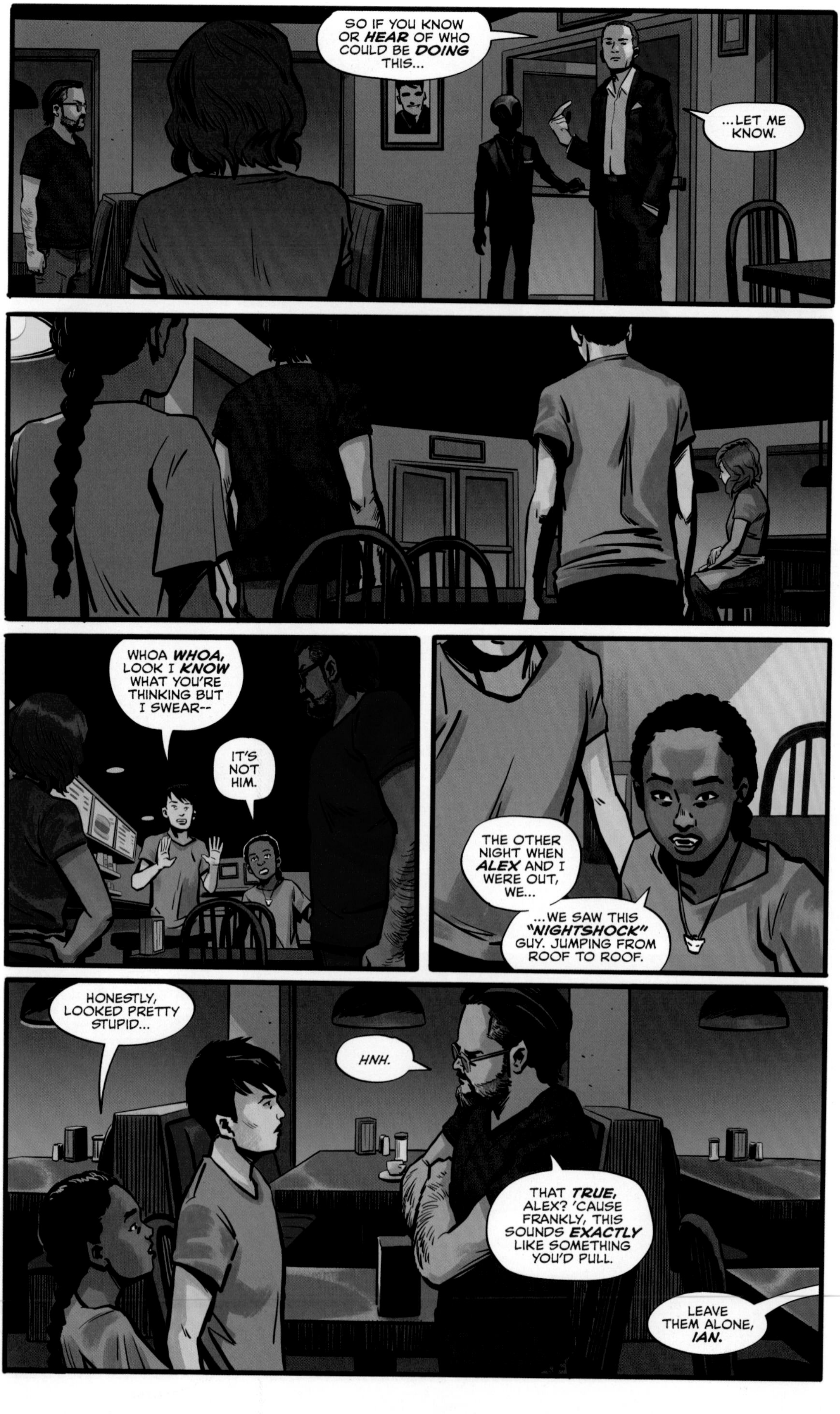
SO IF YOU KNOW OR HEAR OF WHO COULD BE DOING THIS...
...LET ME KNOW.
WHOA WHOA, LOOK I KNOW WHAT YOU'RE THINKING BUT I SWEAR--
IT'S NOT HIM.
THE OTHER NIGHT WHEN ALEX AND I WERE OUT, WE...
...WE SAW THIS "NIGHTSHOCK" GUY. JUMPING FROM ROOF TO ROOF.
HONESTLY, LOOKED PRETTY STUPID...
HNH.
THAT TRUE, ALEX? 'CAUSE FRANKLY, THIS SOUNDS EXACTLY LIKE SOMETHING YOU'D PULL.
LEAVE THEM ALONE, IAN.

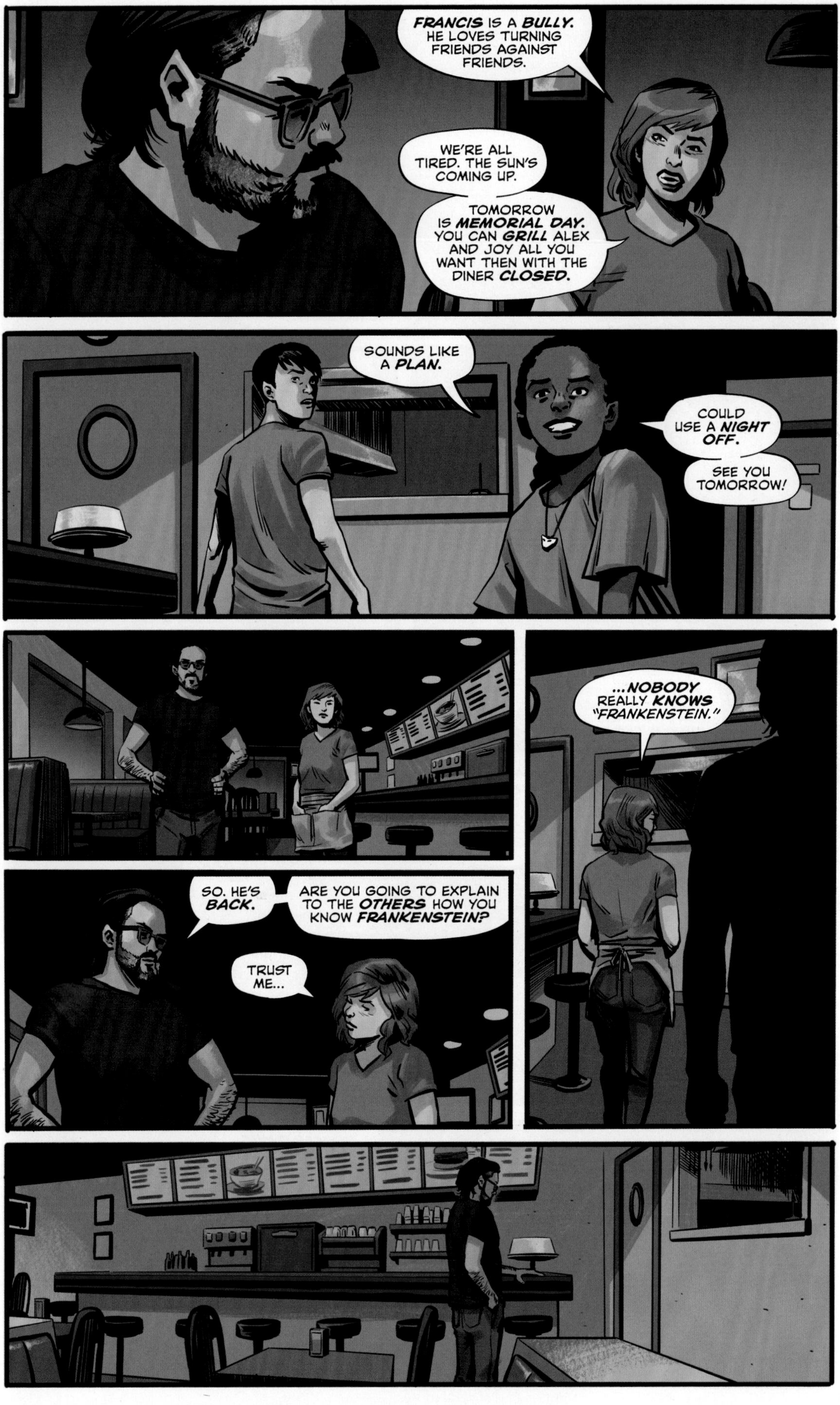

FRANCIS IS A BULLY. HE LOVES TURNING FRIENDS AGAINST FRIENDS.
WE'RE ALL TIRED. THE SUN'S COMING UP.
TOMORROW IS MEMORIAL DAY. YOU CAN GRILL ALEX AND JOY ALL YOU WANT THEN WITH THE DINER CLOSED.
SOUNDS LIKE A PLAN.
COULD USE A NIGHT OFF.
SEE YOU TOMORROW!
SO. HE'S BACK.
ARE YOU GOING TO EXPLAIN TO THE OTHERS HOW YOU KNOW FRANKENSTEIN?
TRUST ME...
...NOBODY REALLY KNOWS "FRANKENSTEIN."

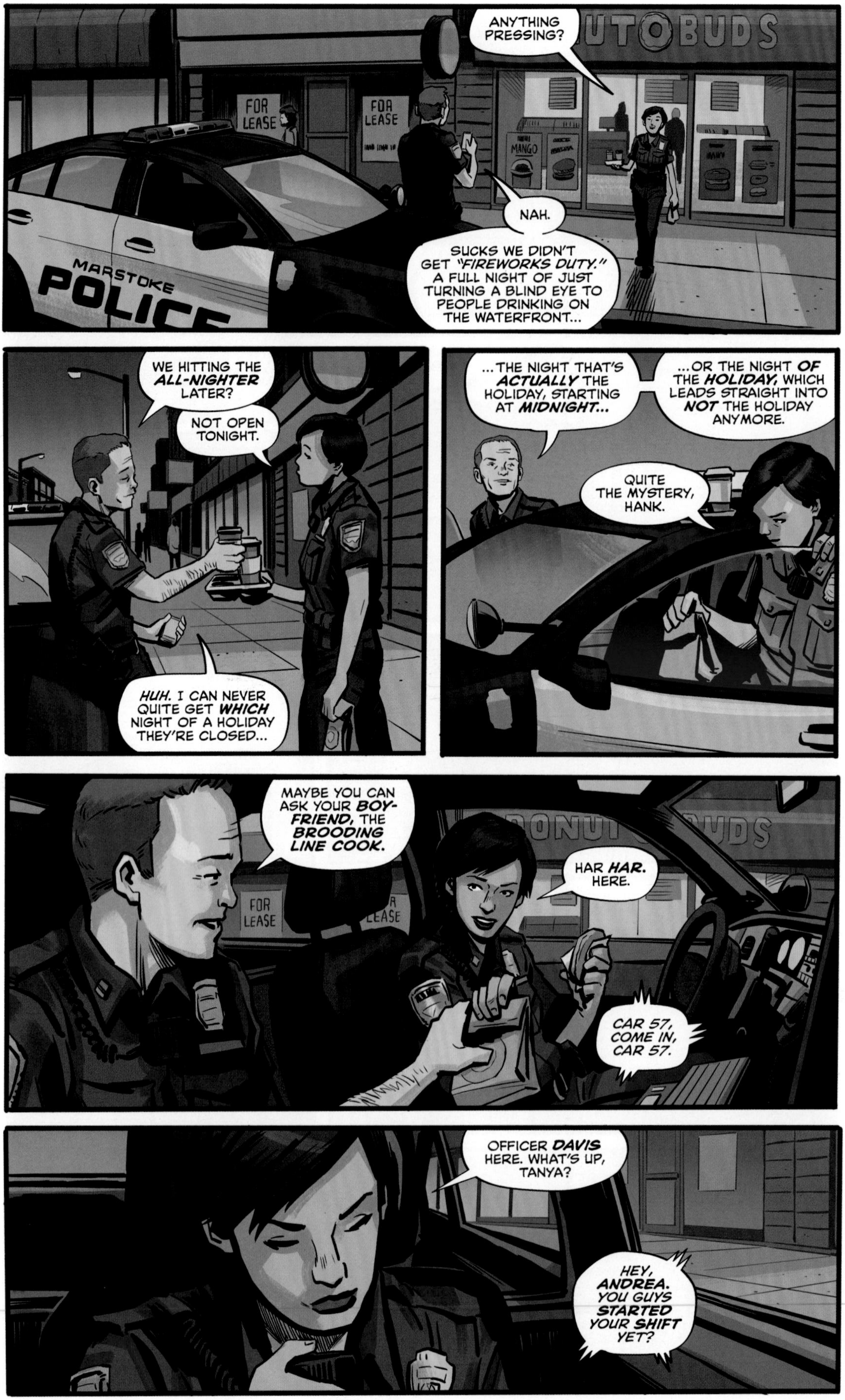
ANYTHING PRESSING?
UTOBUDS
FOR LEASE
FOR LEASE
MANGO
MARSTOKE POLICE
NAH.
SUCKS WE DIDN'T GET "FIREWORKS DUTY." A FULL NIGHT OF JUST TURNING A BLIND EYE TO PEOPLE DRINKING ON THE WATERFRONT...
WE HITTING THE ALL-NIGHTER LATER?
NOT OPEN TONIGHT.
HUH. I CAN NEVER QUITE GET WHICH NIGHT OF A HOLIDAY THEY'RE CLOSED...
...THE NIGHT THAT'S ACTUALLY THE HOLIDAY, STARTING AT MIDNIGHT...
...OR THE NIGHT OF THE HOLIDAY, WHICH LEADS STRAIGHT INTO NOT THE HOLIDAY ANYMORE.
QUITE THE MYSTERY, HANK.
MAYBE YOU CAN ASK YOUR BOY-FRIEND, THE BROODING LINE COOK.
FOR LEASE
HAR HAR. HERE.
CAR 57, COME IN, CAR 57.
OFFICER DAVIS HERE. WHAT'S UP, TANYA?
HEY, ANDREA. YOU GUYS STARTED YOUR SHIFT YET?

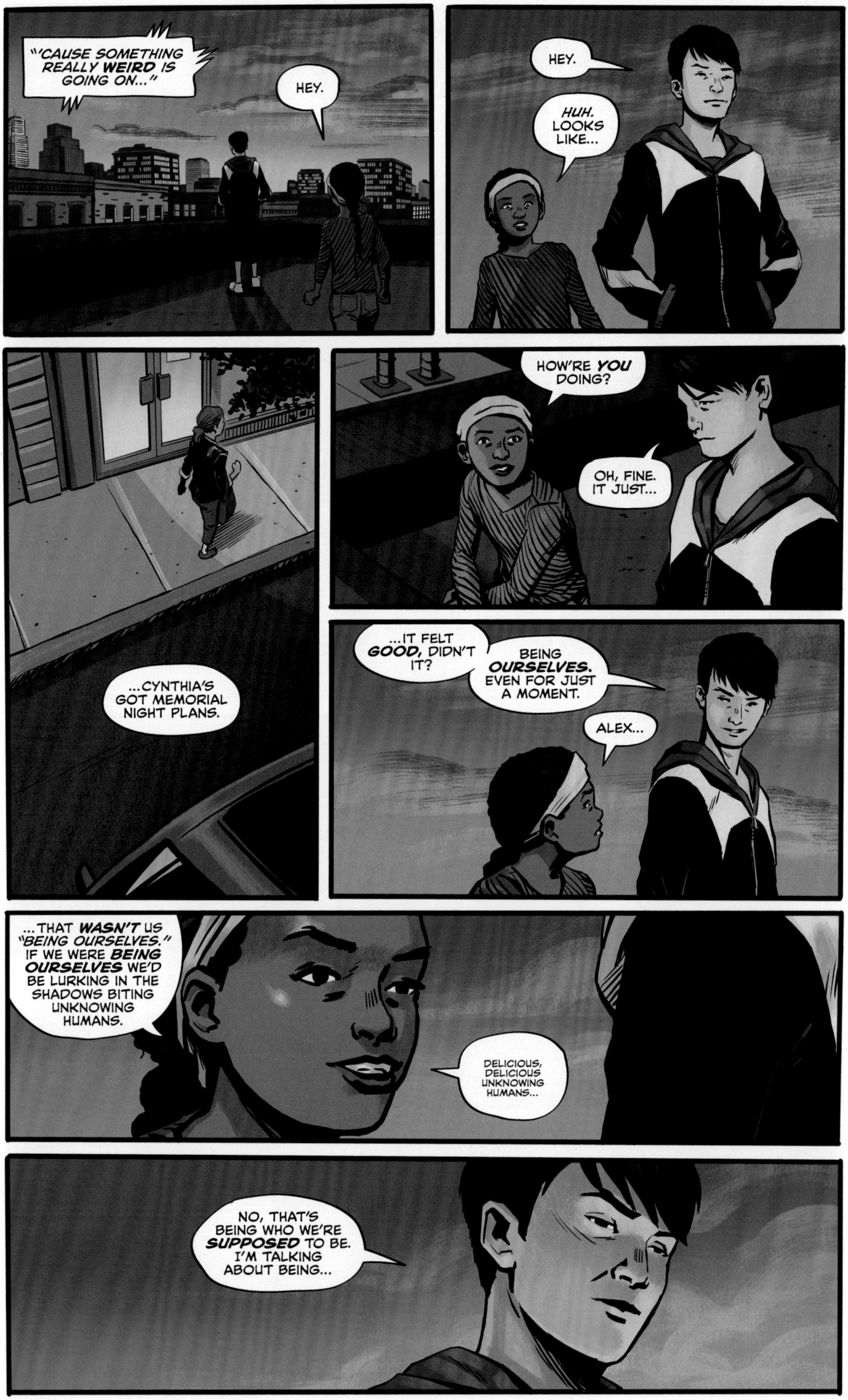
"'CAUSE SOMETHING REALLY WEIRD IS GOING ON..."
HEY.
HEY.
HUH. LOOKS LIKE...
...CYNTHIA'S GOT MEMORIAL NIGHT PLANS.
HOW'RE YOU DOING?
OH, FINE. IT JUST...
...IT FELT GOOD, DIDN'T IT?
BEING OURSELVES. EVEN FOR JUST A MOMENT.
ALEX...
...THAT WASN'T US "BEING OURSELVES." IF WE WERE BEING OURSELVES WE'D BE LURKING IN THE SHADOWS BITING UNKNOWING HUMANS.
DELICIOUS, DELICIOUS UNKNOWING HUMANS...
NO, THAT'S BEING WHO WE'RE SUPPOSED TO BE. I'M TALKING ABOUT BEING...

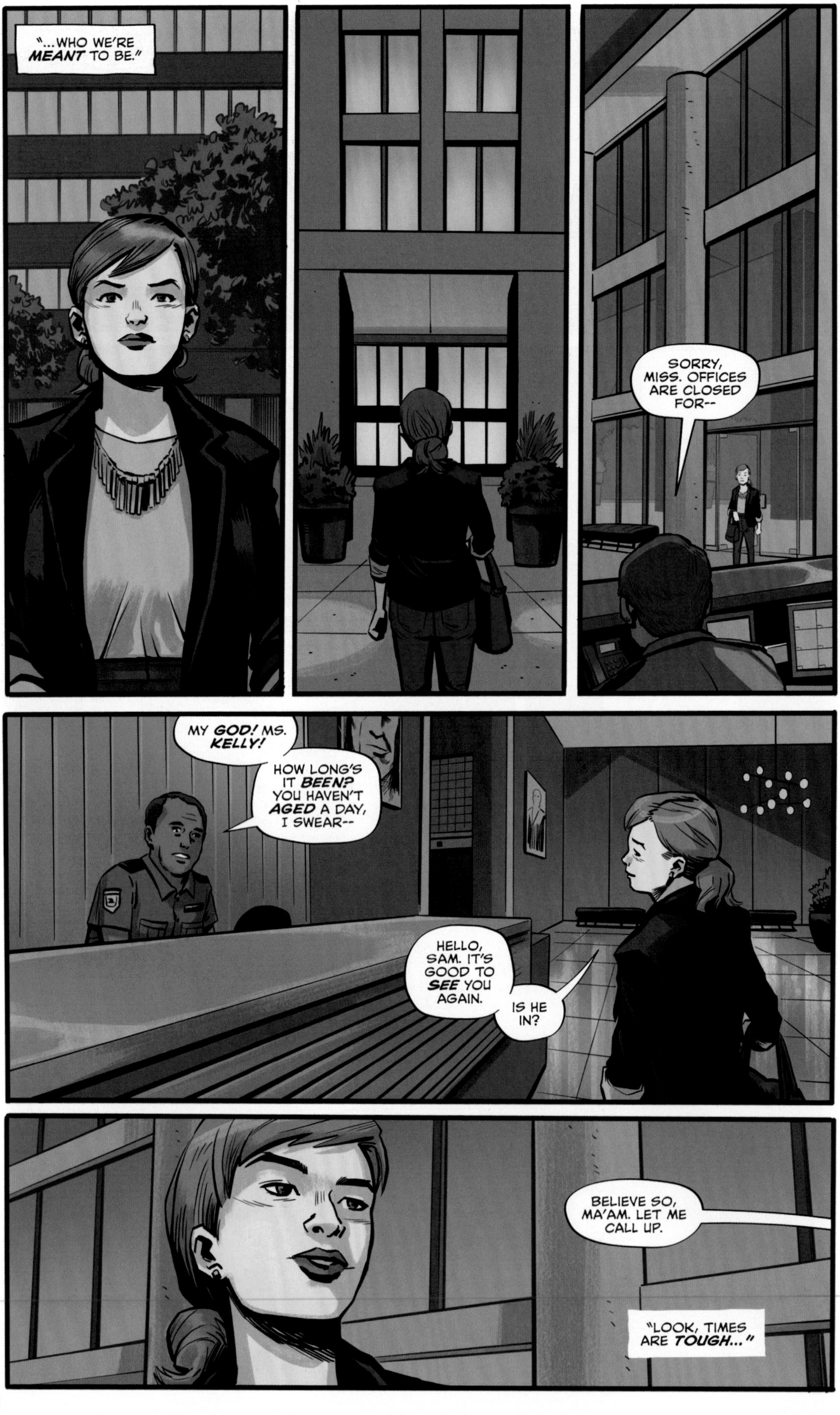
"...WHO WE'RE **MEANT** TO BE."
SORRY, MISS. OFFICES ARE CLOSED FOR--
MY **GOD!** MS. **KELLY!**
HOW LONG'S IT **BEEN?** YOU HAVEN'T **AGED** A DAY, I SWEAR--
HELLO, SAM. IT'S GOOD TO **SEE** YOU AGAIN.
IS HE IN?
BELIEVE SO, MA'AM. LET ME CALL UP.
"LOOK, TIMES ARE **TOUGH...**"

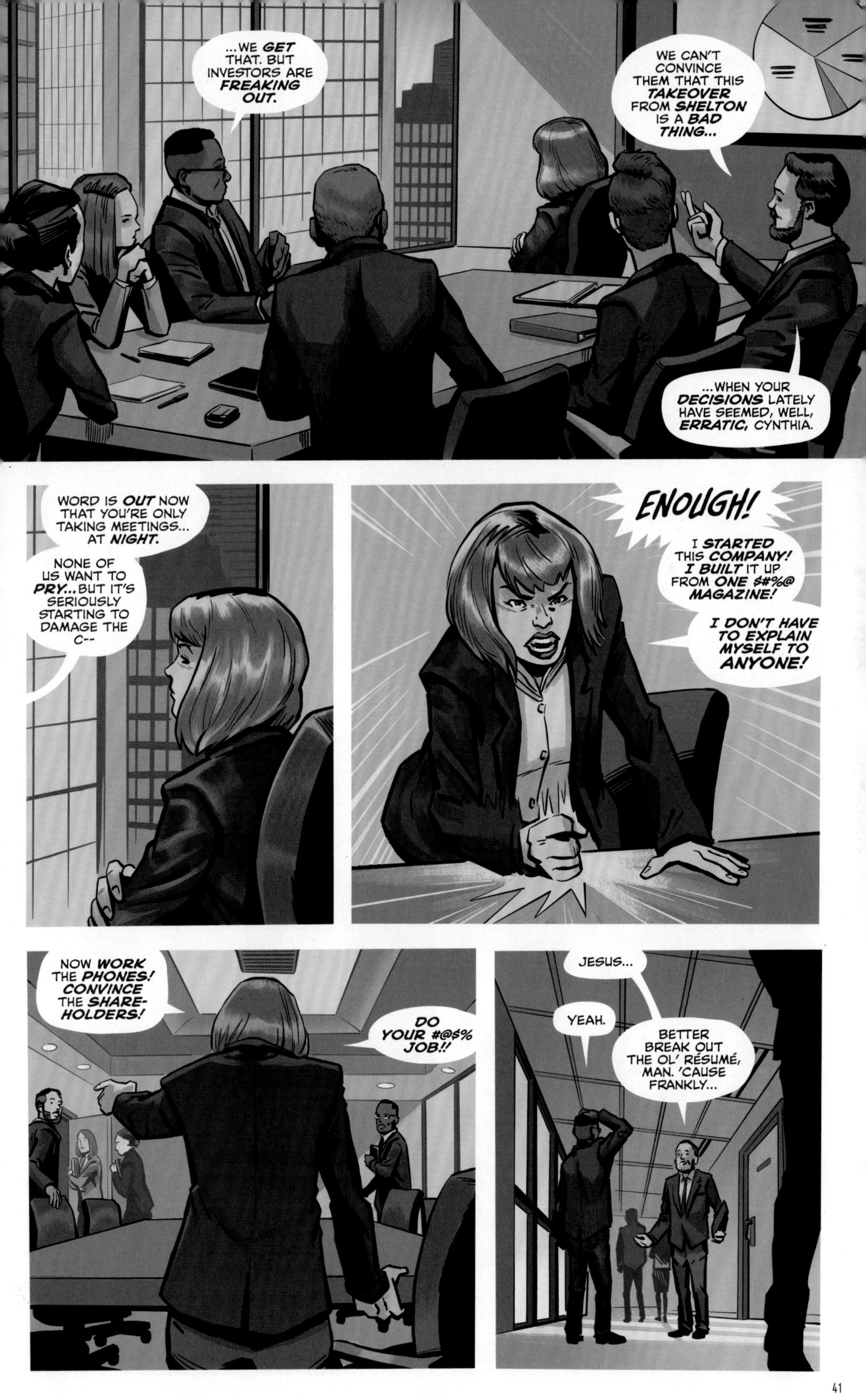
...WE GET THAT. BUT INVESTORS ARE FREAKING OUT.
WE CAN'T CONVINCE THEM THAT THIS TAKEOVER FROM SHELTON IS A BAD THING...
...WHEN YOUR DECISIONS LATELY HAVE SEEMED, WELL, ERRATIC, CYNTHIA.
WORD IS OUT NOW THAT YOU'RE ONLY TAKING MEETINGS... AT NIGHT.
NONE OF US WANT TO PRY...BUT IT'S SERIOUSLY STARTING TO DAMAGE THE C--
ENOUGH!
I STARTED THIS COMPANY! I BUILT IT UP FROM ONE $#%@ MAGAZINE!
I DON'T HAVE TO EXPLAIN MYSELF TO ANYONE!
NOW WORK THE PHONES! CONVINCE THE SHARE-HOLDERS!
DO YOUR #@$% JOB!!
JESUS...
YEAH.
BETTER BREAK OUT THE OL' RÉSUMÉ, MAN. 'CAUSE FRANKLY...

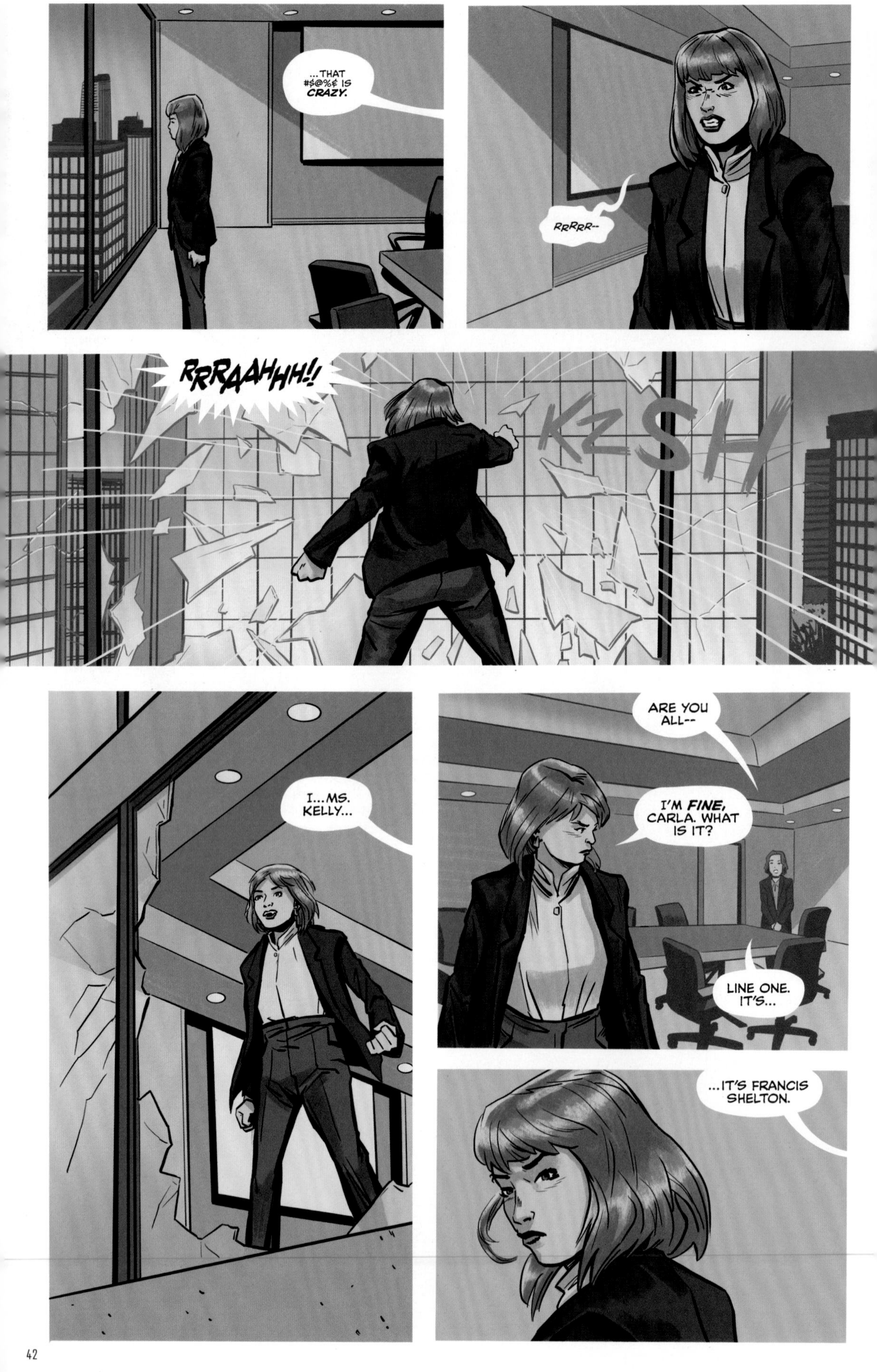
...THAT #$@%¢ IS *CRAZY.*
RRRRR--
RRRAAHHH!!
KZSH
I...MS. KELLY...
ARE YOU ALL--
I'M *FINE,* CARLA. WHAT IS IT?
LINE ONE. IT'S...
...IT'S FRANCIS SHELTON.

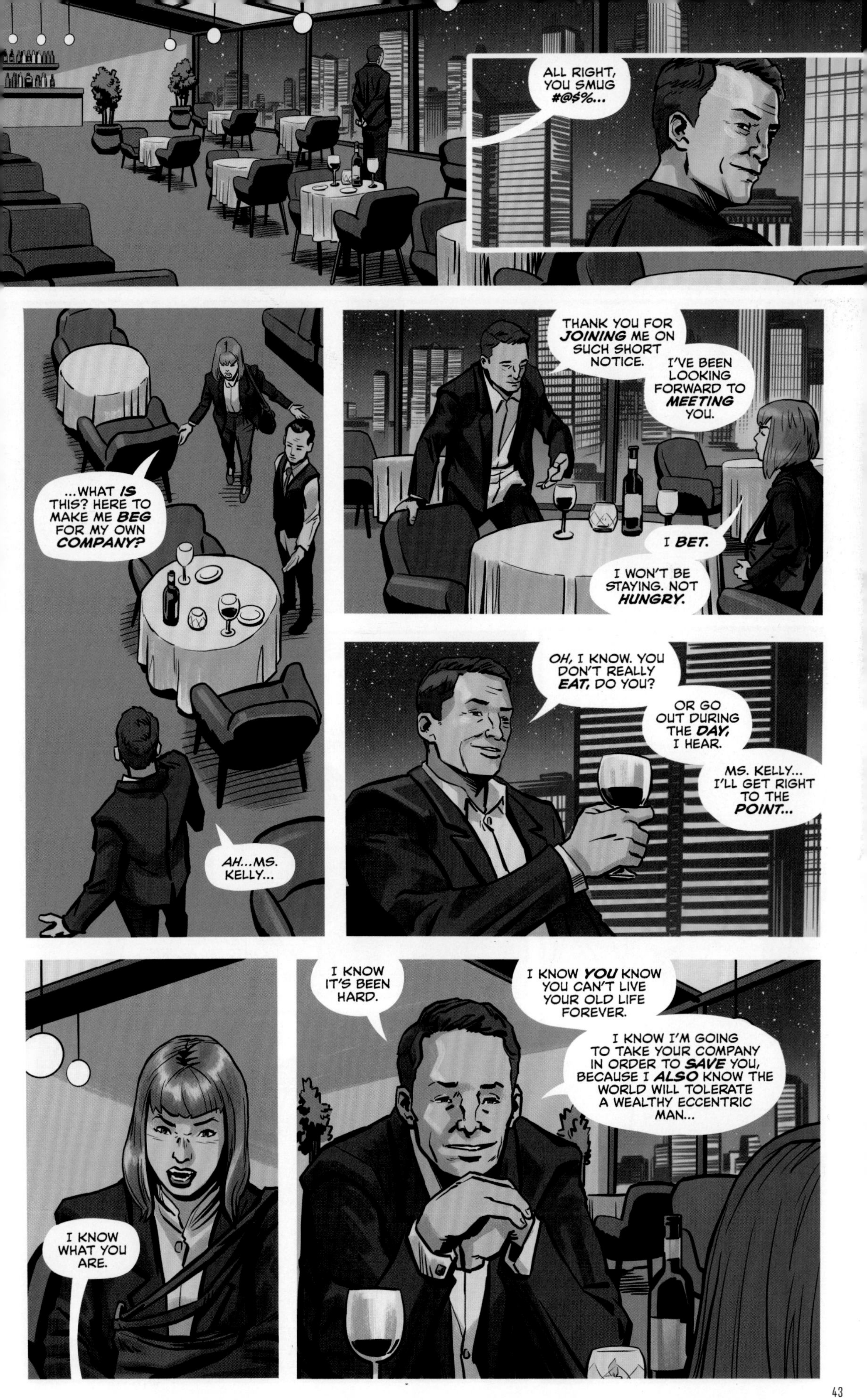
ALL RIGHT, YOU SMUG #@$%...
...WHAT IS THIS? HERE TO MAKE ME BEG FOR MY OWN COMPANY?
AH...MS. KELLY...
THANK YOU FOR JOINING ME ON SUCH SHORT NOTICE.
I'VE BEEN LOOKING FORWARD TO MEETING YOU.
I BET.
I WON'T BE STAYING. NOT HUNGRY.
OH, I KNOW. YOU DON'T REALLY EAT, DO YOU?
OR GO OUT DURING THE DAY, I HEAR.
MS. KELLY... I'LL GET RIGHT TO THE POINT...
I KNOW WHAT YOU ARE.
I KNOW IT'S BEEN HARD.
I KNOW YOU KNOW YOU CAN'T LIVE YOUR OLD LIFE FOREVER.
I KNOW I'M GOING TO TAKE YOUR COMPANY IN ORDER TO SAVE YOU, BECAUSE I ALSO KNOW THE WORLD WILL TOLERATE A WEALTHY ECCENTRIC MAN...

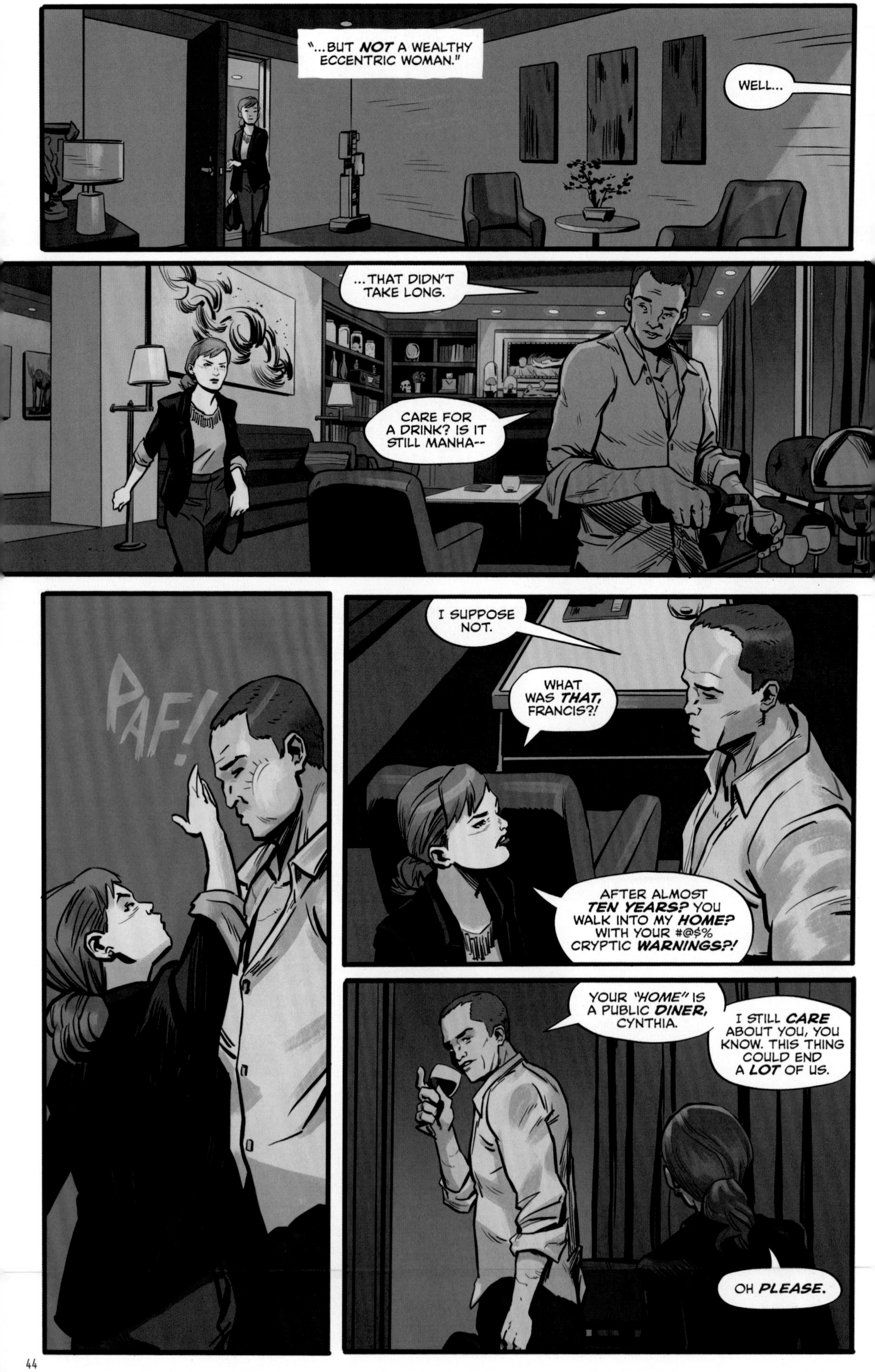
"...BUT NOT A WEALTHY ECCENTRIC WOMAN."
WELL...
...THAT DIDN'T TAKE LONG.
CARE FOR A DRINK? IS IT STILL MANHA--
PAF!
I SUPPOSE NOT.
WHAT WAS THAT, FRANCIS?!
AFTER ALMOST TEN YEARS? YOU WALK INTO MY HOME? WITH YOUR #@$% CRYPTIC WARNINGS?!
YOUR "HOME" IS A PUBLIC DINER, CYNTHIA.
I STILL CARE ABOUT YOU, YOU KNOW. THIS THING COULD END A LOT OF US.
OH PLEASE.

IT'S TRUE. I'VE BEEN *AROUND* LONGER THAN YOU. I CAN *SENSE* THESE THINGS.

I'M *HERE* TO TELL YOU TO LEAVE MY FRIENDS *ALONE*, NOT TO HEAR ABOUT SOME #@$¢--

IT'S IMPORTANT.

IT'S FUNNY. ALL OUR TIME TOGETHER AND YOU NEVER ONCE ASKED ME ABOUT THE *BOOK.*

ABOUT *FRANKEN-STEIN.*

I ASSUME YOU NEVER ASKED BECAUSE YOU THOUGHT THE BOOK WAS WRITTEN *ABOUT* ME.

IT'S FUNNY HOW WE NEVER THINK TO ASK THE QUESTIONS THAT WE'RE SURE WE HAVE THE ANSWERS TO.

BUT YOU WERE WRONG.

MARY WROTE THE BOOK. CREATED THE CHARACTERS. THE FIRST "*SCIENCE FICTION*" NOVEL.

IT CHANGED THE WORLD, IMBUED IT WITH *INDELIBLE MAGIC.*

AND *THEN* I CAME TO BE.

I WOKE IN A FOREST, SCARED. MEMORIES OF THINGS THAT NEVER HAPPENED, THAT I KNEW IN MY ECLECTIC *BONES* HADN'T HAPPENED.

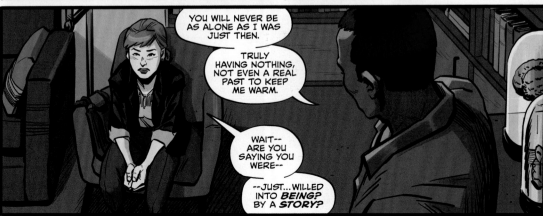

YOU WILL NEVER BE AS ALONE AS I WAS JUST THEN.

TRULY HAVING NOTHING, NOT EVEN A REAL PAST TO KEEP ME WARM.

WAIT-- ARE YOU SAYING YOU WERE--

--JUST...WILLED INTO *BEING?* BY A *STORY?*

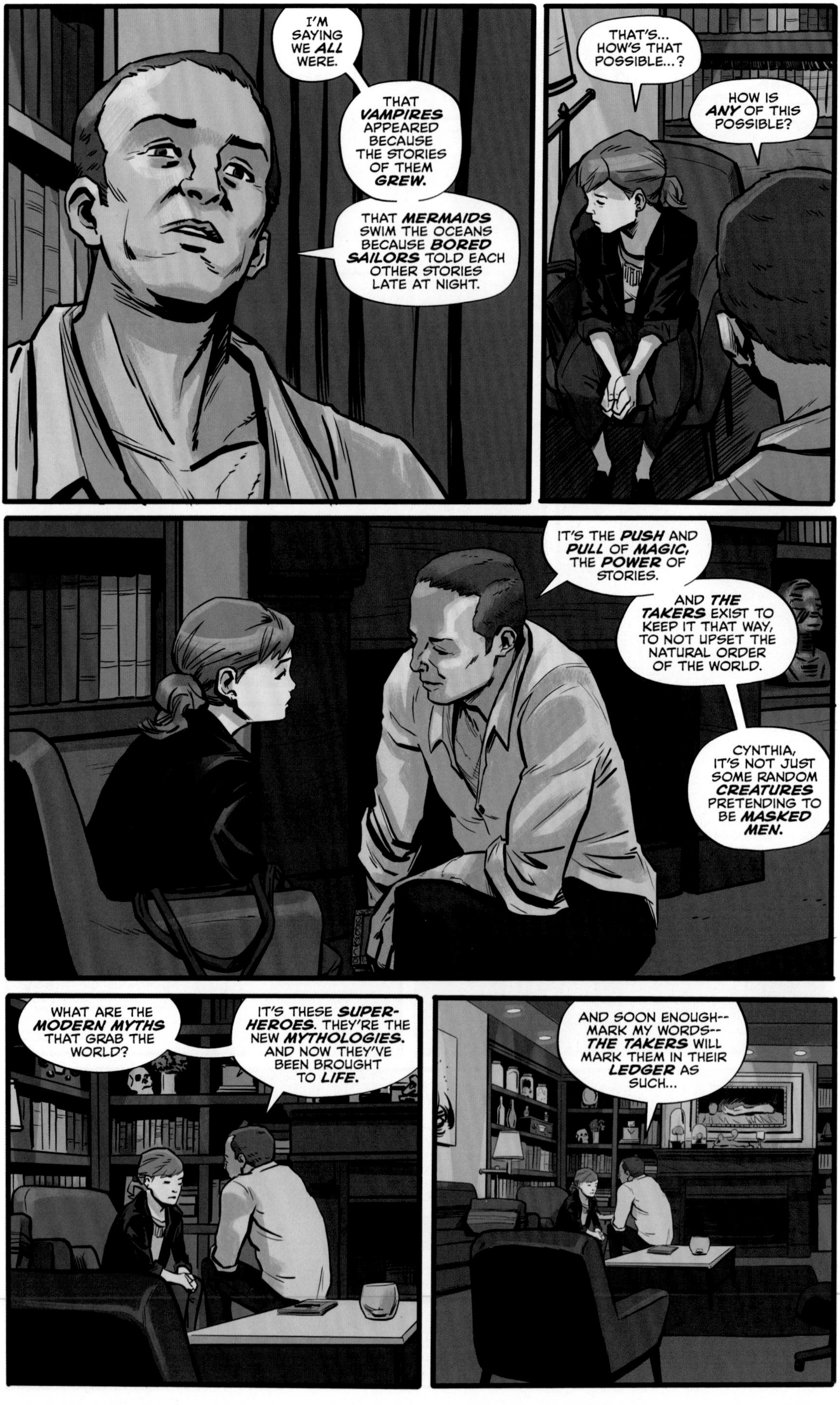
I'M SAYING WE ALL WERE.
THAT VAMPIRES APPEARED BECAUSE THE STORIES OF THEM GREW.
THAT MERMAIDS SWIM THE OCEANS BECAUSE BORED SAILORS TOLD EACH OTHER STORIES LATE AT NIGHT.
THAT'S... HOW'S THAT POSSIBLE...?
HOW IS ANY OF THIS POSSIBLE?
IT'S THE PUSH AND PULL OF MAGIC, THE POWER OF STORIES.
AND THE TAKERS EXIST TO KEEP IT THAT WAY, TO NOT UPSET THE NATURAL ORDER OF THE WORLD.
CYNTHIA, IT'S NOT JUST SOME RANDOM CREATURES PRETENDING TO BE MASKED MEN.
WHAT ARE THE MODERN MYTHS THAT GRAB THE WORLD?
IT'S THESE SUPER-HEROES. THEY'RE THE NEW MYTHOLOGIES. AND NOW THEY'VE BEEN BROUGHT TO LIFE.
AND SOON ENOUGH-- MARK MY WORDS-- THE TAKERS WILL MARK THEM IN THEIR LEDGER AS SUCH...

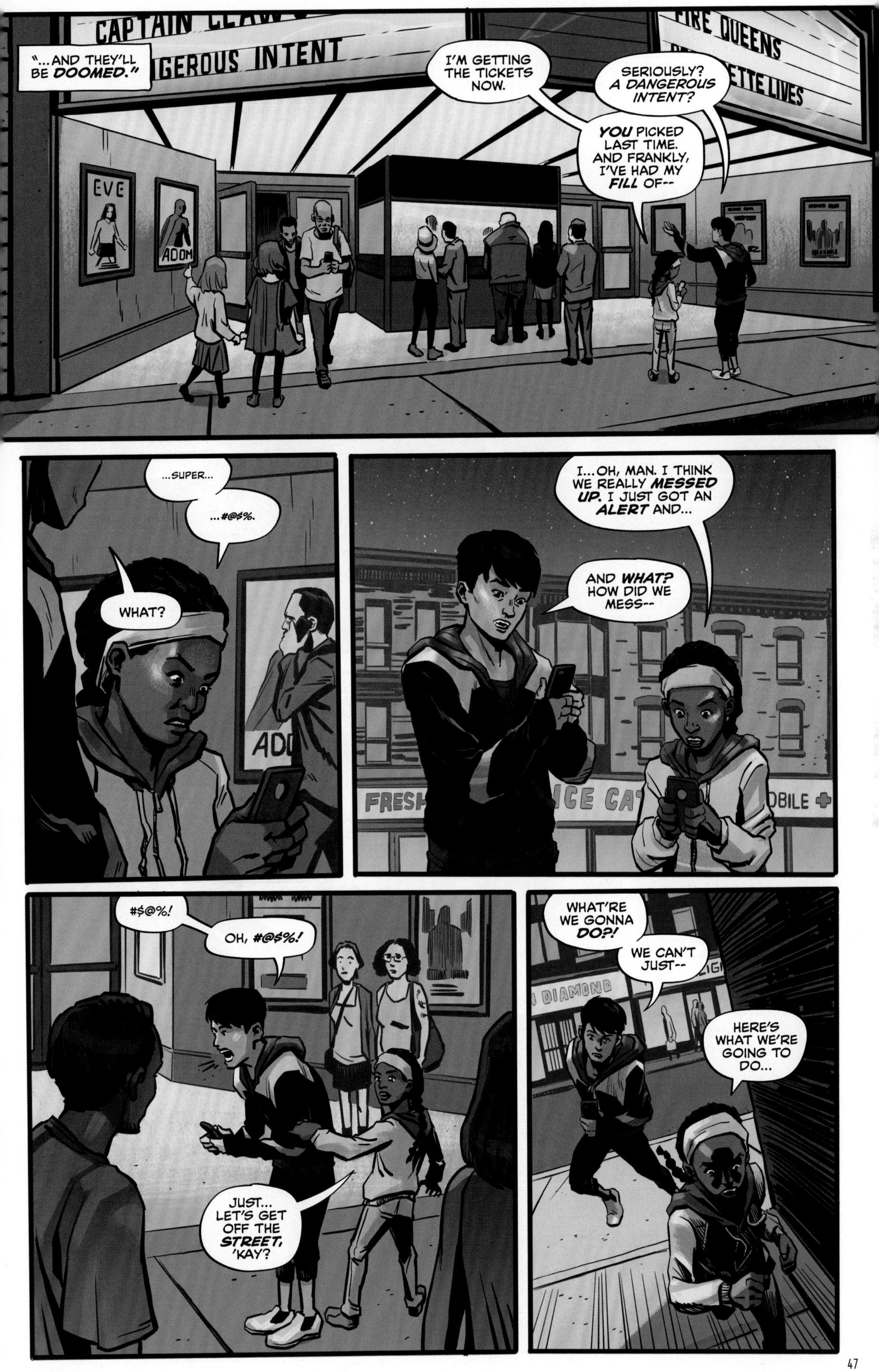

"...AND THEY'LL BE *DOOMED.*"
I'M GETTING THE TICKETS NOW.
SERIOUSLY? A *DANGEROUS INTENT*?
YOU PICKED LAST TIME. AND FRANKLY, I'VE HAD MY *FILL* OF--
FIRE QUEENS
EVE
ADOM
...SUPER...
...#@$%.
WHAT?
I...OH, MAN. I THINK WE REALLY *MESSED UP.* I JUST GOT AN *ALERT* AND...
AND *WHAT?* HOW DID WE MESS--
#$@%!
OH, *#@$%!*
JUST... LET'S GET OFF THE *STREET,* 'KAY?
WHAT'RE WE GONNA *DO?!*
WE CAN'T JUST--
HERE'S WHAT WE'RE GOING TO DO...

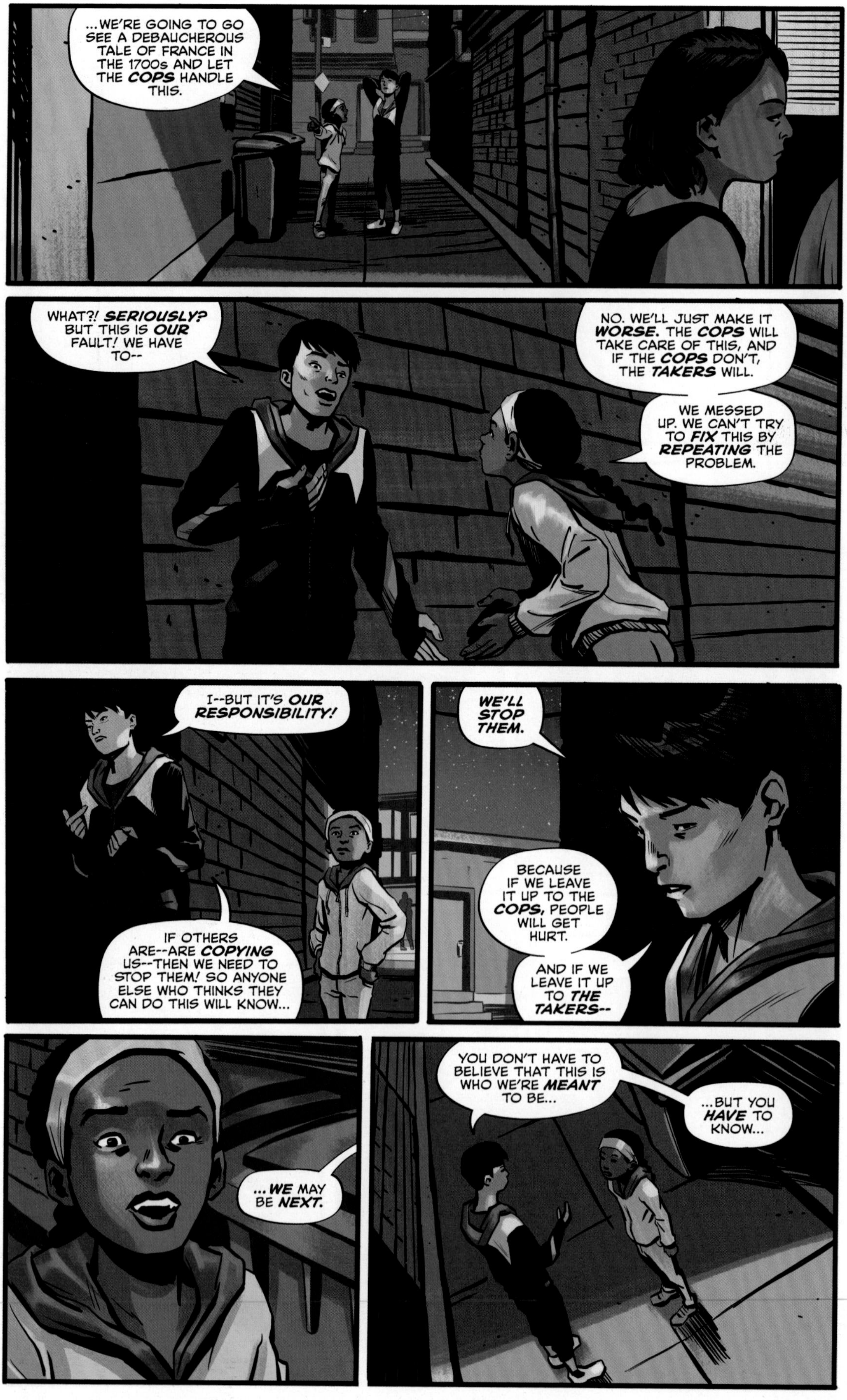
...WE'RE GOING TO GO SEE A DEBAUCHEROUS TALE OF FRANCE IN THE 1700s AND LET THE COPS HANDLE THIS.
WHAT?! SERIOUSLY? BUT THIS IS OUR FAULT! WE HAVE TO--
NO. WE'LL JUST MAKE IT WORSE. THE COPS WILL TAKE CARE OF THIS, AND IF THE COPS DON'T, THE TAKERS WILL.
WE MESSED UP. WE CAN'T TRY TO FIX THIS BY REPEATING THE PROBLEM.
I--BUT IT'S OUR RESPONSIBILITY!
IF OTHERS ARE--ARE COPYING US--THEN WE NEED TO STOP THEM! SO ANYONE ELSE WHO THINKS THEY CAN DO THIS WILL KNOW...
WE'LL STOP THEM.
BECAUSE IF WE LEAVE IT UP TO THE COPS, PEOPLE WILL GET HURT.
AND IF WE LEAVE IT UP TO THE TAKERS--
...WE MAY BE NEXT.
YOU DON'T HAVE TO BELIEVE THAT THIS IS WHO WE'RE MEANT TO BE...
...BUT YOU HAVE TO KNOW...

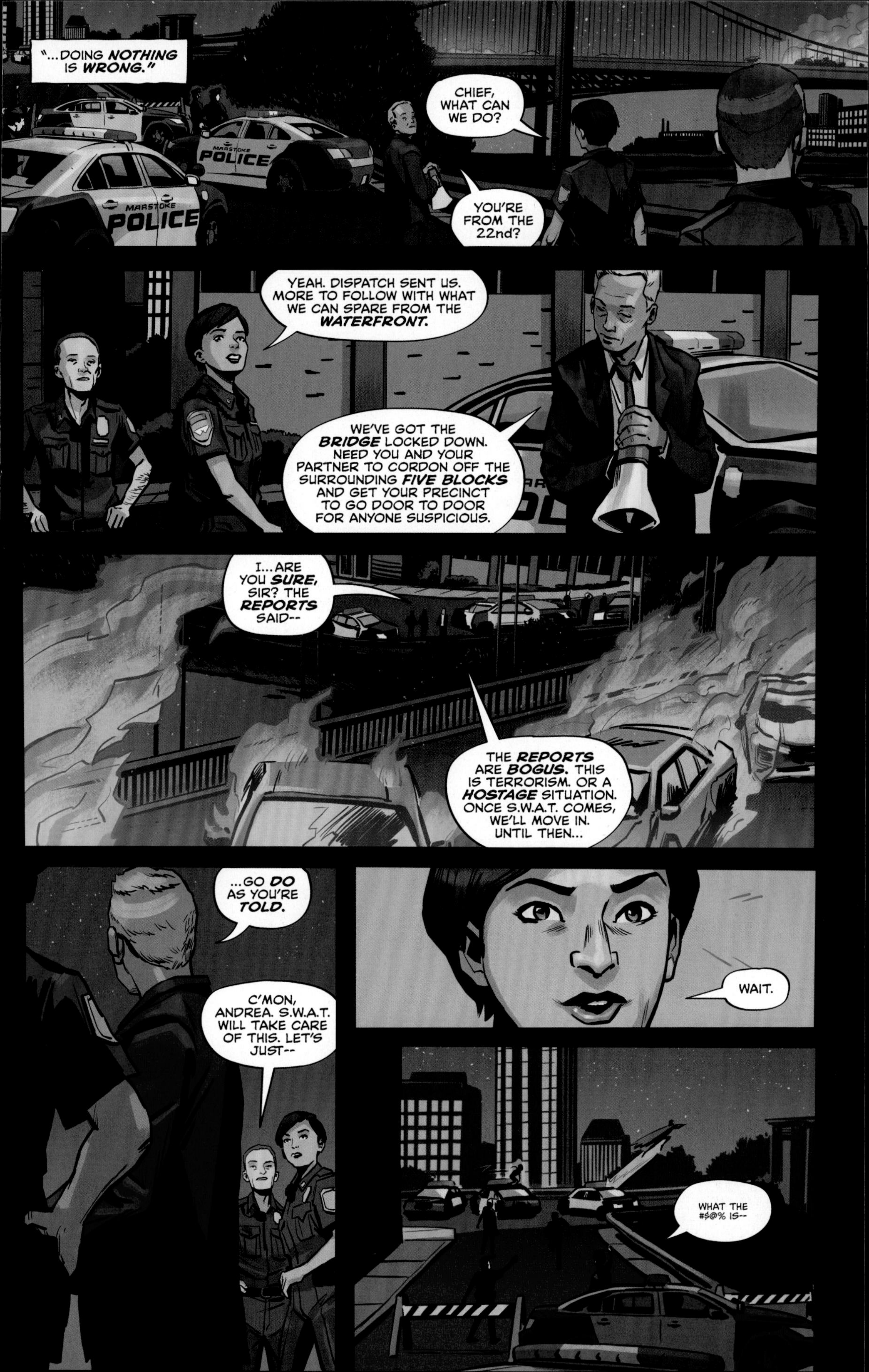
"...DOING NOTHING IS WRONG."
CHIEF, WHAT CAN WE DO?
YOU'RE FROM THE 22nd?
MARSTOKE POLICE
YEAH. DISPATCH SENT US. MORE TO FOLLOW WITH WHAT WE CAN SPARE FROM THE WATERFRONT.
WE'VE GOT THE BRIDGE LOCKED DOWN. NEED YOU AND YOUR PARTNER TO CORDON OFF THE SURROUNDING FIVE BLOCKS AND GET YOUR PRECINCT TO GO DOOR TO DOOR FOR ANYONE SUSPICIOUS.
I...ARE YOU SURE, SIR? THE REPORTS SAID--
THE REPORTS ARE BOGUS. THIS IS TERRORISM. OR A HOSTAGE SITUATION. ONCE S.W.A.T. COMES, WE'LL MOVE IN. UNTIL THEN...
...GO DO AS YOU'RE TOLD.
C'MON, ANDREA. S.W.A.T. WILL TAKE CARE OF THIS. LET'S JUST--
WAIT.
WHAT THE #$@% IS--

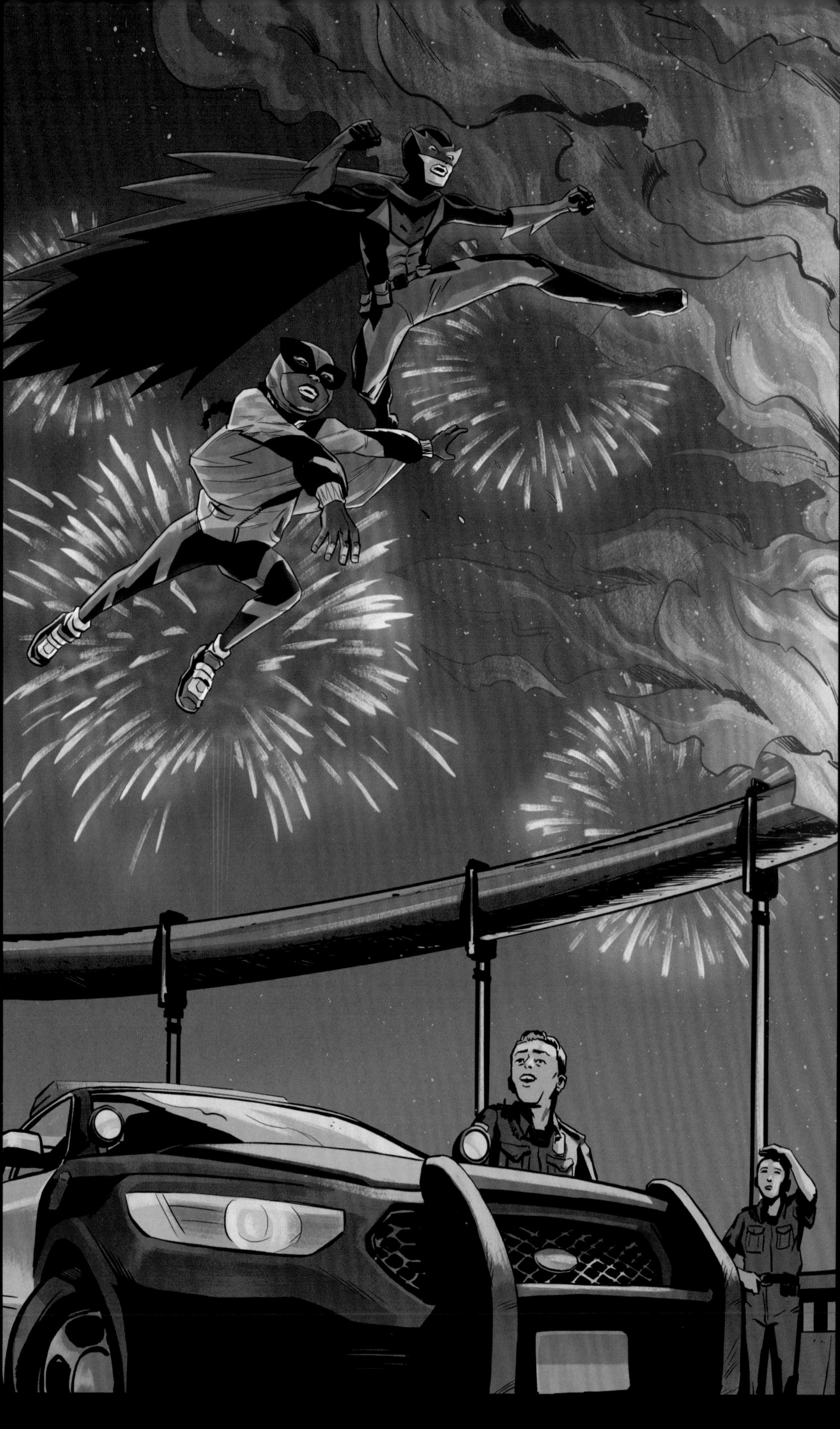

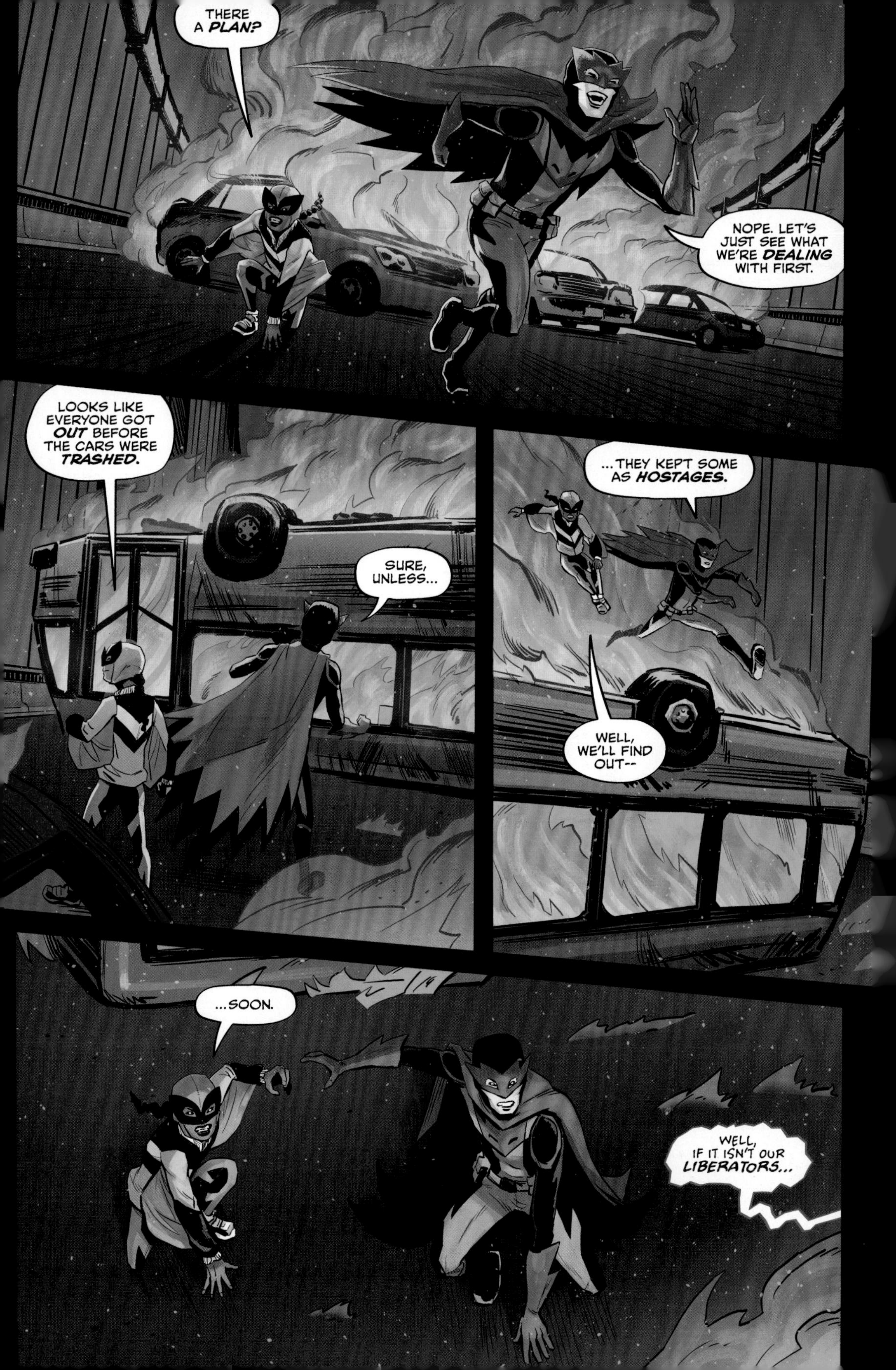
THERE A PLAN?
NOPE. LET'S JUST SEE WHAT WE'RE DEALING WITH FIRST.
LOOKS LIKE EVERYONE GOT OUT BEFORE THE CARS WERE TRASHED.
SURE, UNLESS...
...THEY KEPT SOME AS HOSTAGES.
WELL, WE'LL FIND OUT--
...SOON.
WELL, IF IT ISN'T OUR LIBERATORS...

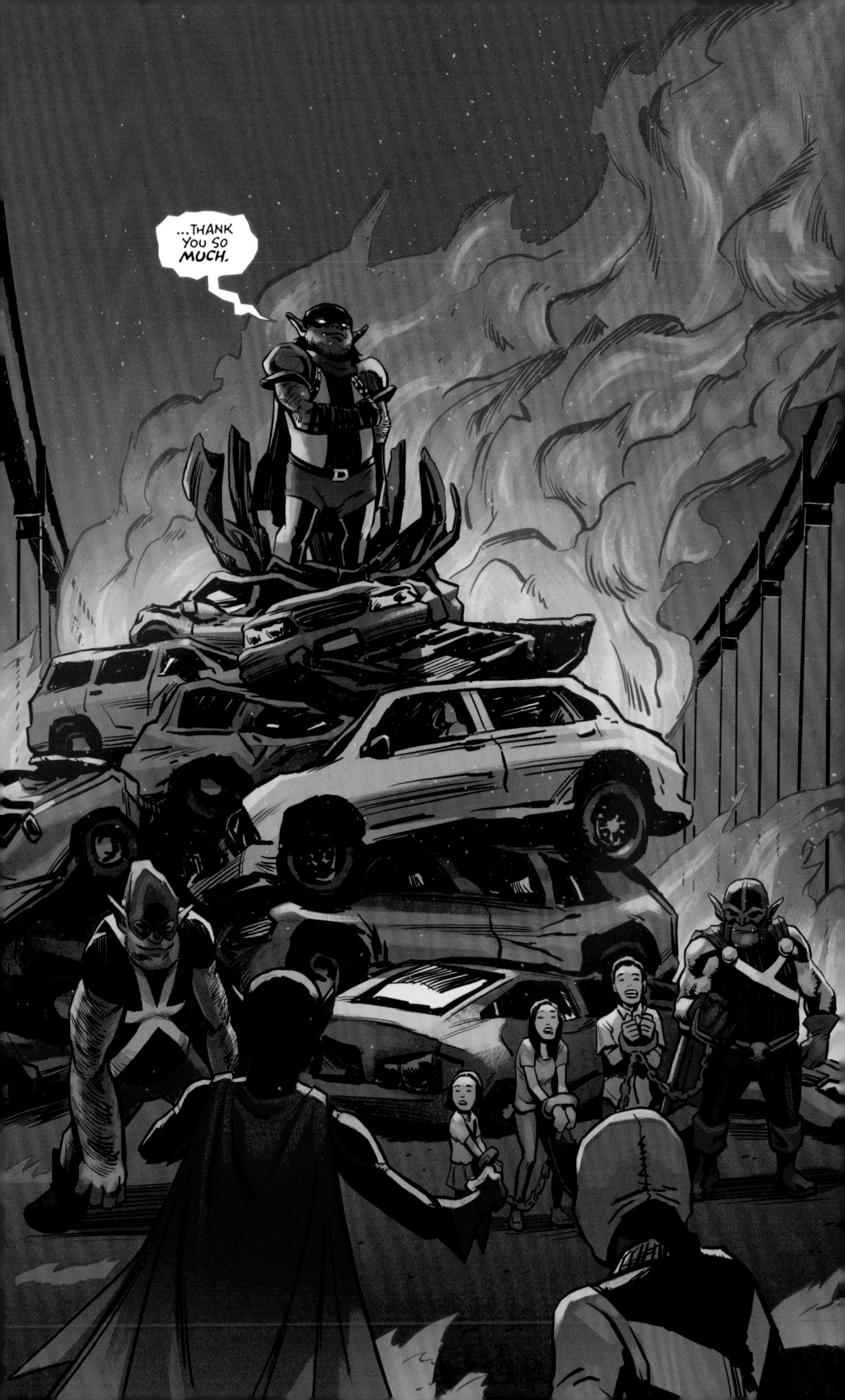
...THANK YOU SO MUCH.

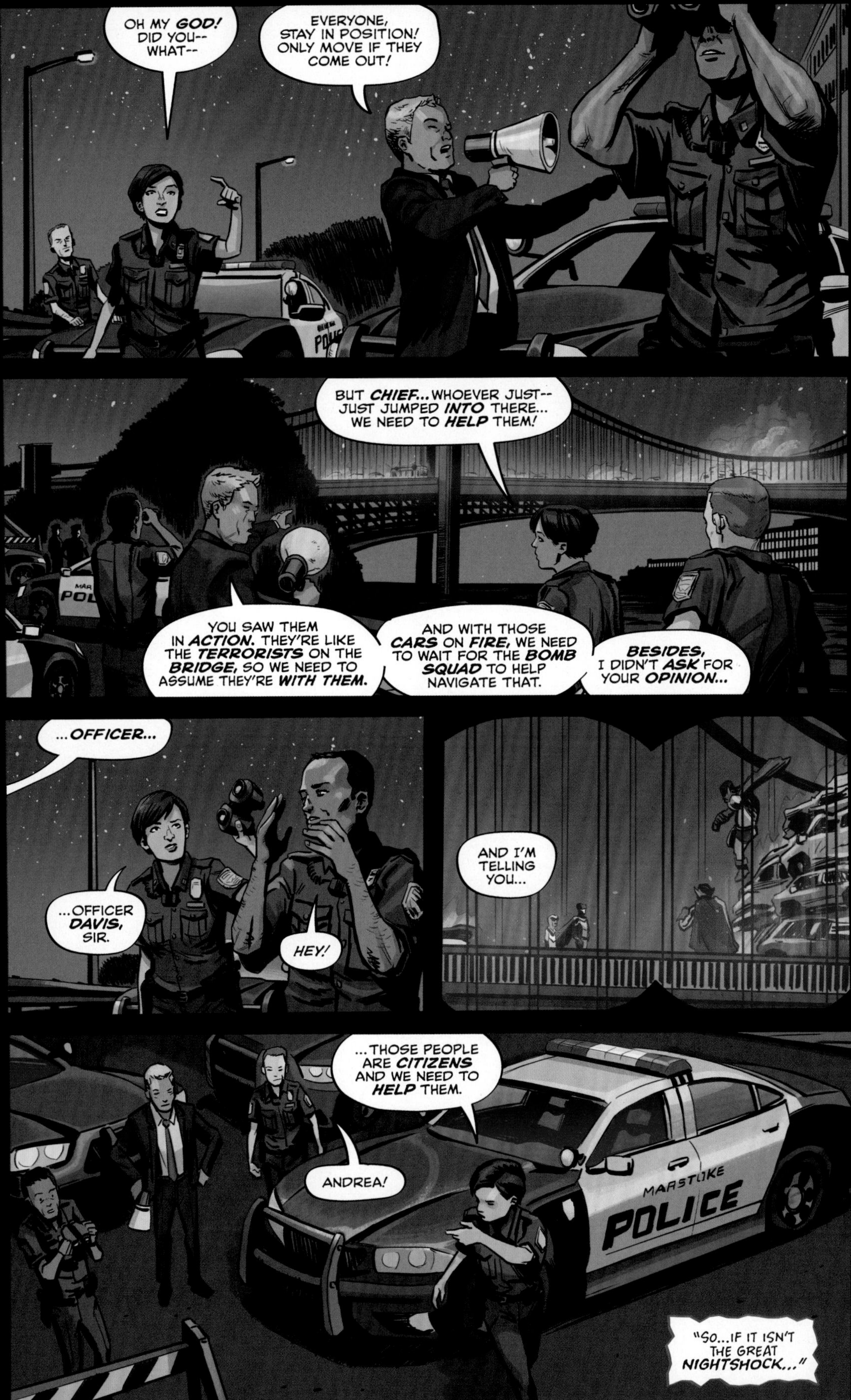
OH MY GOD! DID YOU-- WHAT--
EVERYONE, STAY IN POSITION! ONLY MOVE IF THEY COME OUT!
BUT CHIEF... WHOEVER JUST-- JUST JUMPED INTO THERE... WE NEED TO HELP THEM!
YOU SAW THEM IN ACTION. THEY'RE LIKE THE TERRORISTS ON THE BRIDGE, SO WE NEED TO ASSUME THEY'RE WITH THEM.
AND WITH THOSE CARS ON FIRE, WE NEED TO WAIT FOR THE BOMB SQUAD TO HELP NAVIGATE THAT.
BESIDES, I DIDN'T ASK FOR YOUR OPINION...
...OFFICER...
...OFFICER DAVIS, SIR.
HEY!
AND I'M TELLING YOU...
...THOSE PEOPLE ARE CITIZENS AND WE NEED TO HELP THEM.
ANDREA!
MARSTLKE
POLICE
"SO...IF IT ISN'T THE GREAT NIGHTSHOCK..."

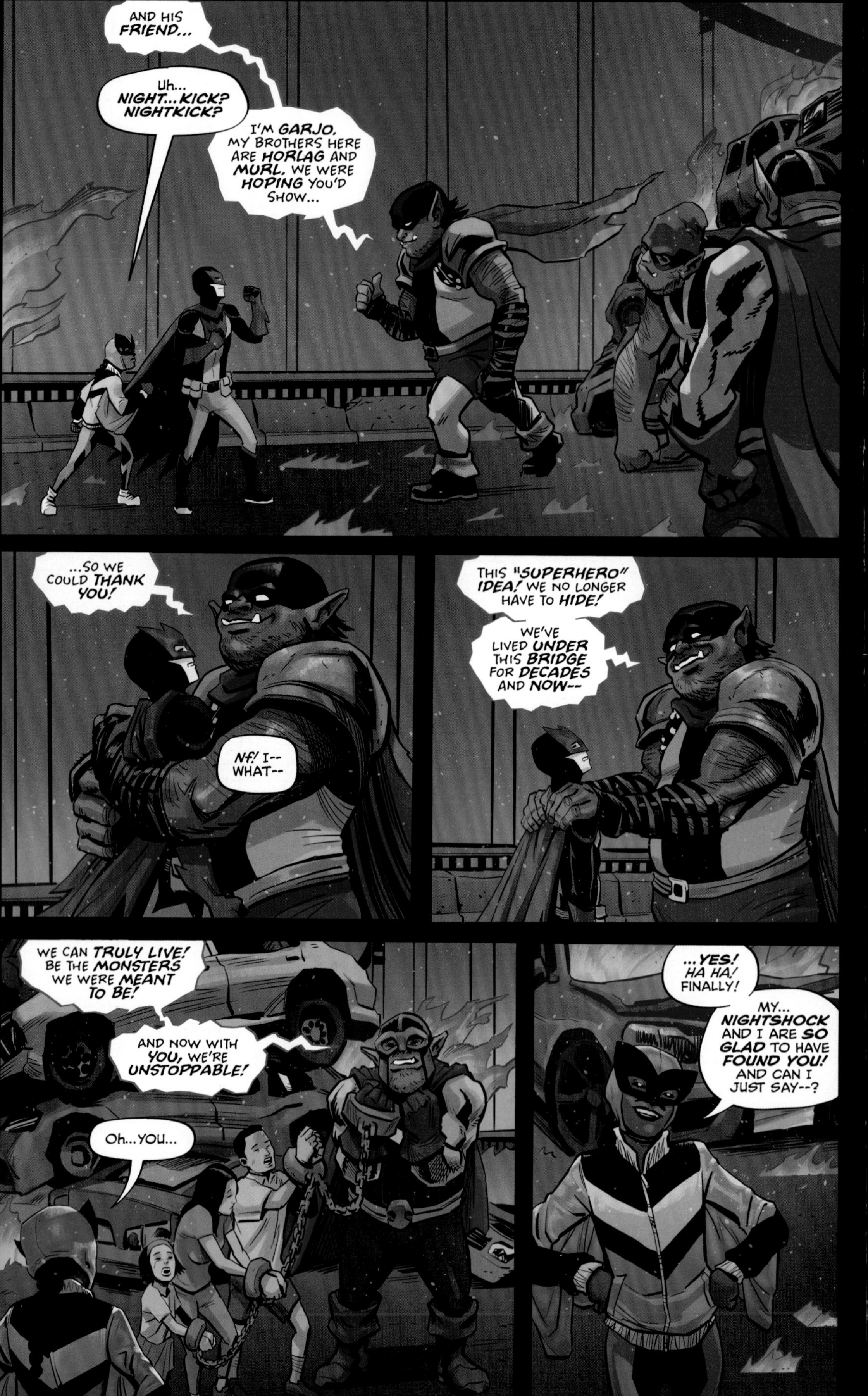
AND HIS FRIEND...
Uh... NIGHT...KICK? NIGHTKICK?
I'M GARJO. MY BROTHERS HERE ARE HORLAG AND MURL. WE WERE HOPING YOU'D SHOW...
...SO WE COULD THANK YOU!
Nf! I-- WHAT--
THIS "SUPERHERO" IDEA! WE NO LONGER HAVE TO HIDE!
WE'VE LIVED UNDER THIS BRIDGE FOR DECADES AND NOW--
WE CAN TRULY LIVE! BE THE MONSTERS WE WERE MEANT TO BE!
AND NOW WITH YOU, WE'RE UNSTOPPABLE!
Oh...YOU...
...YES! HA HA! FINALLY!
MY... NIGHTSHOCK AND I ARE SO GLAD TO HAVE FOUND YOU! AND CAN I JUST SAY--?

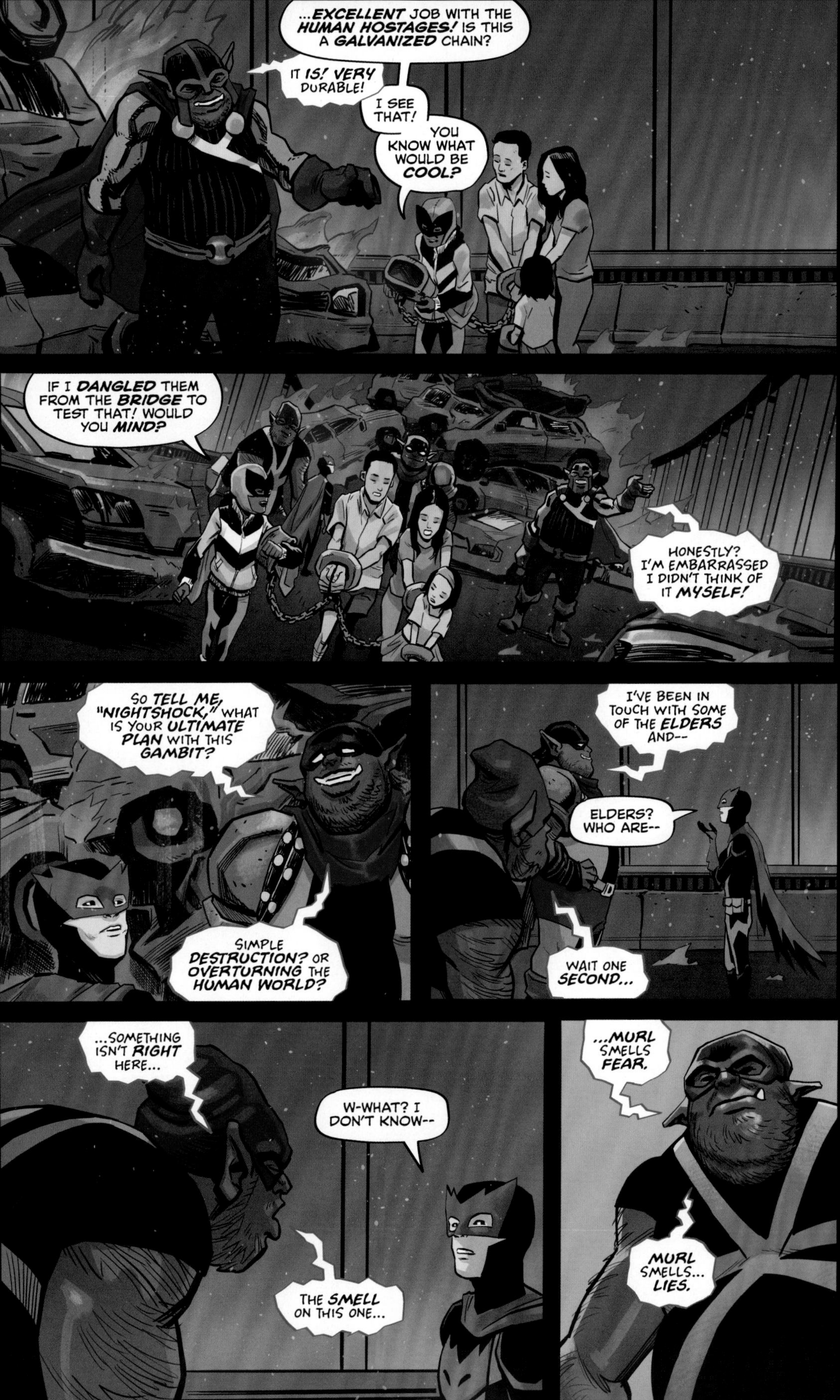
...EXCELLENT JOB WITH THE HUMAN HOSTAGES! IS THIS A GALVANIZED CHAIN?
IT IS! VERY DURABLE!
I SEE THAT!
YOU KNOW WHAT WOULD BE COOL?
IF I DANGLED THEM FROM THE BRIDGE TO TEST THAT! WOULD YOU MIND?
HONESTLY? I'M EMBARRASSED I DIDN'T THINK OF IT MYSELF!
SO TELL ME, "NIGHTSHOCK," WHAT IS YOUR ULTIMATE PLAN WITH THIS GAMBIT?
SIMPLE DESTRUCTION? OR OVERTURNING THE HUMAN WORLD?
I'VE BEEN IN TOUCH WITH SOME OF THE ELDERS AND--
ELDERS? WHO ARE--
WAIT ONE SECOND...
...SOMETHING ISN'T RIGHT HERE...
W-WHAT? I DON'T KNOW--
THE SMELL ON THIS ONE...
...MURL SMELLS FEAR.
MURL SMELLS... LIES.

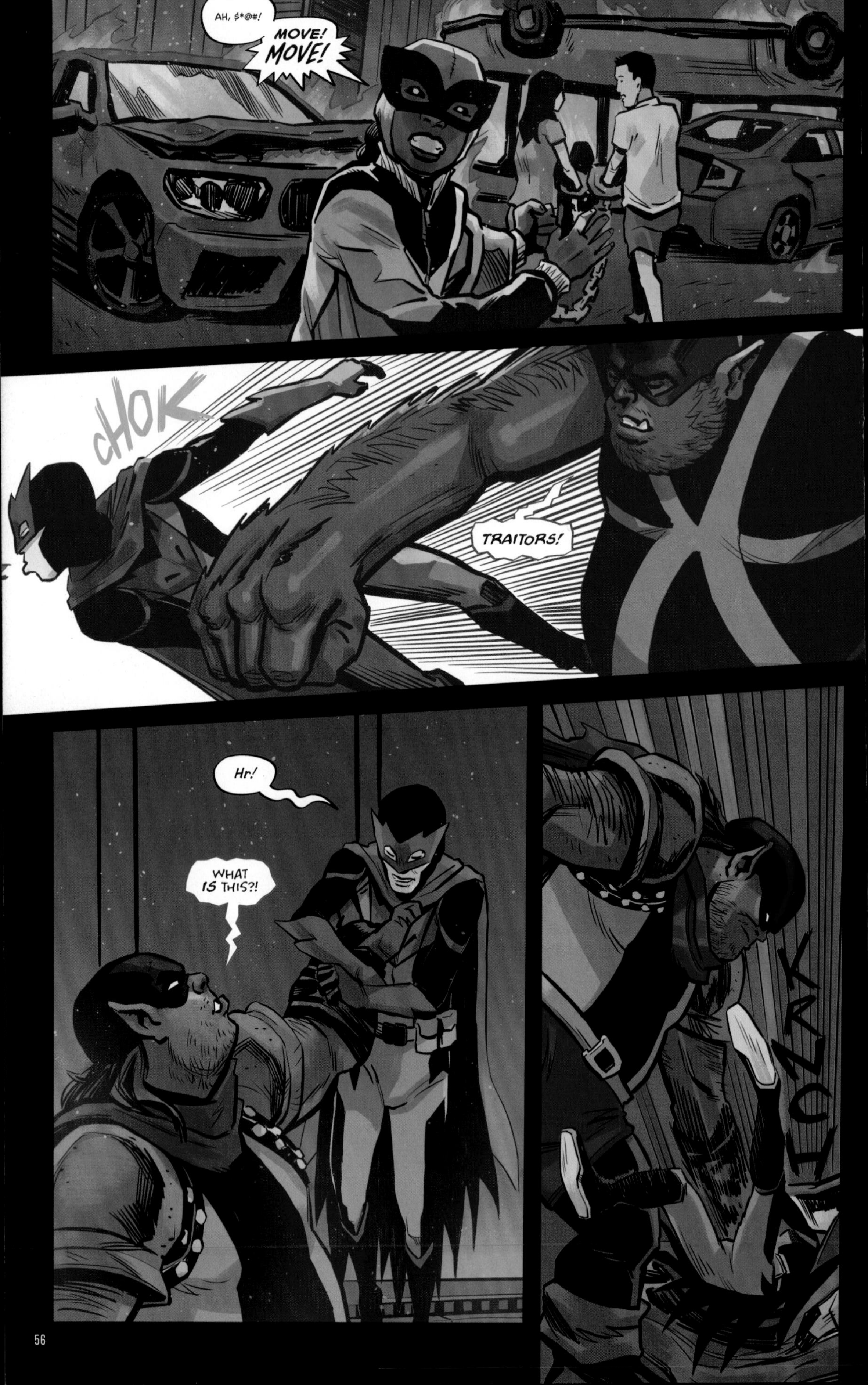
AH, $*@#!
MOVE! MOVE!
CHOK
TRAITORS!
Hr!
WHAT IS THIS?!
KRNCH

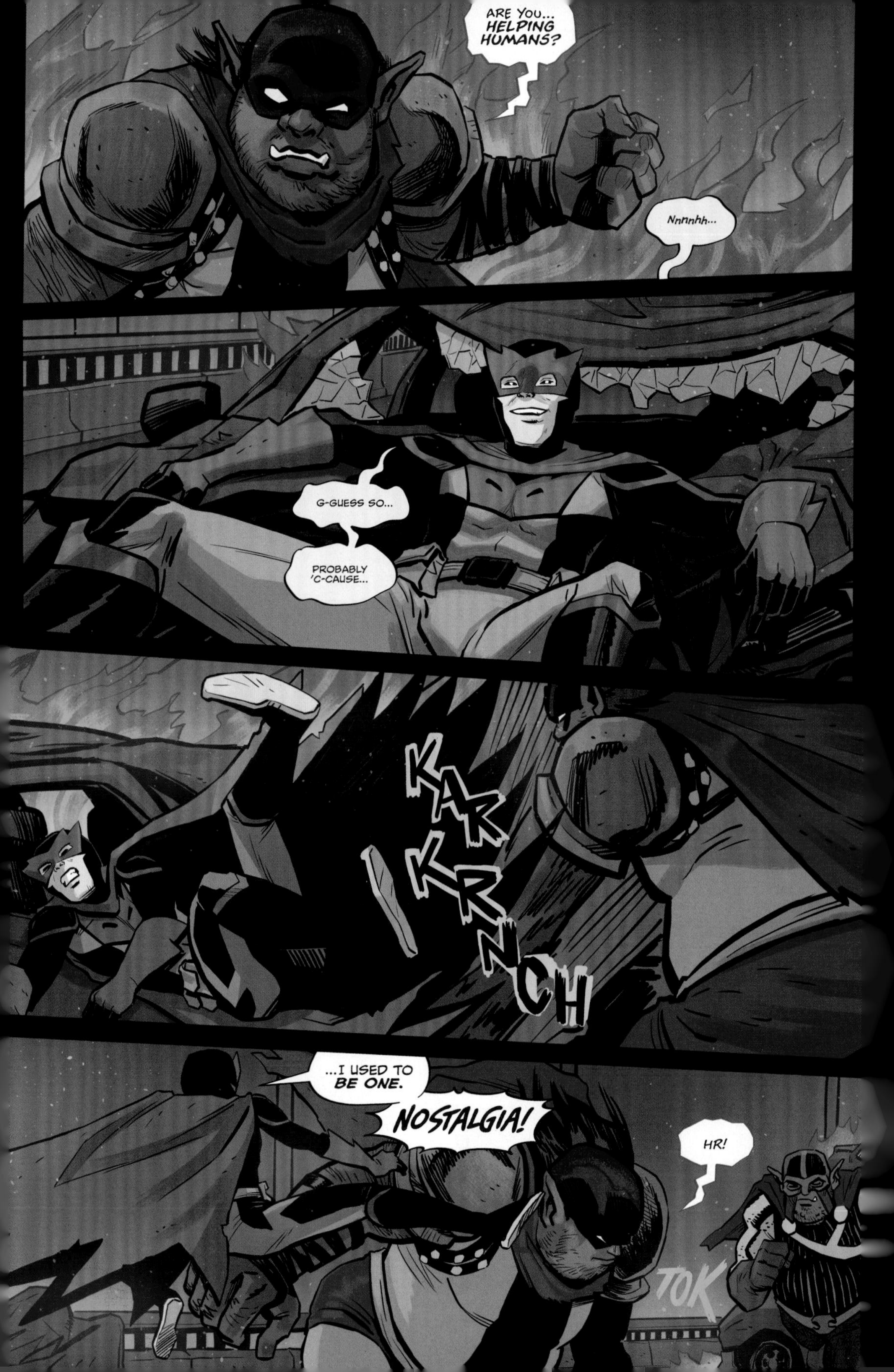

ARE YOU... HELPING HUMANS?
Nnnnhh...
G-GUESS SO...
PROBABLY 'C-CAUSE...
KAR KRNCH
...I USED TO BE ONE.
NOSTALGIA!
HR!
TOK

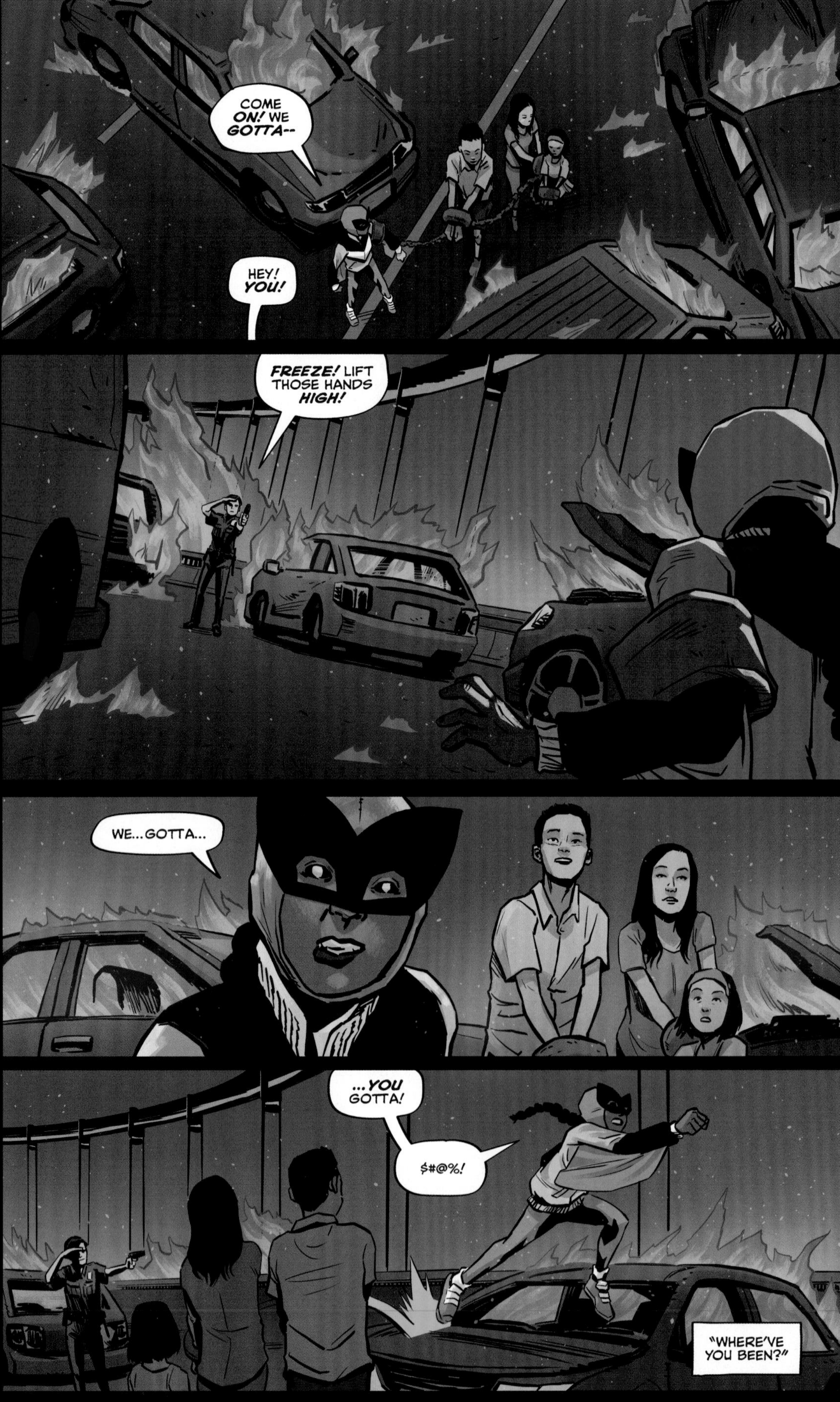
COME ON! WE GOTTA--
HEY! YOU!
FREEZE! LIFT THOSE HANDS HIGH!
WE...GOTTA...
...YOU GOTTA!
$#@%!
"WHERE'VE YOU BEEN?"

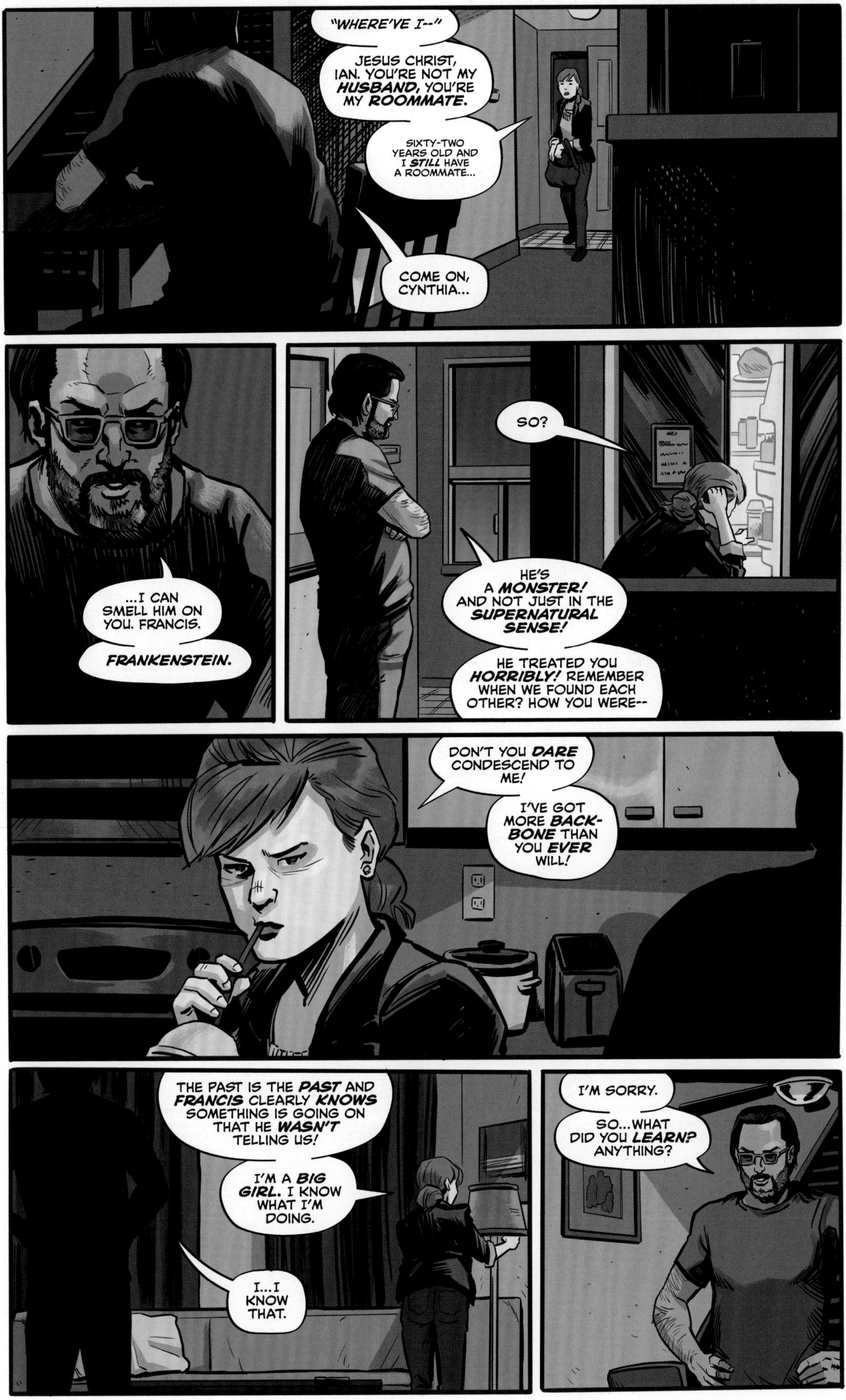
"WHERE'VE I--"
JESUS CHRIST, IAN. YOU'RE NOT MY HUSBAND, YOU'RE MY ROOMMATE.
SIXTY-TWO YEARS OLD AND I STILL HAVE A ROOMMATE...
COME ON, CYNTHIA...
...I CAN SMELL HIM ON YOU. FRANCIS.
FRANKENSTEIN.
SO?
HE'S A MONSTER! AND NOT JUST IN THE SUPERNATURAL SENSE!
HE TREATED YOU HORRIBLY! REMEMBER WHEN WE FOUND EACH OTHER? HOW YOU WERE--
DON'T YOU DARE CONDESCEND TO ME!
I'VE GOT MORE BACK-BONE THAN YOU EVER WILL!
THE PAST IS THE PAST AND FRANCIS CLEARLY KNOWS SOMETHING IS GOING ON THAT HE WASN'T TELLING US!
I'M A BIG GIRL. I KNOW WHAT I'M DOING.
I...I KNOW THAT.
I'M SORRY.
SO...WHAT DID YOU LEARN? ANYTHING?

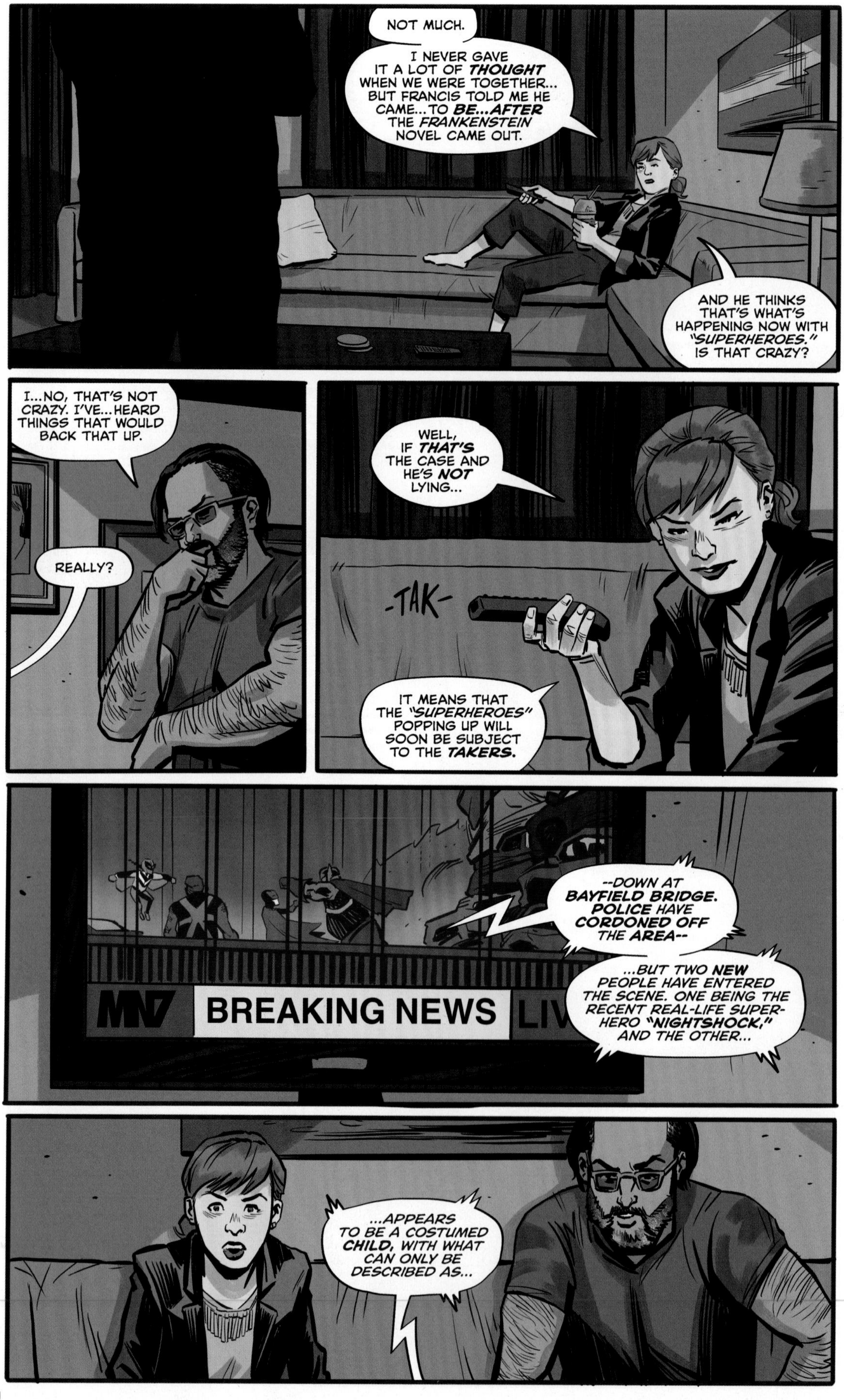
NOT MUCH.
I NEVER GAVE IT A LOT OF THOUGHT WHEN WE WERE TOGETHER... BUT FRANCIS TOLD ME HE CAME...TO BE...AFTER THE FRANKENSTEIN NOVEL CAME OUT.
AND HE THINKS THAT'S WHAT'S HAPPENING NOW WITH "SUPERHEROES." IS THAT CRAZY?
I...NO, THAT'S NOT CRAZY. I'VE...HEARD THINGS THAT WOULD BACK THAT UP.
REALLY?
WELL, IF THAT'S THE CASE AND HE'S NOT LYING...
-TAK-
IT MEANS THAT THE "SUPERHEROES" POPPING UP WILL SOON BE SUBJECT TO THE TAKERS.
MN7 BREAKING NEWS LIV
--DOWN AT BAYFIELD BRIDGE. POLICE HAVE CORDONED OFF THE AREA--
...BUT TWO NEW PEOPLE HAVE ENTERED THE SCENE. ONE BEING THE RECENT REAL-LIFE SUPER-HERO "NIGHTSHOCK," AND THE OTHER...
...APPEARS TO BE A COSTUMED CHILD, WITH WHAT CAN ONLY BE DESCRIBED AS...

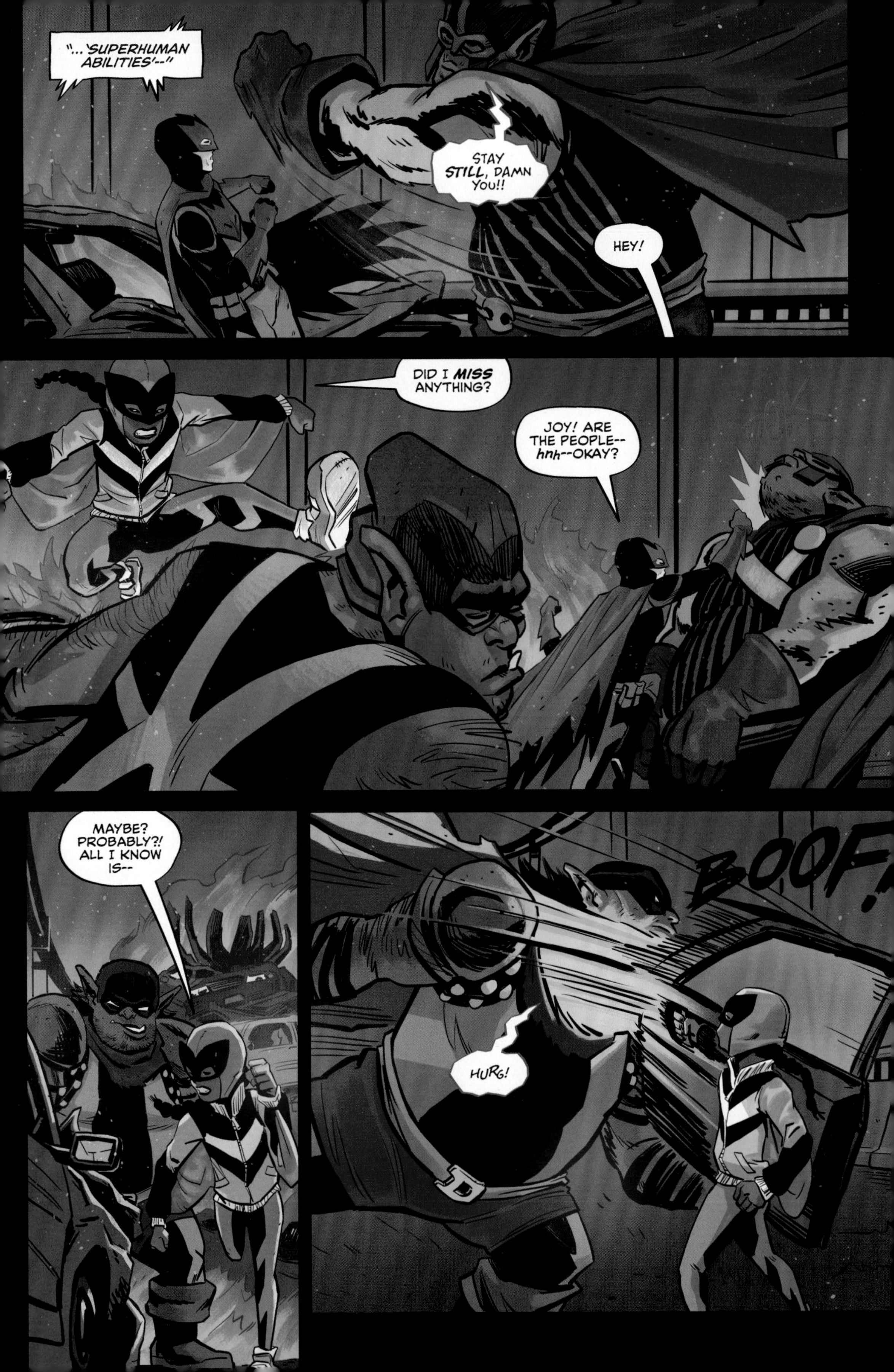
"...'SUPERHUMAN ABILITIES'--"
STAY STILL, DAMN YOU!!
HEY!
DID I MISS ANYTHING?
JOY! ARE THE PEOPLE-- hnh--OKAY?
MAYBE? PROBABLY?! ALL I KNOW IS--
BOOF!!
HURG!

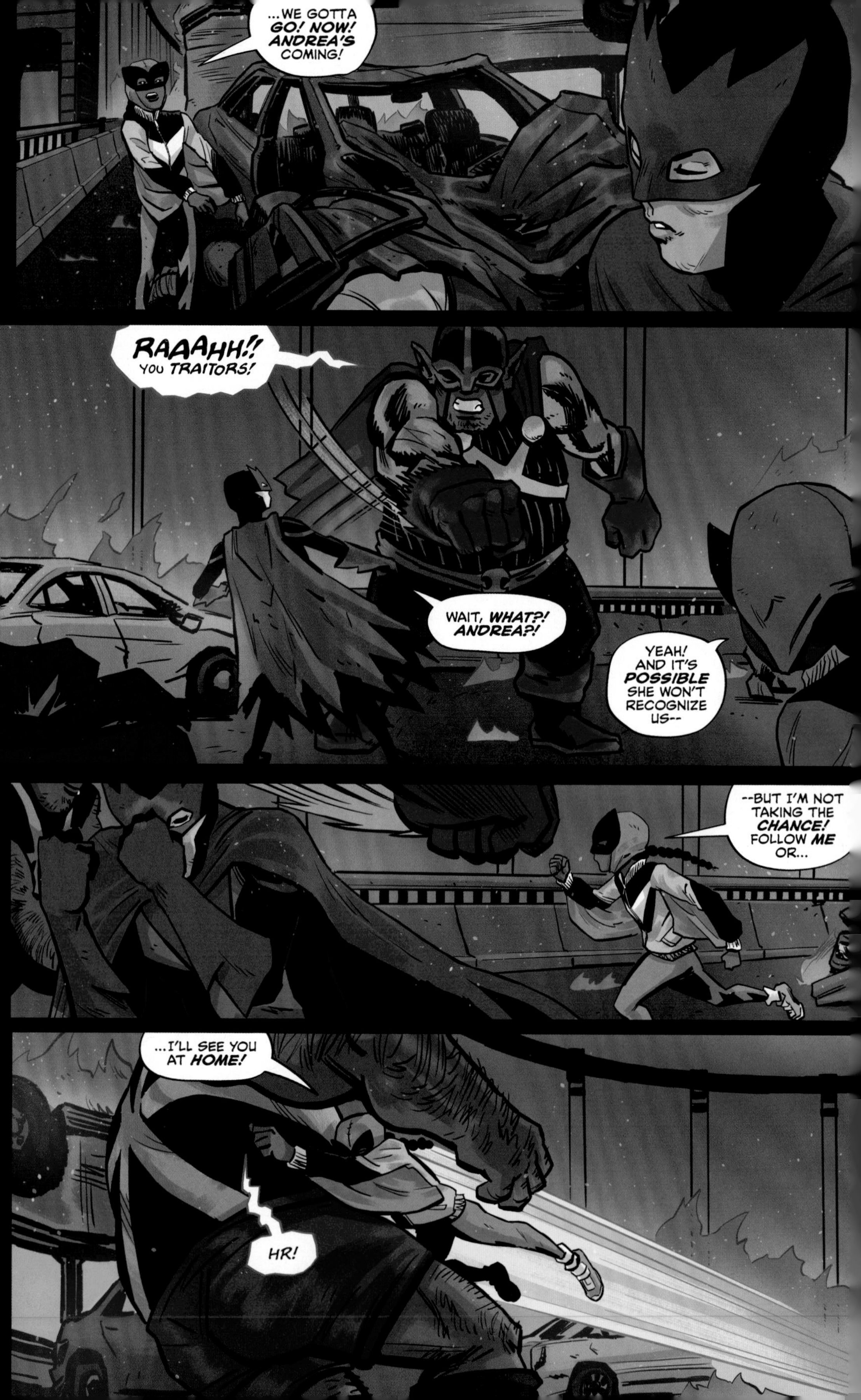
...WE GOTTA GO! NOW! ANDREA'S COMING!
RAAAHH!! YOU TRAITORS!
WAIT, WHAT?! ANDREA?!
YEAH! AND IT'S POSSIBLE SHE WON'T RECOGNIZE US--
--BUT I'M NOT TAKING THE CHANCE! FOLLOW ME OR...
...I'LL SEE YOU AT HOME!
HR!

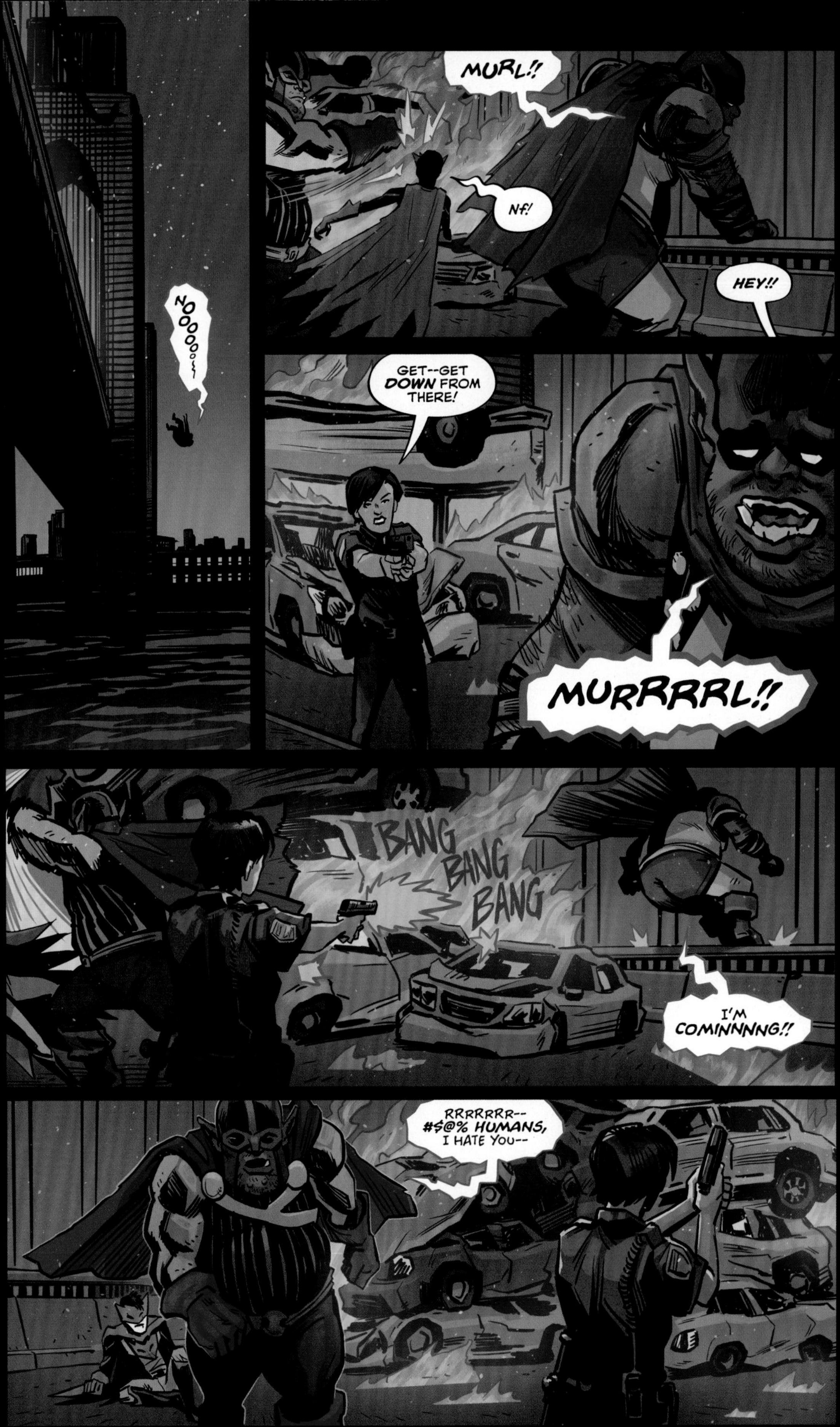
NOOOOo~~
MURL!!
Nf!
HEY!!
GET--GET DOWN FROM THERE!
MURRRRL!!
BANG BANG BANG
I'M COMINNNNG!!
RRRRRRR-- #$@% HUMANS, I HATE YOU--

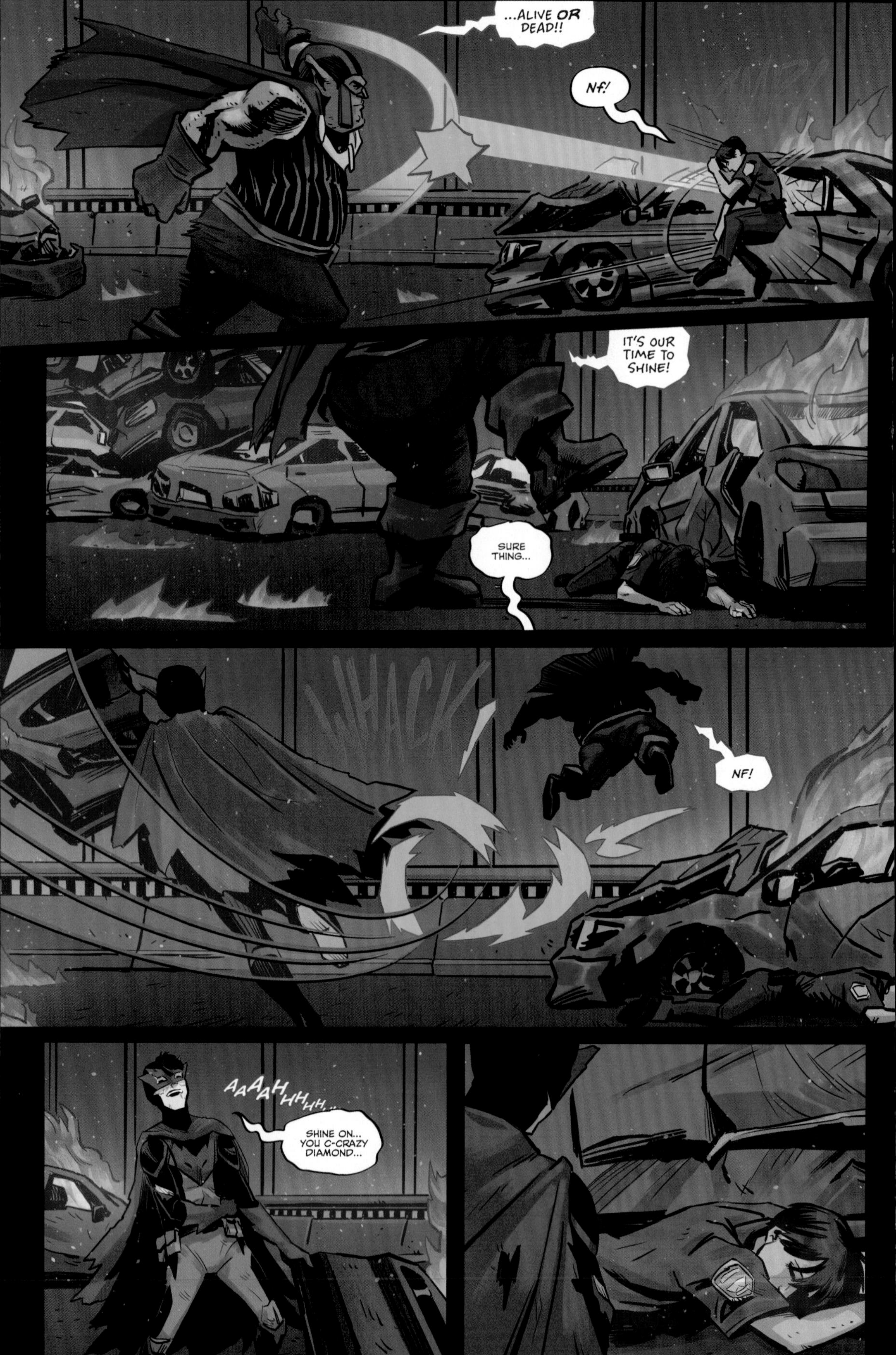
...ALIVE OR DEAD!!
Nf!
IT'S OUR TIME TO SHINE!
SURE THING...
WHACK!
NF!
AAAAHHHH...
SHINE ON... YOU C-CRAZY DIAMOND...

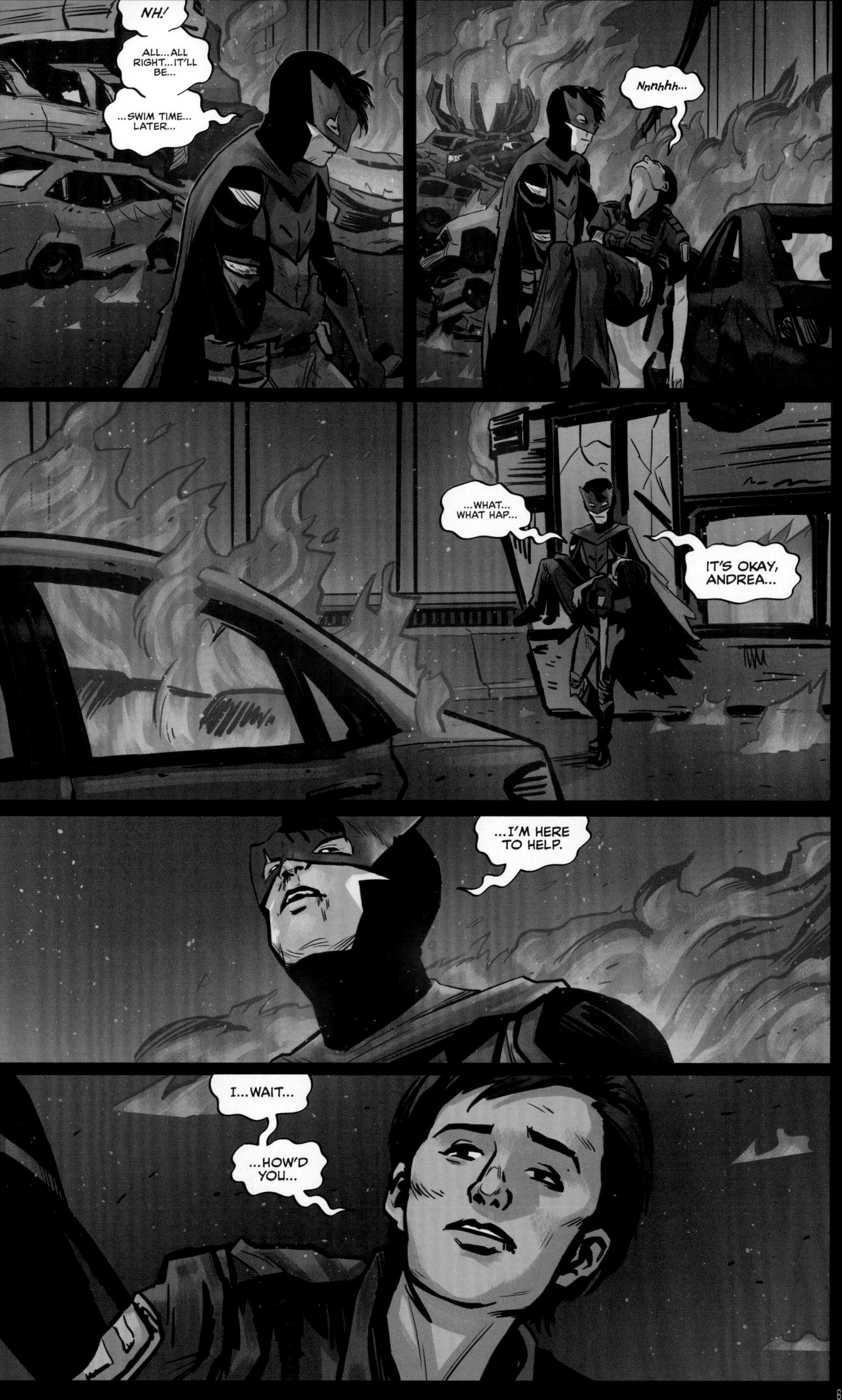
NH!
ALL...ALL RIGHT...IT'LL BE...
...SWIM TIME... LATER...
Nnnhhh...
...WHAT... WHAT HAP...
IT'S OKAY, ANDREA...
...I'M HERE TO HELP.
I...WAIT...
...HOW'D YOU...

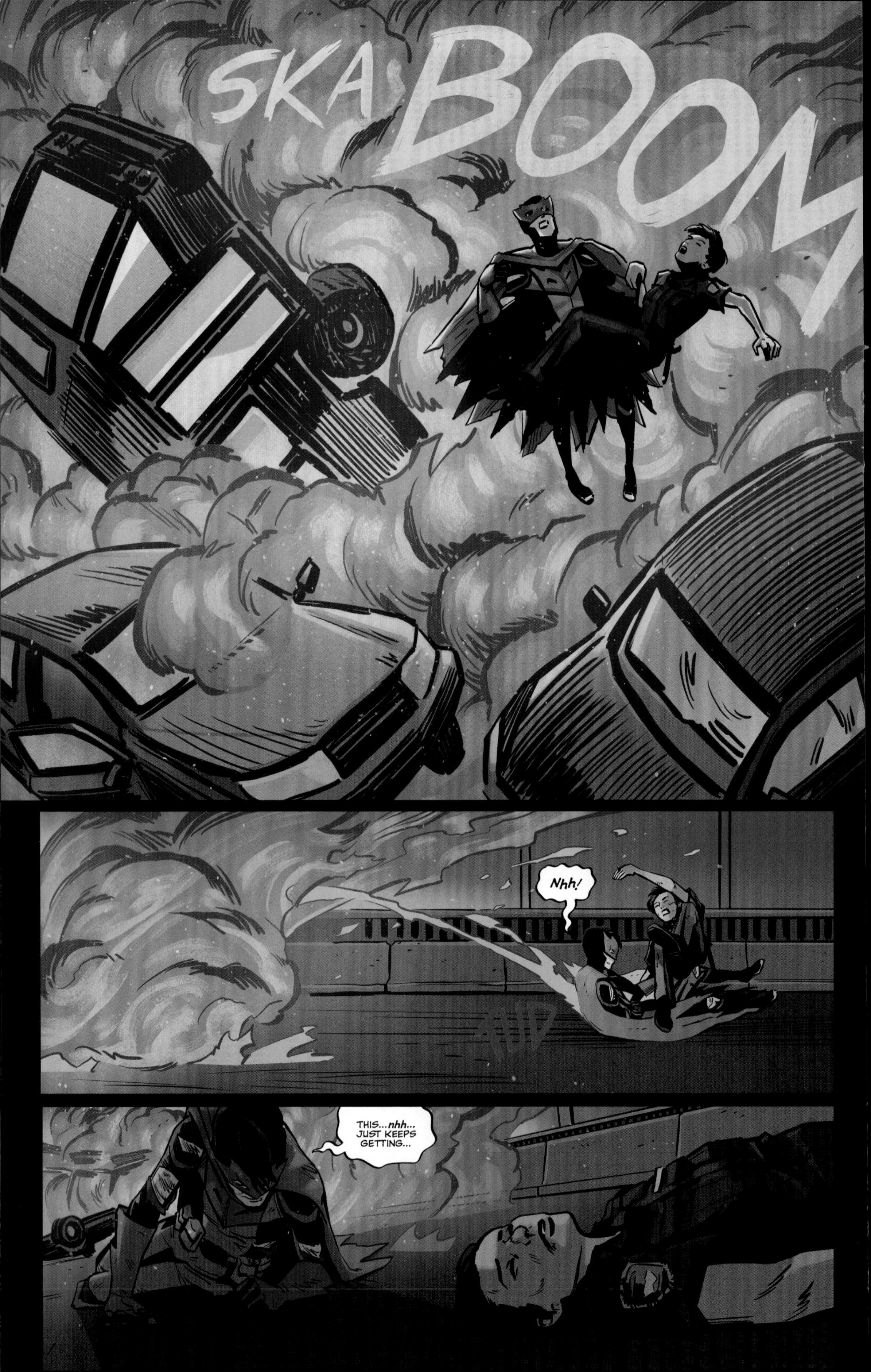
SKA BOOM
Nhh!
THIS...nhh... JUST KEEPS GETTING...

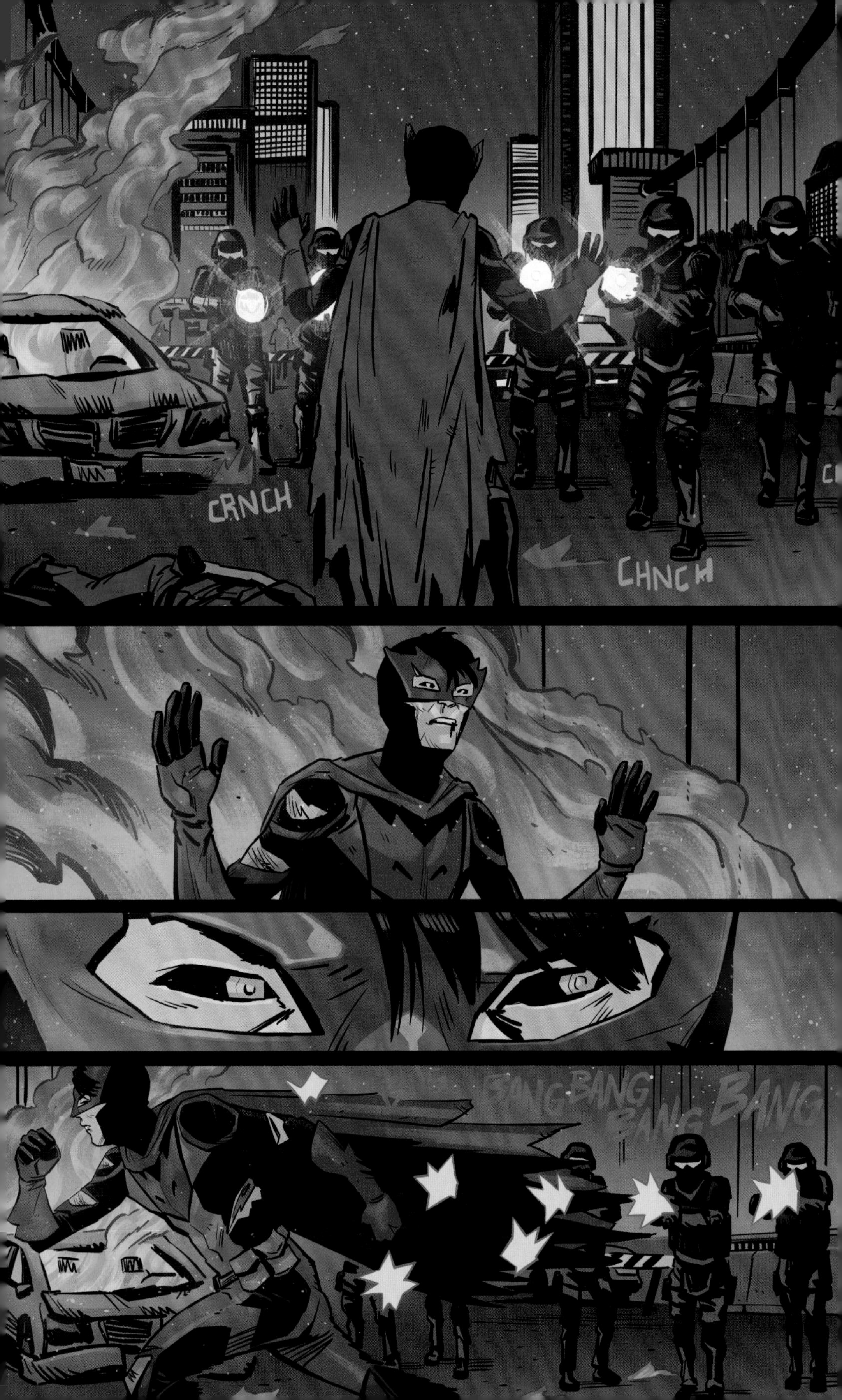
CRNCH
CHNCH
BANG BANG
BANG BANG

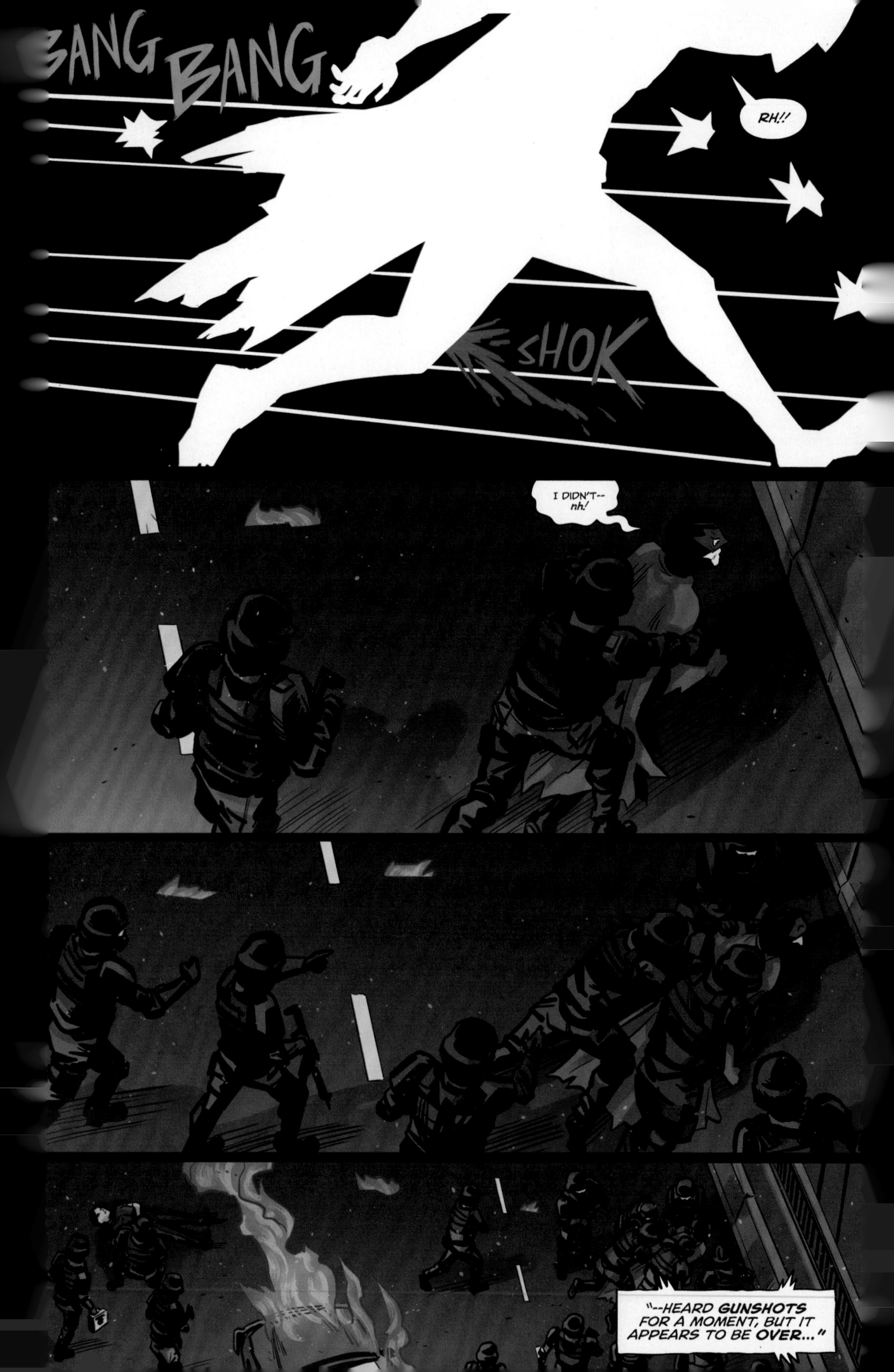
BANG BANG
RH!!
SHOK
I DIDN'T-- nh!
"--HEARD GUNSHOTS FOR A MOMENT, BUT IT APPEARS TO BE OVER..."

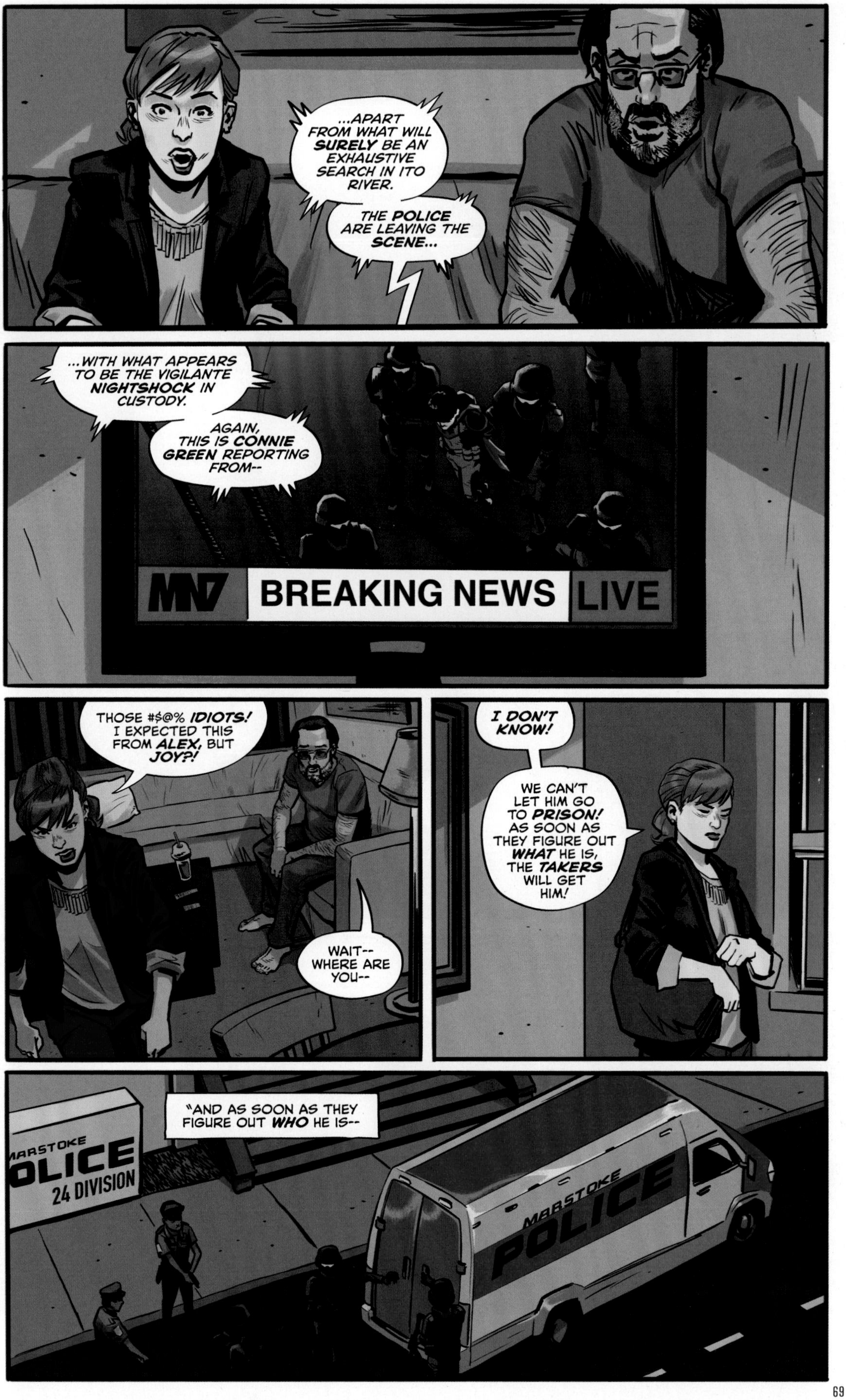

...APART FROM WHAT WILL SURELY BE AN EXHAUSTIVE SEARCH IN ITO RIVER.
THE POLICE ARE LEAVING THE SCENE...
...WITH WHAT APPEARS TO BE THE VIGILANTE NIGHTSHOCK IN CUSTODY.
AGAIN, THIS IS CONNIE GREEN REPORTING FROM--
MN7
BREAKING NEWS
LIVE
THOSE #$@% IDIOTS! I EXPECTED THIS FROM ALEX, BUT JOY?!
WAIT-- WHERE ARE YOU--
I DON'T KNOW!
WE CAN'T LET HIM GO TO PRISON! AS SOON AS THEY FIGURE OUT WHAT HE IS, THE TAKERS WILL GET HIM!
"AND AS SOON AS THEY FIGURE OUT WHO HE IS--
MARSTOKE
OLICE
24 DIVISION
MARSTOKE
POLICE

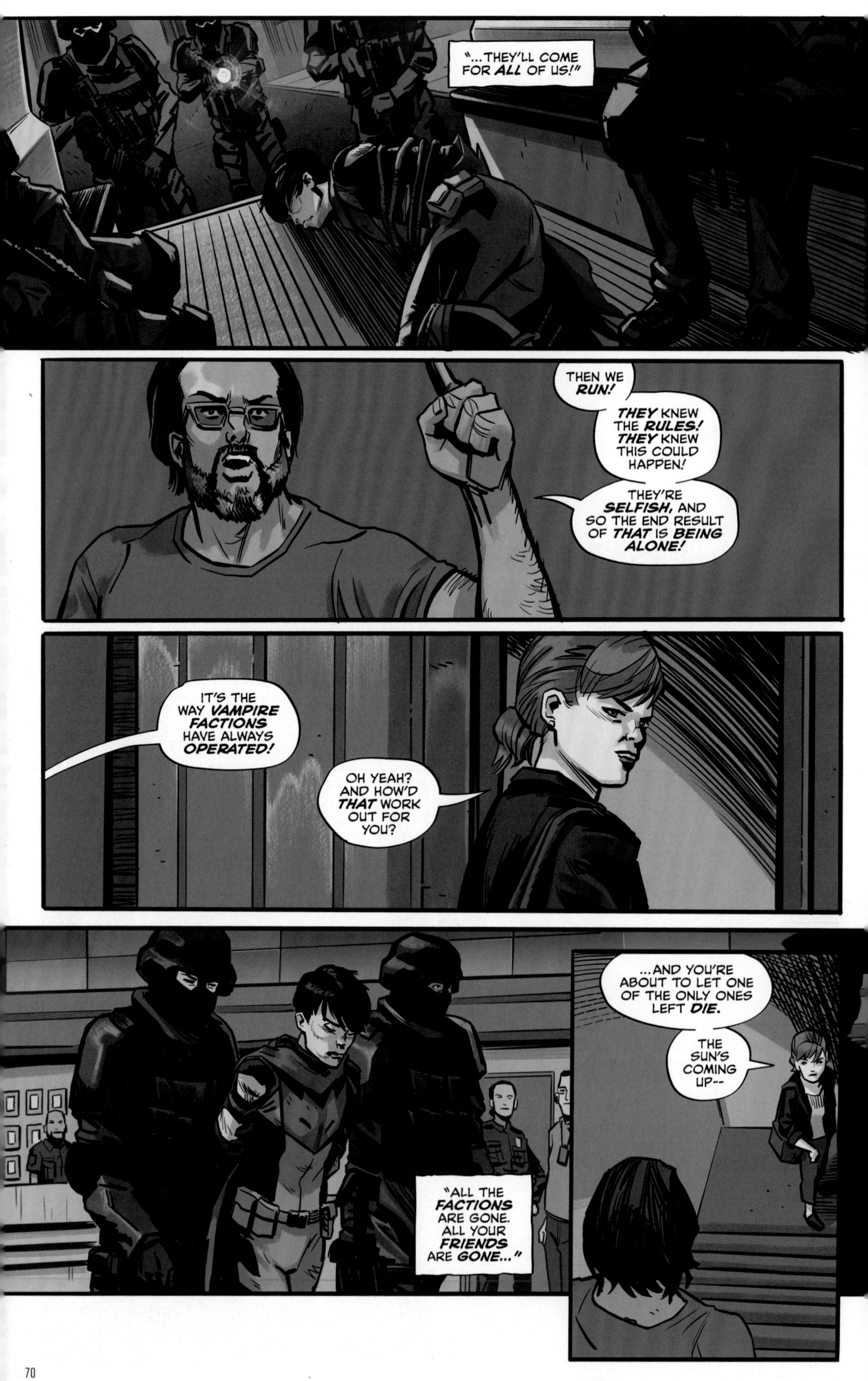
"...THEY'LL COME FOR ALL OF US!"
THEN WE RUN!
THEY KNEW THE RULES! THEY KNEW THIS COULD HAPPEN!
THEY'RE SELFISH, AND SO THE END RESULT OF THAT IS BEING ALONE!
IT'S THE WAY VAMPIRE FACTIONS HAVE ALWAYS OPERATED!
OH YEAH? AND HOW'D THAT WORK OUT FOR YOU?
"ALL THE FACTIONS ARE GONE. ALL YOUR FRIENDS ARE GONE..."
...AND YOU'RE ABOUT TO LET ONE OF THE ONLY ONES LEFT DIE.
THE SUN'S COMING UP--

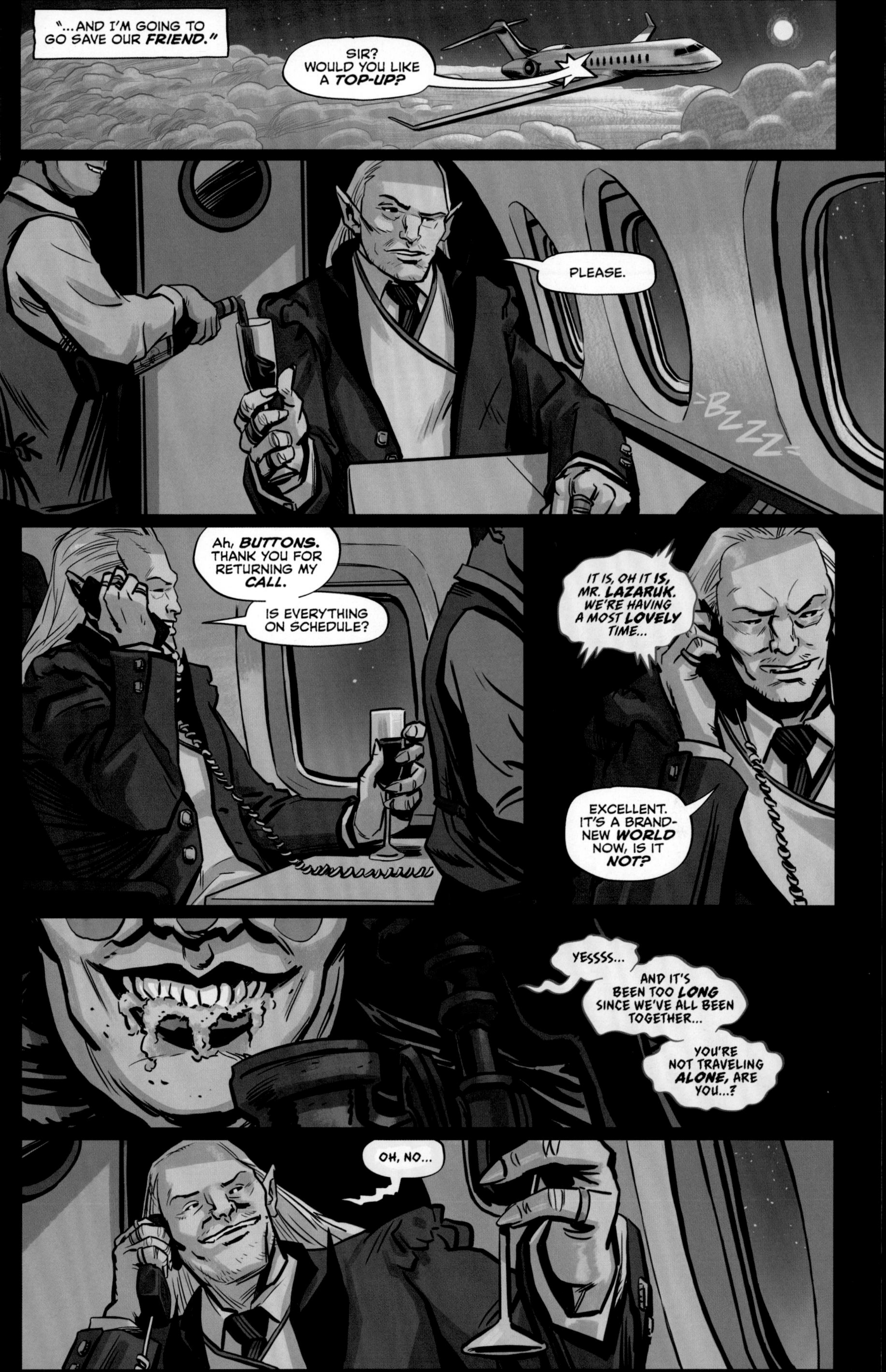
"...AND I'M GOING TO GO SAVE OUR FRIEND."
SIR? WOULD YOU LIKE A TOP-UP?
PLEASE.
BZZZZ
Ah, BUTTONS. THANK YOU FOR RETURNING MY CALL.
IS EVERYTHING ON SCHEDULE?
IT IS, OH IT IS, MR. LAZARUK. WE'RE HAVING A MOST LOVELY TIME...
EXCELLENT. IT'S A BRAND-NEW WORLD NOW, IS IT NOT?
YESSSS...
AND IT'S BEEN TOO LONG SINCE WE'VE ALL BEEN TOGETHER...
YOU'RE NOT TRAVELING ALONE, ARE YOU...?
OH, NO...

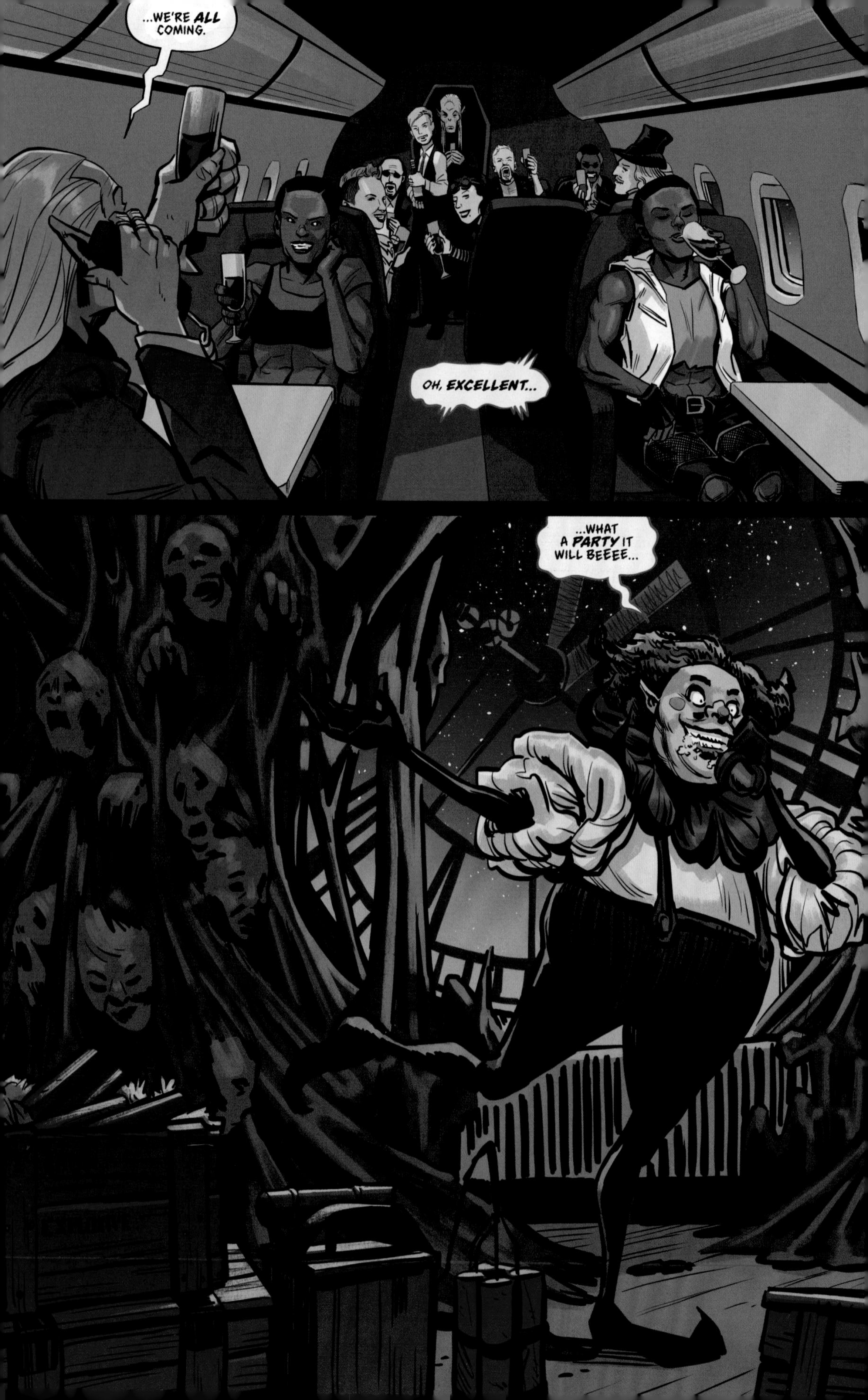
...WE'RE ALL COMING.
OH, EXCELLENT...
...WHAT A PARTY IT WILL BEEEE...

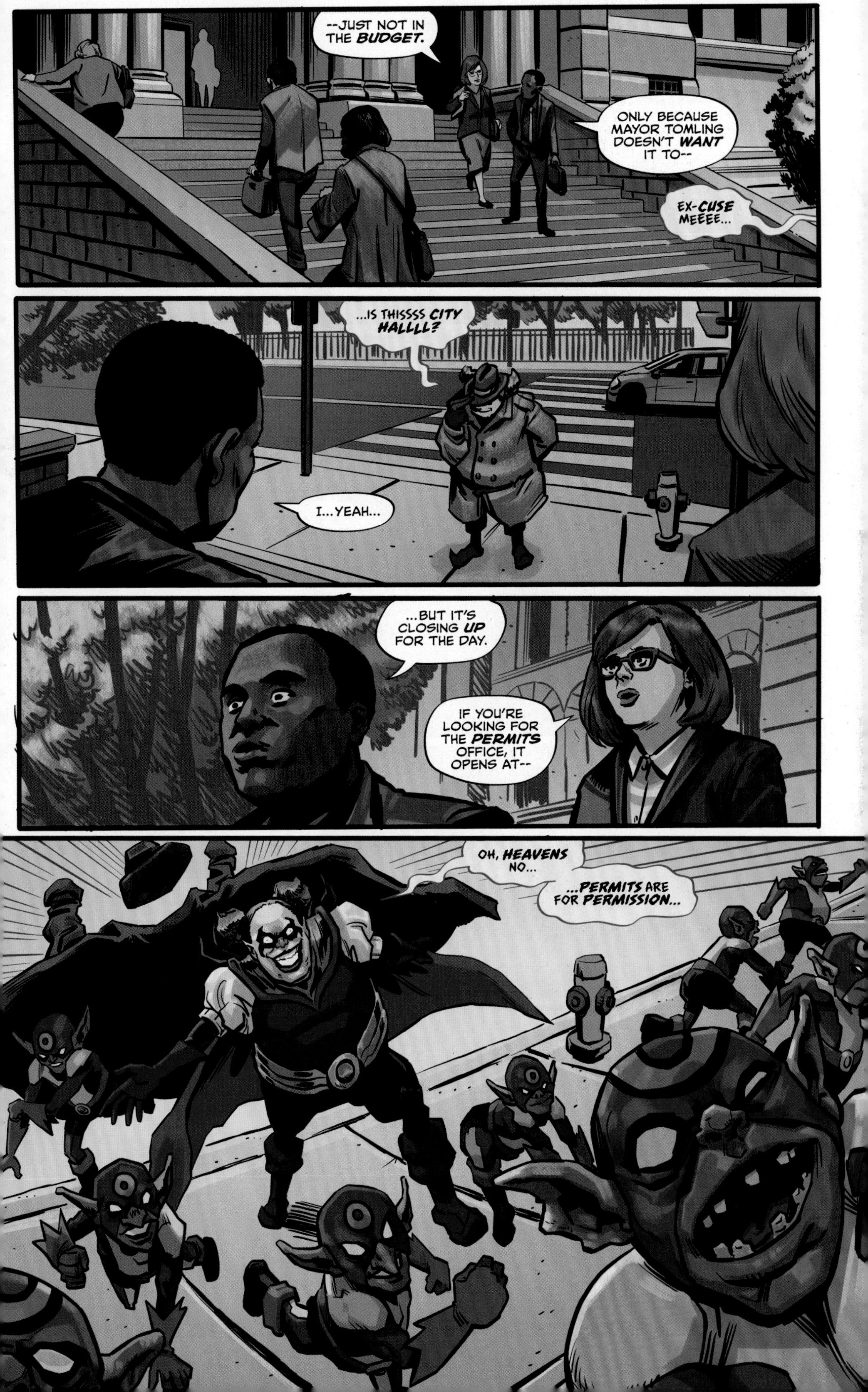
--JUST NOT IN THE BUDGET.
ONLY BECAUSE MAYOR TOMLING DOESN'T WANT IT TO--
EX-CUSE MEEEE...
...IS THISSSS CITY HALLLL?
I...YEAH...
...BUT IT'S CLOSING UP FOR THE DAY.
IF YOU'RE LOOKING FOR THE PERMITS OFFICE, IT OPENS AT--
OH, HEAVENS NO...
...PERMITS ARE FOR PERMISSION...

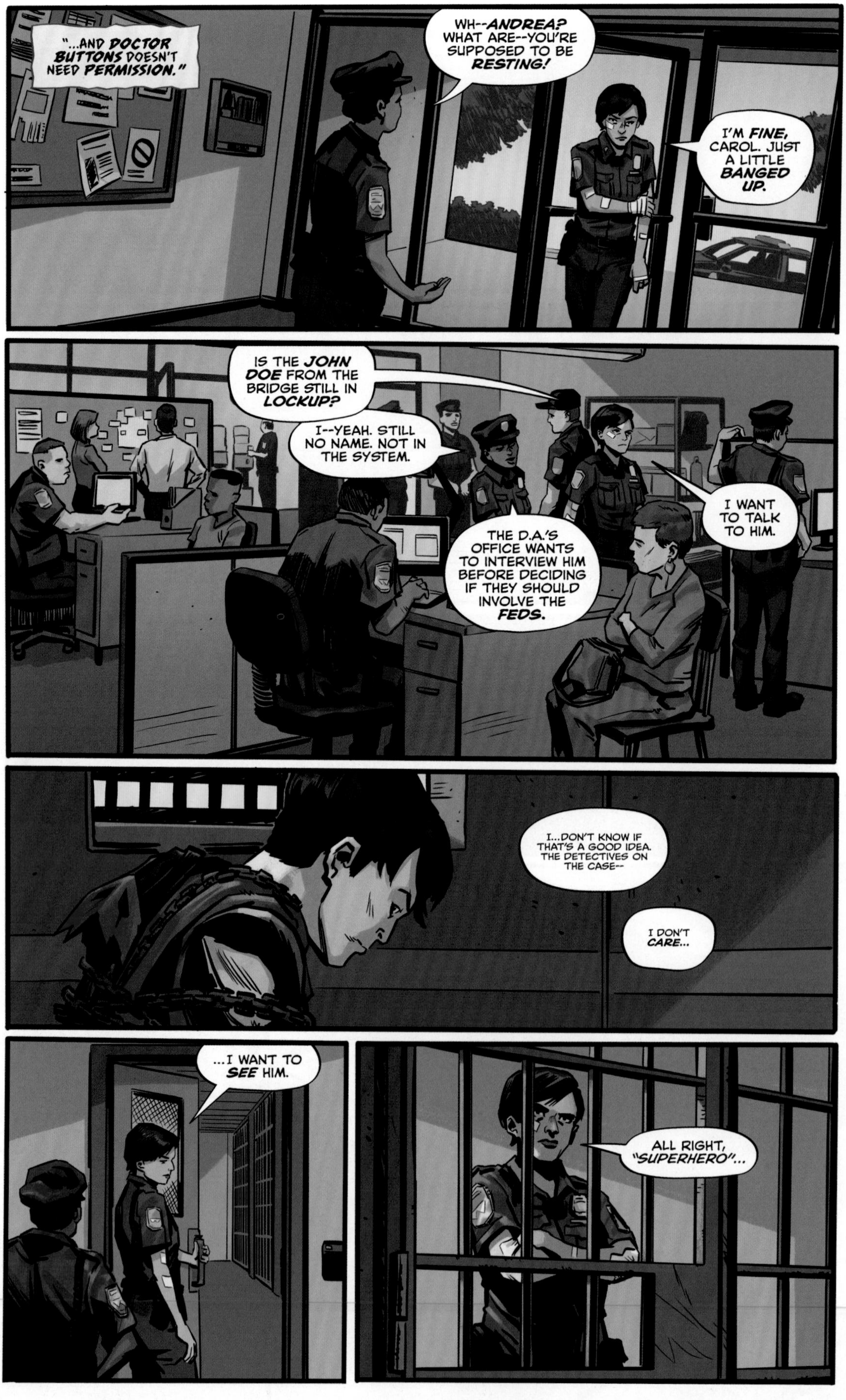
"...AND DOCTOR BUTTONS DOESN'T NEED PERMISSION."
WH--ANDREA? WHAT ARE--YOU'RE SUPPOSED TO BE RESTING!
I'M FINE, CAROL. JUST A LITTLE BANGED UP.
IS THE JOHN DOE FROM THE BRIDGE STILL IN LOCKUP?
I--YEAH. STILL NO NAME. NOT IN THE SYSTEM.
THE D.A.'S OFFICE WANTS TO INTERVIEW HIM BEFORE DECIDING IF THEY SHOULD INVOLVE THE FEDS.
I WANT TO TALK TO HIM.
I...DON'T KNOW IF THAT'S A GOOD IDEA. THE DETECTIVES ON THE CASE--
I DON'T CARE...
...I WANT TO SEE HIM.
ALL RIGHT, "SUPERHERO"...

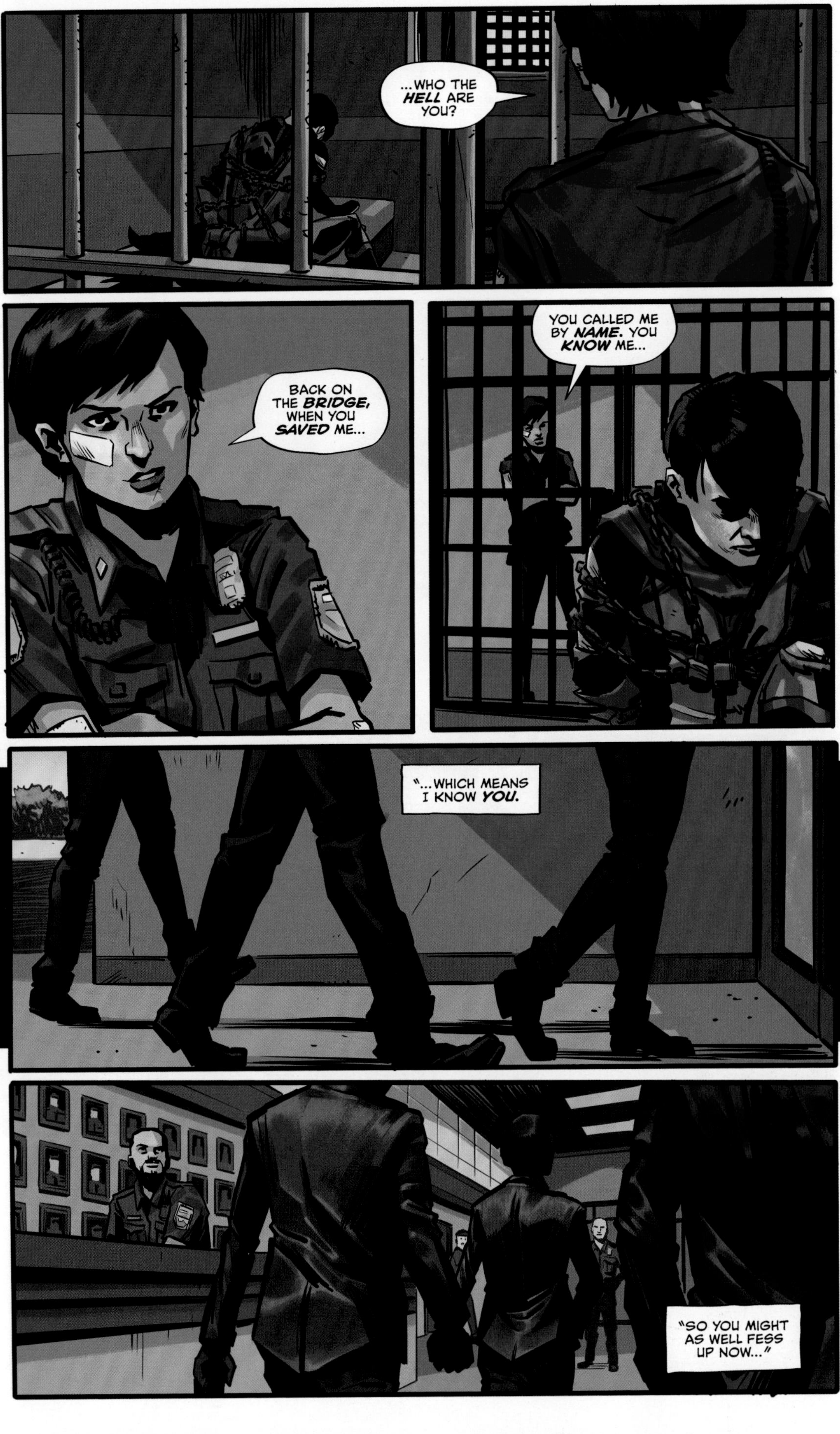
...WHO THE HELL ARE YOU?
BACK ON THE BRIDGE, WHEN YOU SAVED ME...
YOU CALLED ME BY NAME. YOU KNOW ME...
"...WHICH MEANS I KNOW YOU.
"SO YOU MIGHT AS WELL FESS UP NOW..."

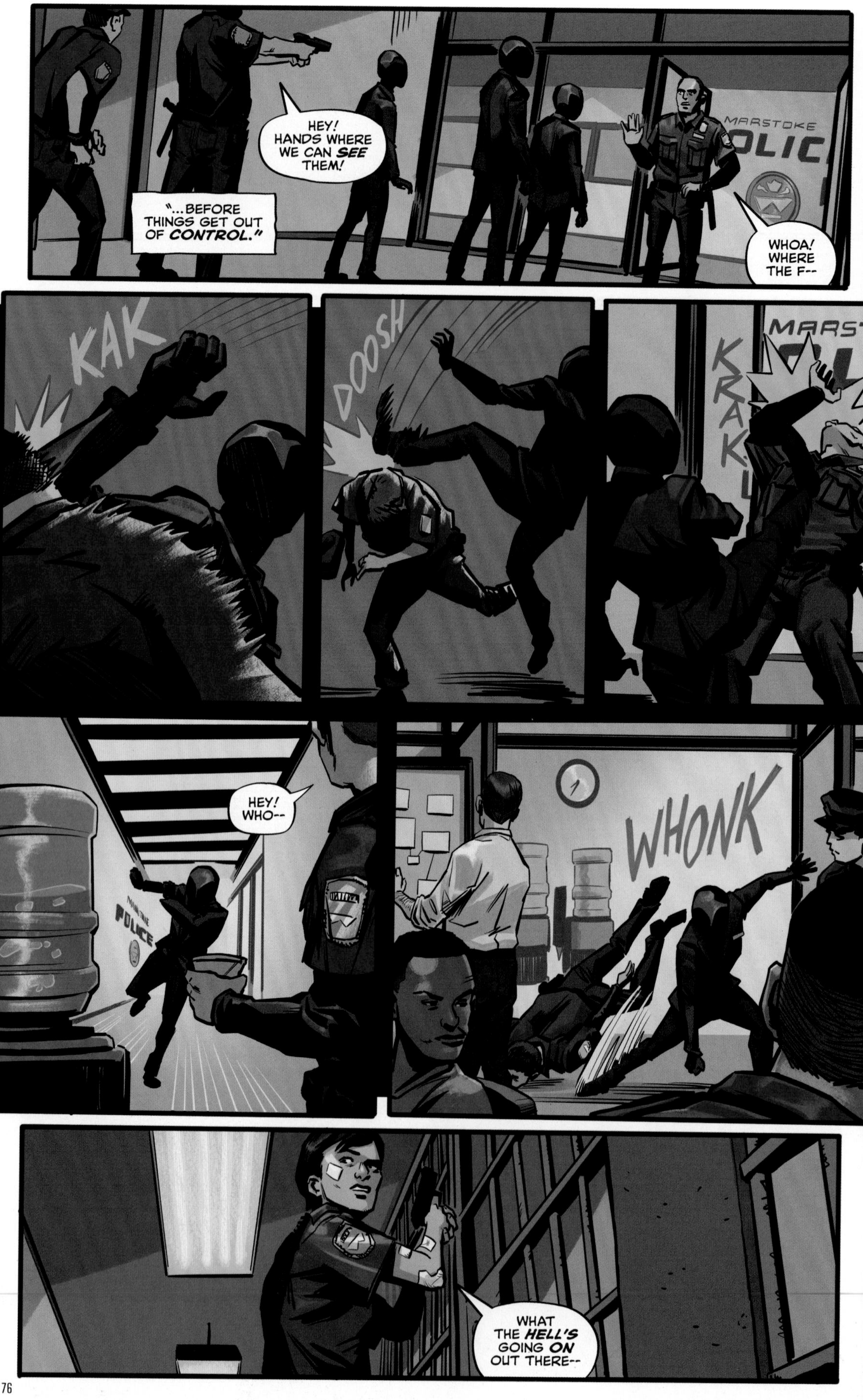

"...BEFORE THINGS GET OUT OF *CONTROL.*"
HEY! HANDS WHERE WE CAN *SEE* THEM!
MARSTOKE
WHOA! WHERE THE F--
KAK
DOOSH
KRAK
HEY! WHO--
WHONK
WHAT THE *HELL'S* GOING *ON* OUT THERE--

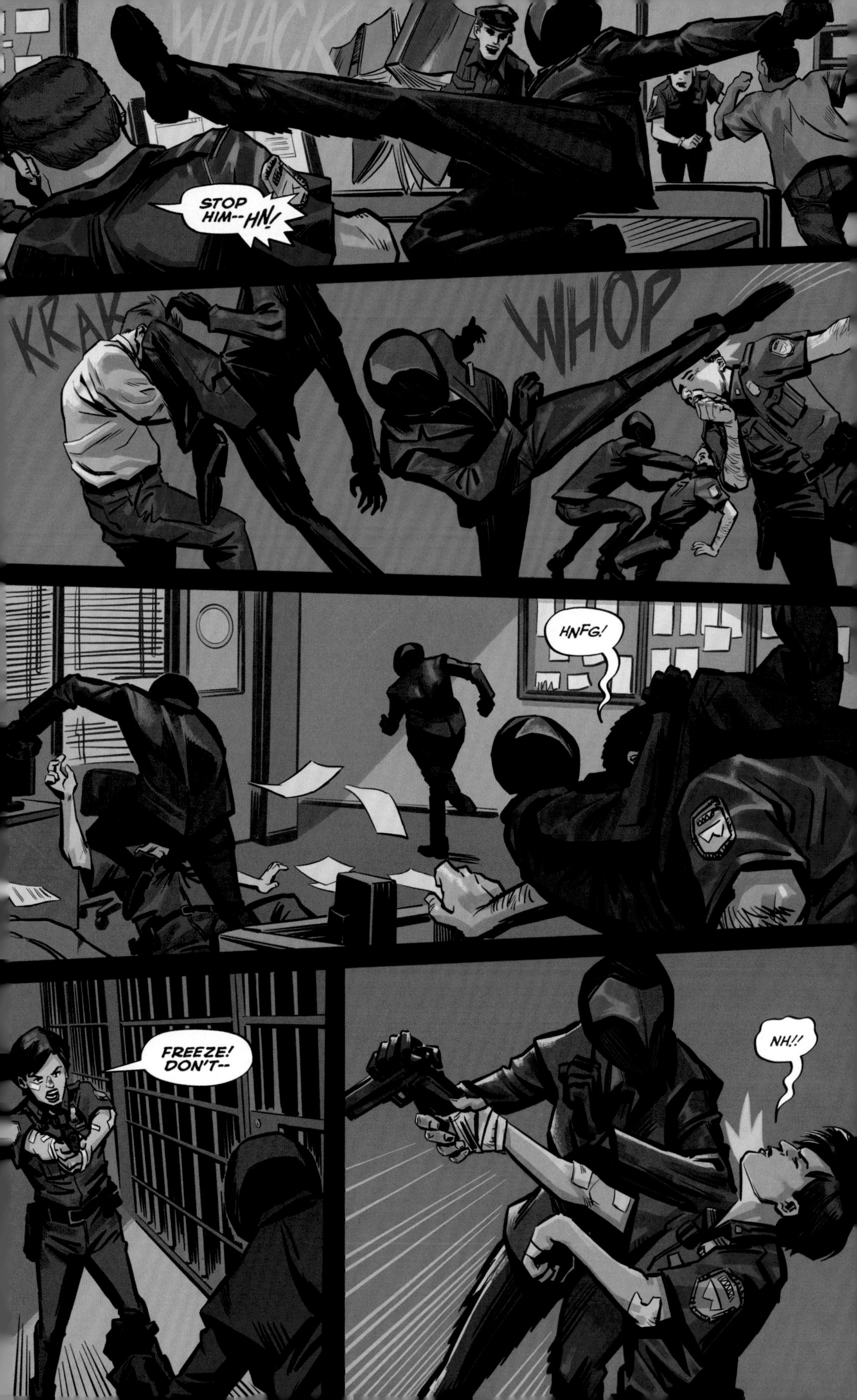
WHACK
STOP HIM--HN!
KRAK
WHOP
HNFG!
FREEZE! DON'T--
NH!!

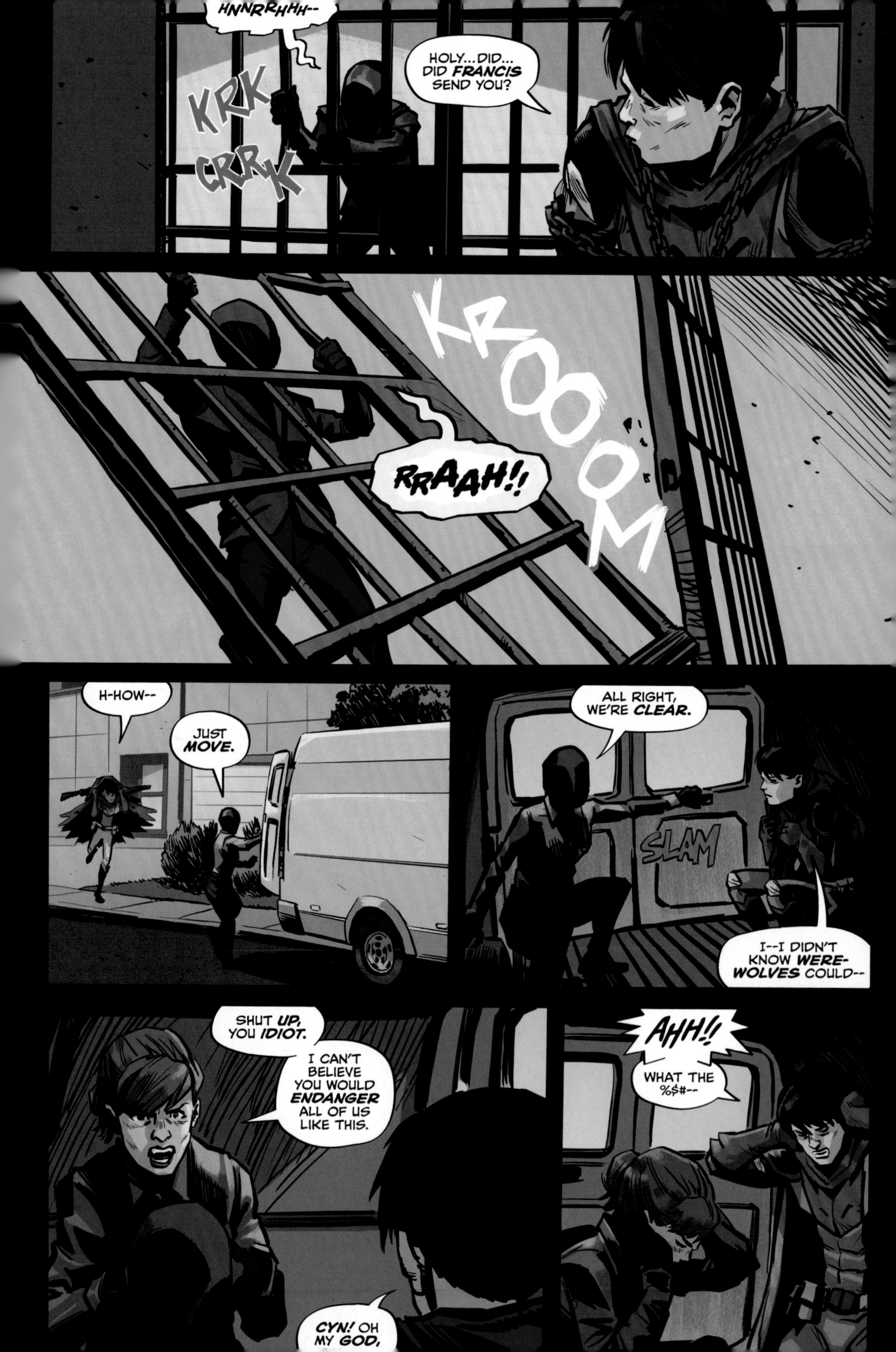
HNNRRHHH--
HOLY...DID... DID FRANCIS SEND YOU?
KRK
CRRK
KROOOOM
RRAAH!!
H-HOW--
JUST MOVE.
ALL RIGHT, WE'RE CLEAR.
SLAM
I--I DIDN'T KNOW WERE-WOLVES COULD--
SHUT UP, YOU IDIOT.
I CAN'T BELIEVE YOU WOULD ENDANGER ALL OF US LIKE THIS.
CYN! OH MY GOD,
AHH!!
WHAT THE %$#--

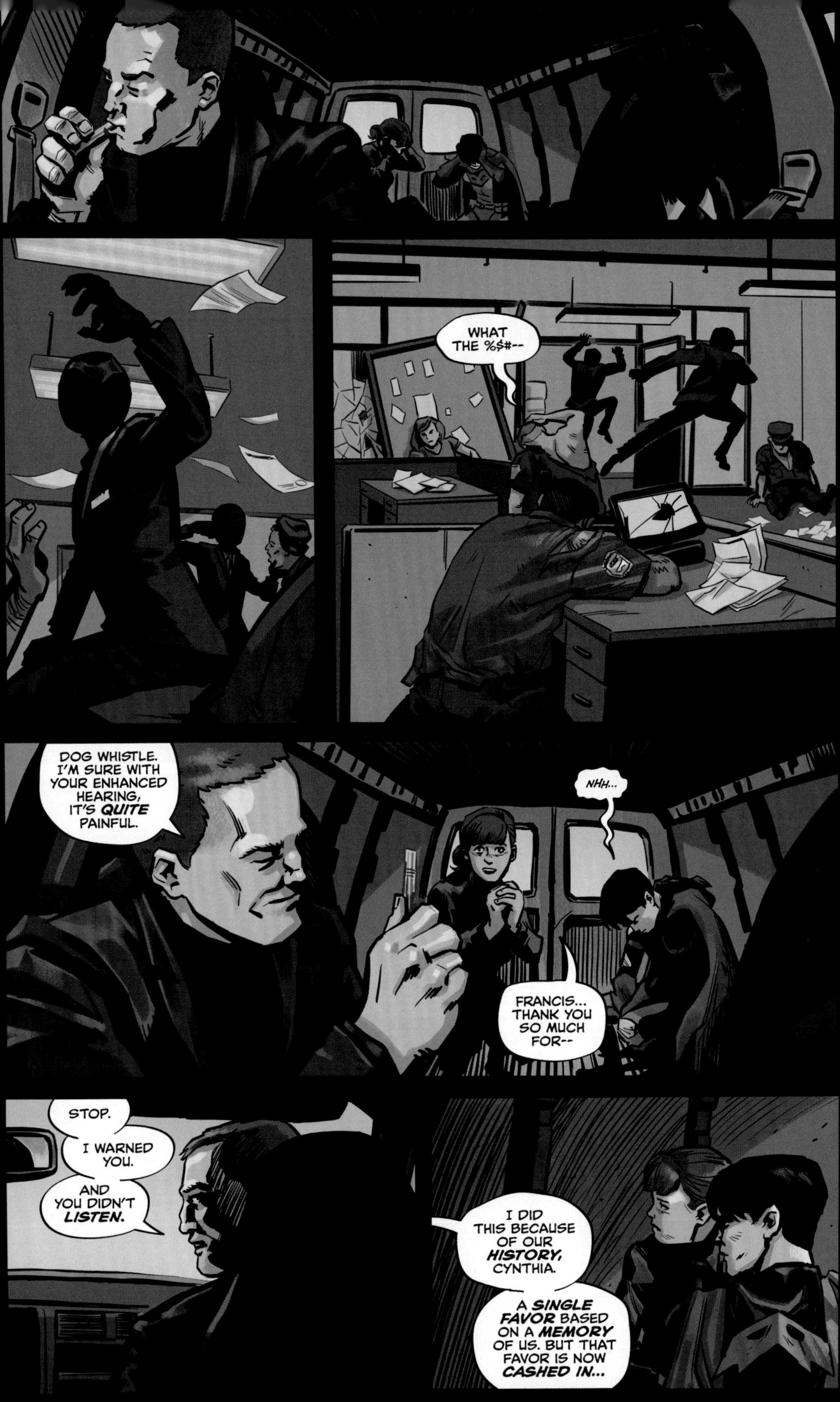
WHAT THE %$#--
DOG WHISTLE. I'M SURE WITH YOUR ENHANCED HEARING, IT'S QUITE PAINFUL.
NHH...
FRANCIS... THANK YOU SO MUCH FOR--
STOP.
I WARNED YOU.
AND YOU DIDN'T LISTEN.
I DID THIS BECAUSE OF OUR HISTORY, CYNTHIA.
A SINGLE FAVOR BASED ON A MEMORY OF US. BUT THAT FAVOR IS NOW CASHED IN...

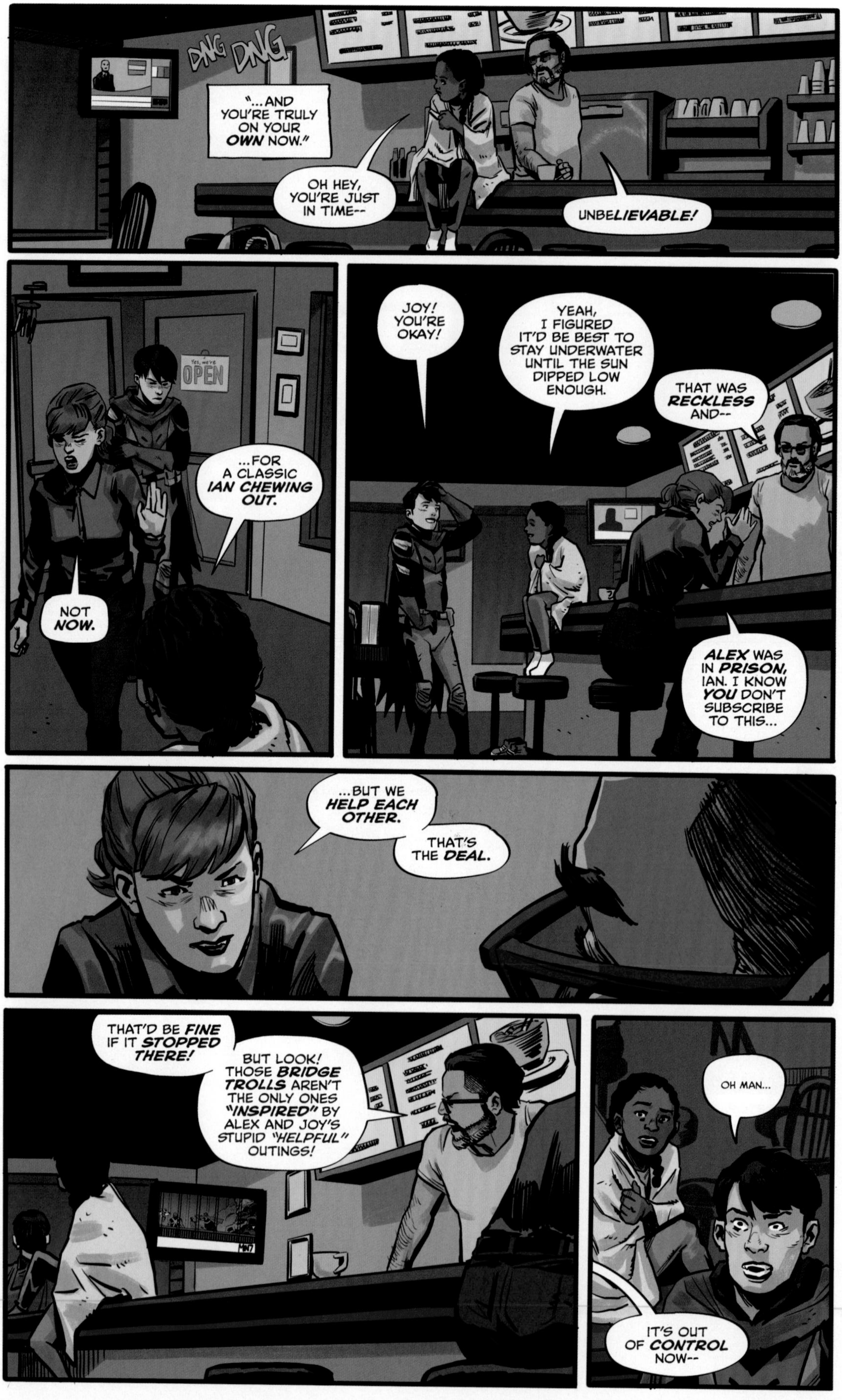
DNG DNG
"...AND YOU'RE TRULY ON YOUR OWN NOW."
OH HEY, YOU'RE JUST IN TIME--
UNBELIEVABLE!
OPEN
...FOR A CLASSIC IAN CHEWING OUT.
NOT NOW.
JOY! YOU'RE OKAY!
YEAH, I FIGURED IT'D BE BEST TO STAY UNDERWATER UNTIL THE SUN DIPPED LOW ENOUGH.
THAT WAS RECKLESS AND--
ALEX WAS IN PRISON, IAN. I KNOW YOU DON'T SUBSCRIBE TO THIS...
...BUT WE HELP EACH OTHER.
THAT'S THE DEAL.
THAT'D BE FINE IF IT STOPPED THERE!
BUT LOOK! THOSE BRIDGE TROLLS AREN'T THE ONLY ONES "INSPIRED" BY ALEX AND JOY'S STUPID "HELPFUL" OUTINGS!
OH MAN...
IT'S OUT OF CONTROL NOW--

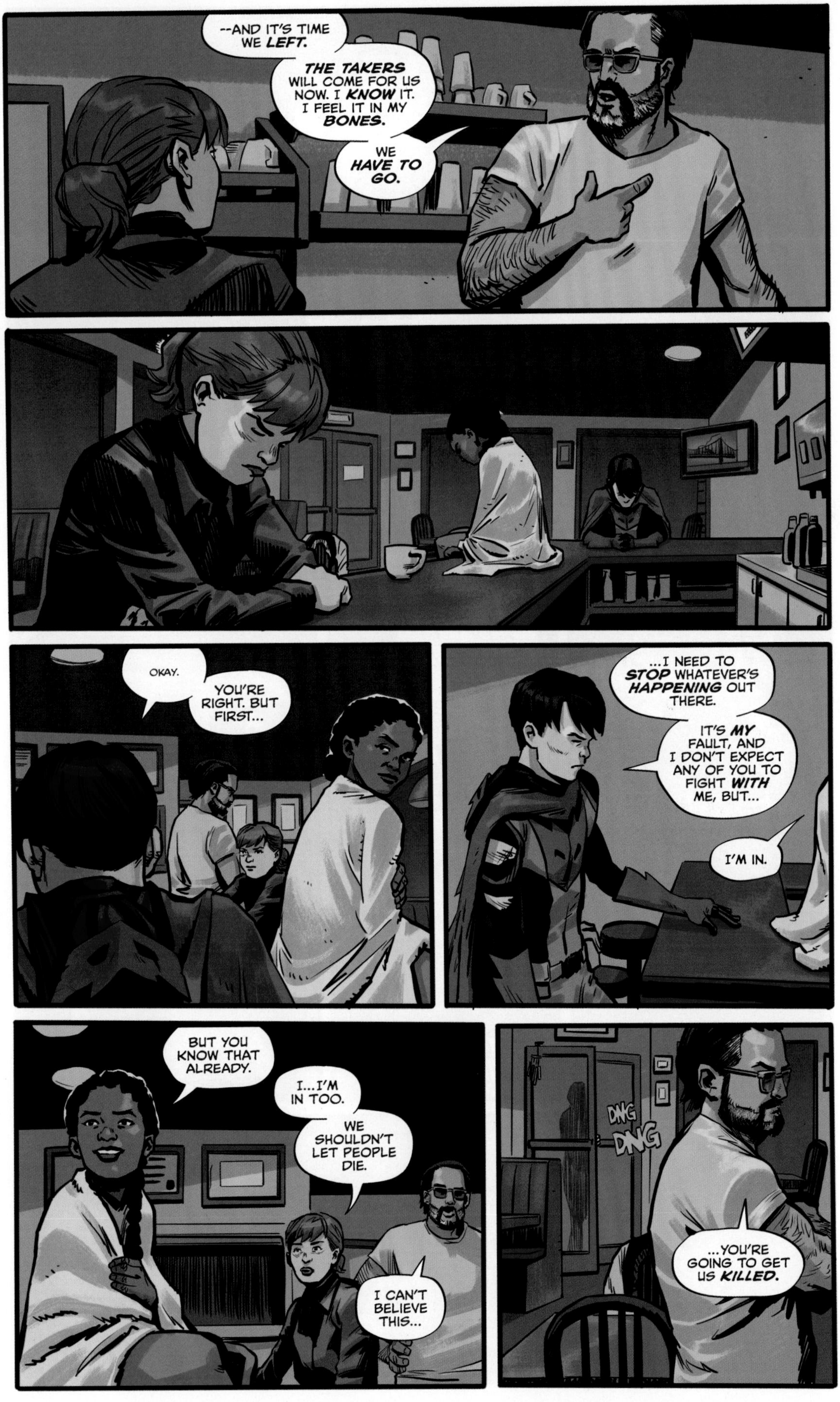
--AND IT'S TIME WE LEFT.
THE TAKERS WILL COME FOR US NOW. I KNOW IT. I FEEL IT IN MY BONES.
WE HAVE TO GO.
OKAY.
YOU'RE RIGHT. BUT FIRST...
...I NEED TO STOP WHATEVER'S HAPPENING OUT THERE.
IT'S MY FAULT, AND I DON'T EXPECT ANY OF YOU TO FIGHT WITH ME, BUT...
I'M IN.
BUT YOU KNOW THAT ALREADY.
I...I'M IN TOO.
WE SHOULDN'T LET PEOPLE DIE.
I CAN'T BELIEVE THIS...
DNG
DNG
...YOU'RE GOING TO GET US KILLED.

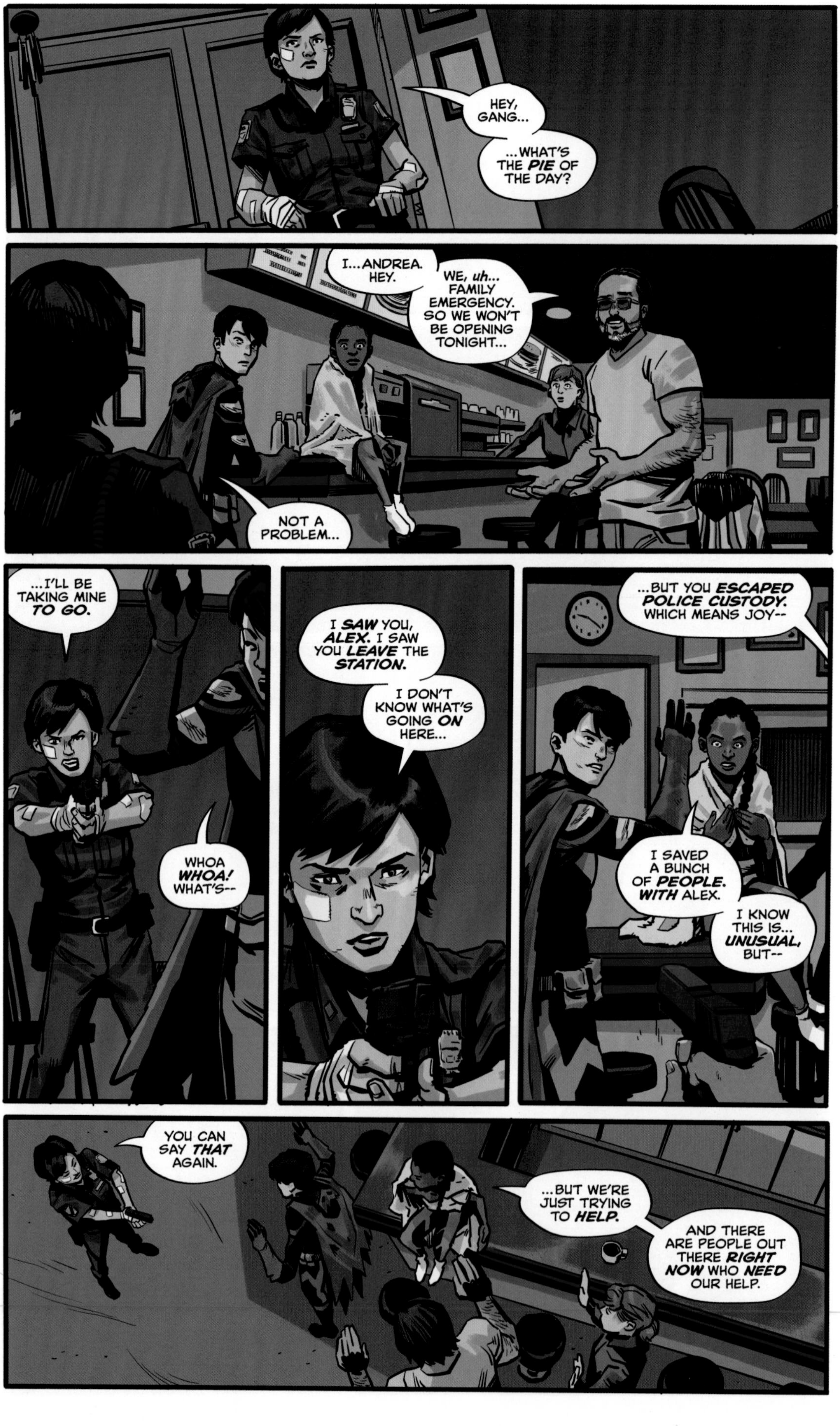
HEY, GANG...
...WHAT'S THE PIE OF THE DAY?
I...ANDREA. HEY.
WE, uh... FAMILY EMERGENCY. SO WE WON'T BE OPENING TONIGHT...
NOT A PROBLEM...
...I'LL BE TAKING MINE TO GO.
WHOA WHOA! WHAT'S--
I SAW YOU, ALEX. I SAW YOU LEAVE THE STATION.
I DON'T KNOW WHAT'S GOING ON HERE...
...BUT YOU ESCAPED POLICE CUSTODY. WHICH MEANS JOY--
I SAVED A BUNCH OF PEOPLE. WITH ALEX.
I KNOW THIS IS... UNUSUAL, BUT--
YOU CAN SAY THAT AGAIN.
...BUT WE'RE JUST TRYING TO HELP.
AND THERE ARE PEOPLE OUT THERE RIGHT NOW WHO NEED OUR HELP.

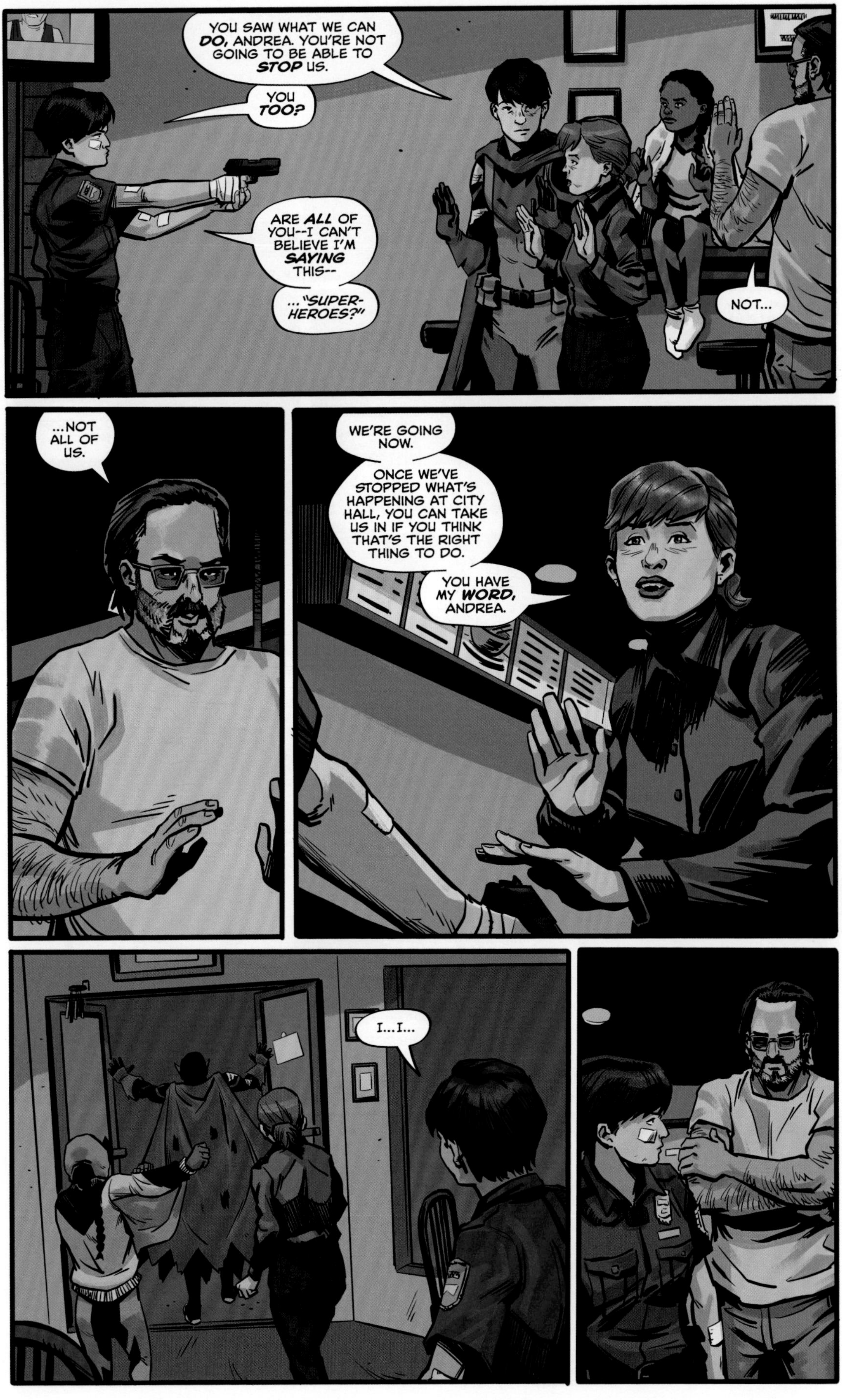
YOU SAW WHAT WE CAN DO, ANDREA. YOU'RE NOT GOING TO BE ABLE TO STOP US.
YOU TOO?
ARE ALL OF YOU--I CAN'T BELIEVE I'M SAYING THIS--
..."SUPER-HEROES?"
NOT...
...NOT ALL OF US.
WE'RE GOING NOW.
ONCE WE'VE STOPPED WHAT'S HAPPENING AT CITY HALL, YOU CAN TAKE US IN IF YOU THINK THAT'S THE RIGHT THING TO DO.
YOU HAVE MY WORD, ANDREA.
I...I...

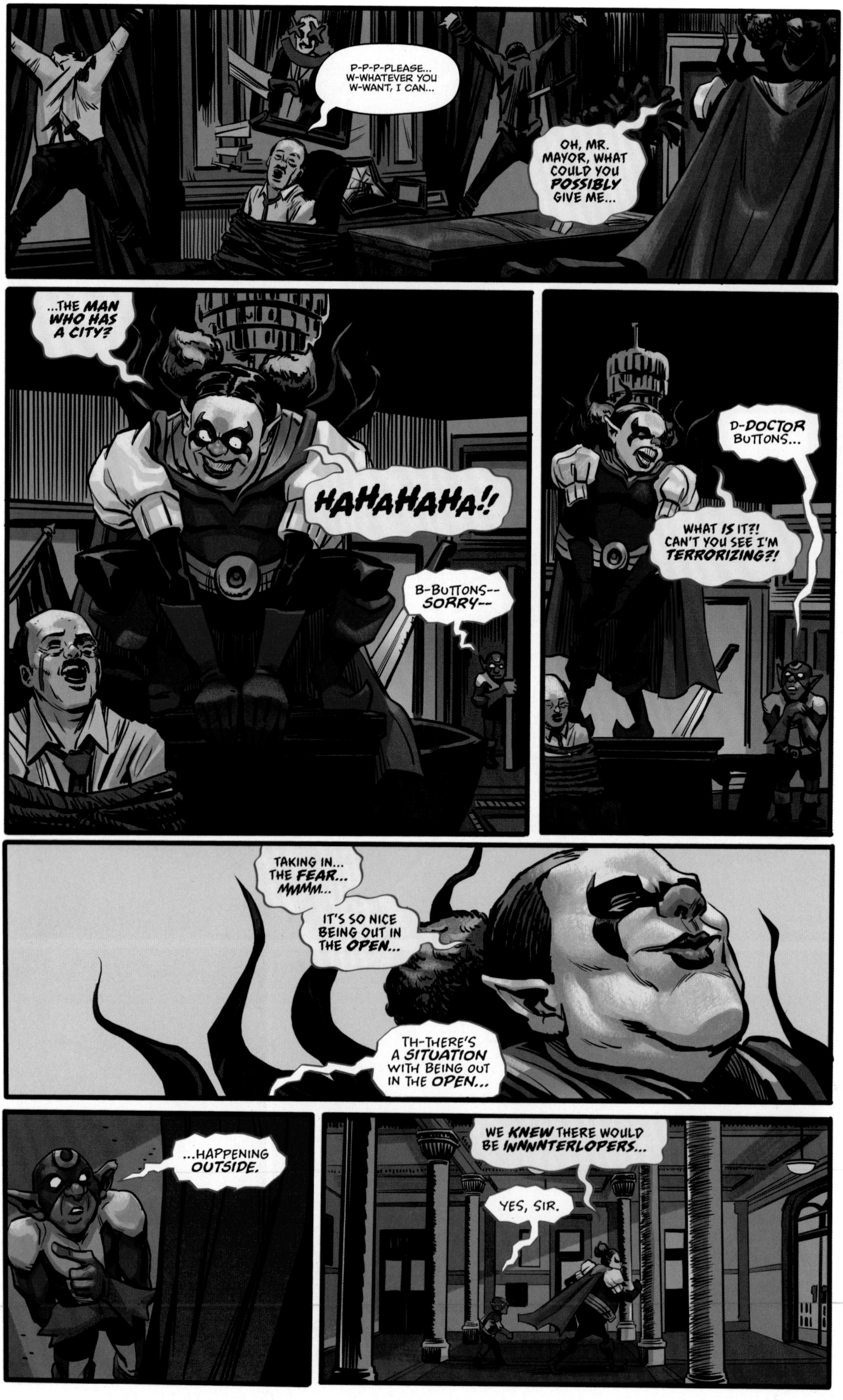
P-P-P-PLEASE... W-WHATEVER YOU W-WANT, I CAN...
OH, MR. MAYOR, WHAT COULD YOU POSSIBLY GIVE ME...
...THE MAN WHO HAS A CITY?
HAHAHAHA!!
B-BUTTONS-- SORRY--
D-DOCTOR BUTTONS...
WHAT IS IT?! CAN'T YOU SEE I'M TERRORIZING?!
TAKING IN... THE FEAR... MMMM...
IT'S SO NICE BEING OUT IN THE OPEN...
TH-THERE'S A SITUATION WITH BEING OUT IN THE OPEN...
...HAPPENING OUTSIDE.
WE KNEW THERE WOULD BE INNNNTERLOPERS...
YES, SIR.

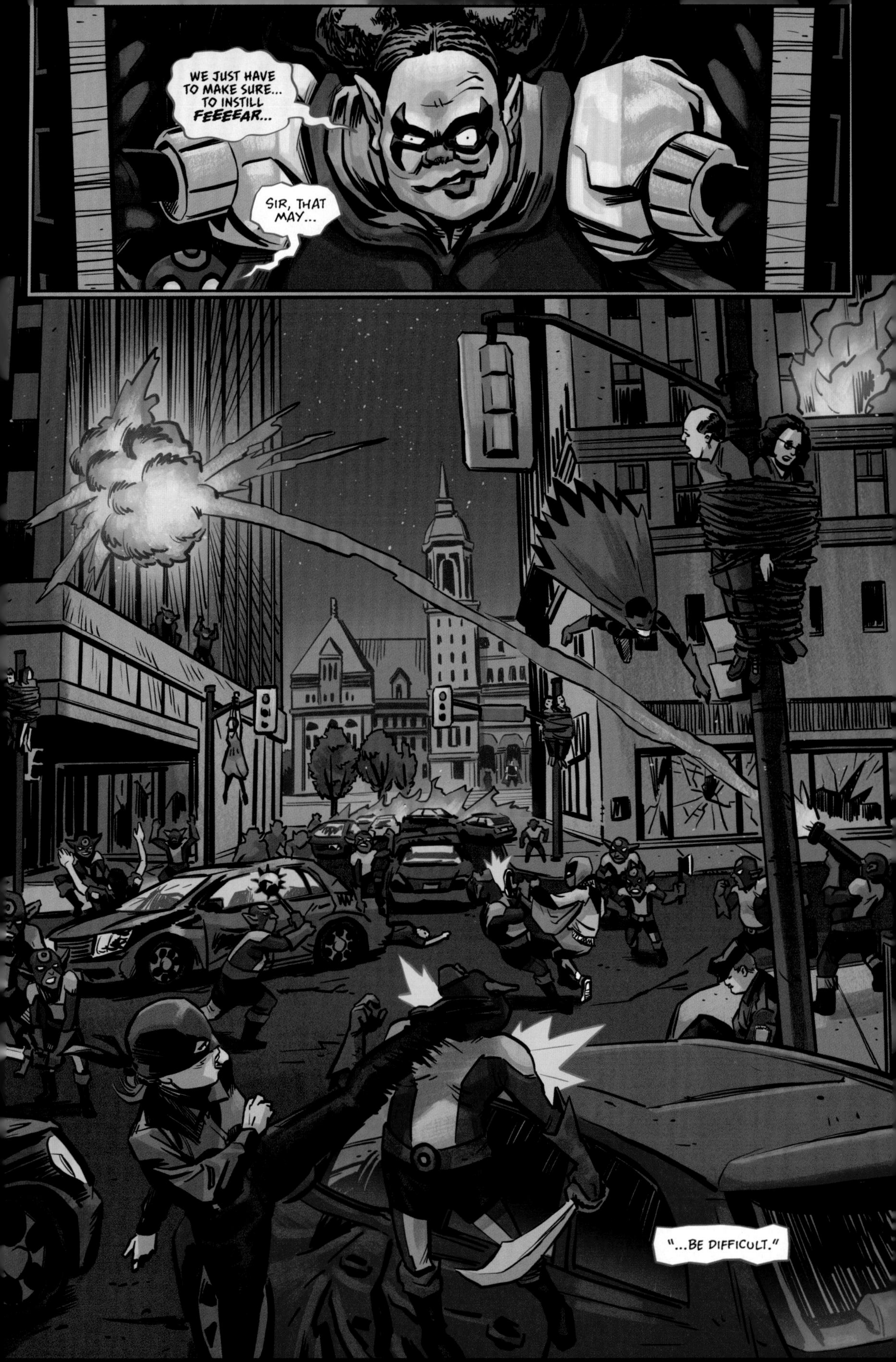
WE JUST HAVE TO MAKE SURE... TO INSTILL FEEEEAR...
SIR, THAT MAY...
"...BE DIFFICULT."

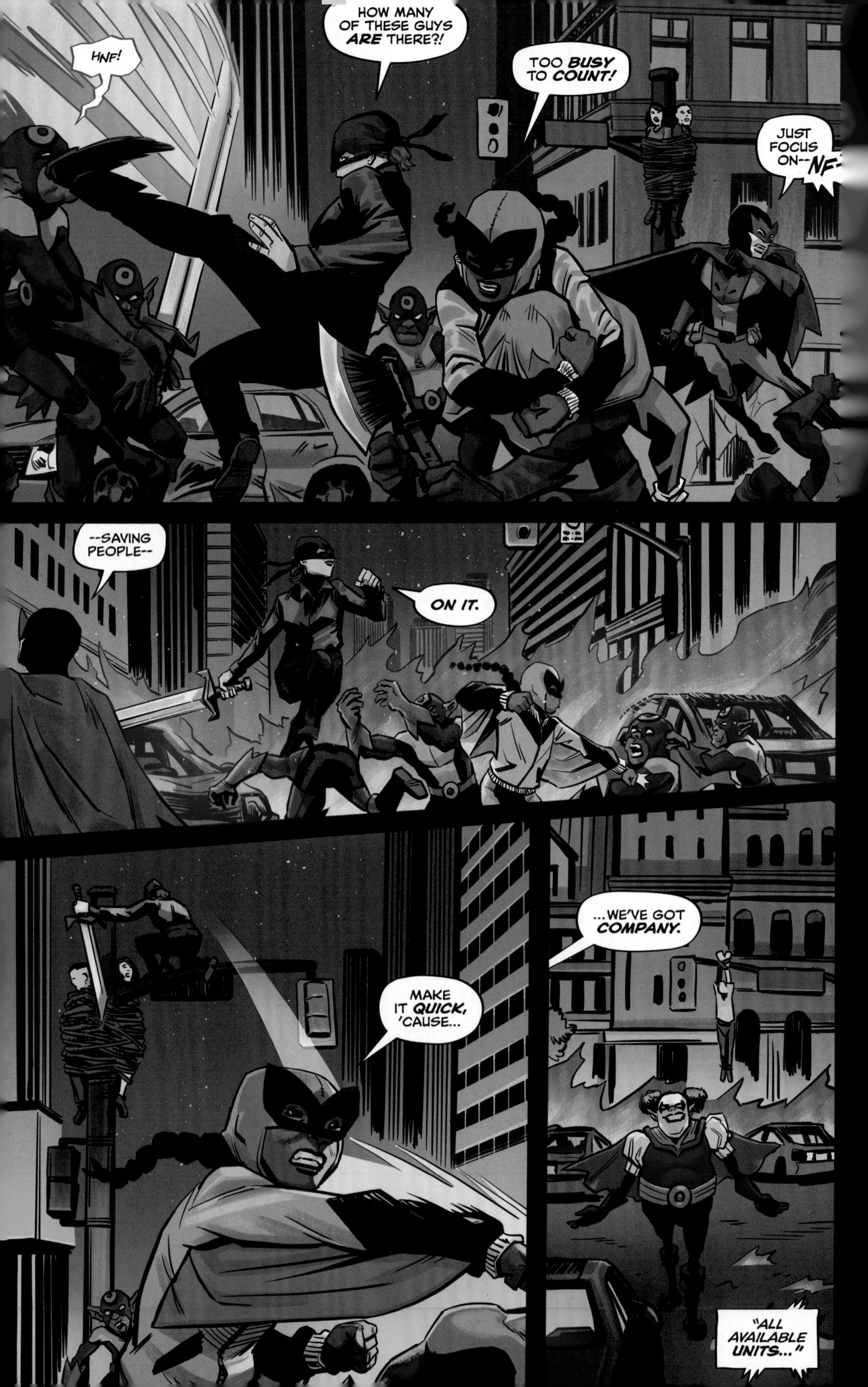
HNF!
HOW MANY OF THESE GUYS ARE THERE?!
TOO BUSY TO COUNT!
JUST FOCUS ON-- NF-
--SAVING PEOPLE--
ON IT.
MAKE IT QUICK, 'CAUSE...
...WE'VE GOT COMPANY.
"ALL AVAILABLE UNITS..."

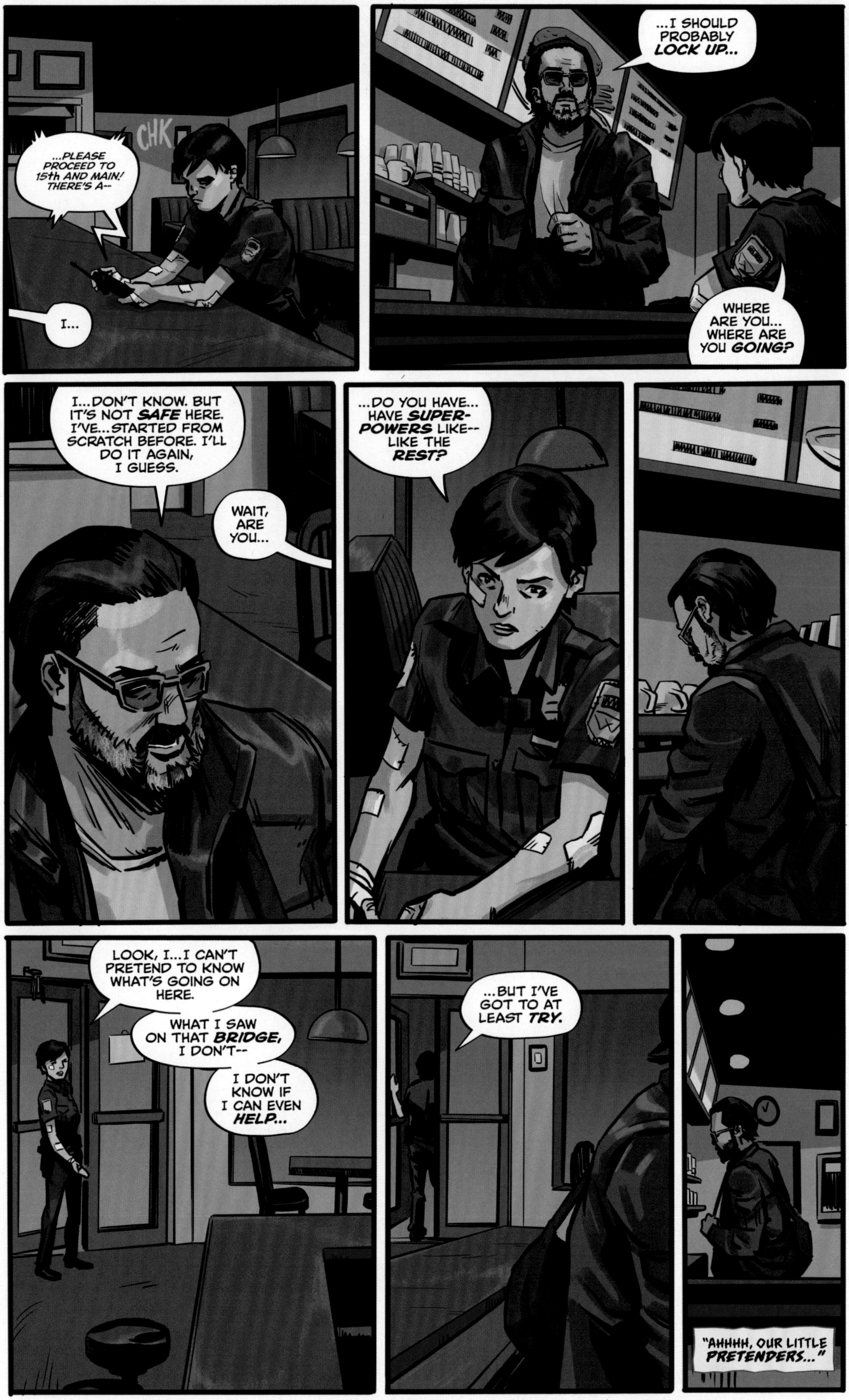

CHK
...PLEASE PROCEED TO 15th AND MAIN! THERE'S A--
I...
...I SHOULD PROBABLY LOCK UP...
WHERE ARE YOU... WHERE ARE YOU GOING?
I...DON'T KNOW. BUT IT'S NOT SAFE HERE. I'VE...STARTED FROM SCRATCH BEFORE. I'LL DO IT AGAIN, I GUESS.
WAIT, ARE YOU...
...DO YOU HAVE... HAVE SUPER-POWERS LIKE--LIKE THE REST?
LOOK, I...I CAN'T PRETEND TO KNOW WHAT'S GOING ON HERE.
WHAT I SAW ON THAT BRIDGE, I DON'T--
I DON'T KNOW IF I CAN EVEN HELP...
...BUT I'VE GOT TO AT LEAST TRY.
"AHHHH, OUR LITTLE PRETENDERS..."

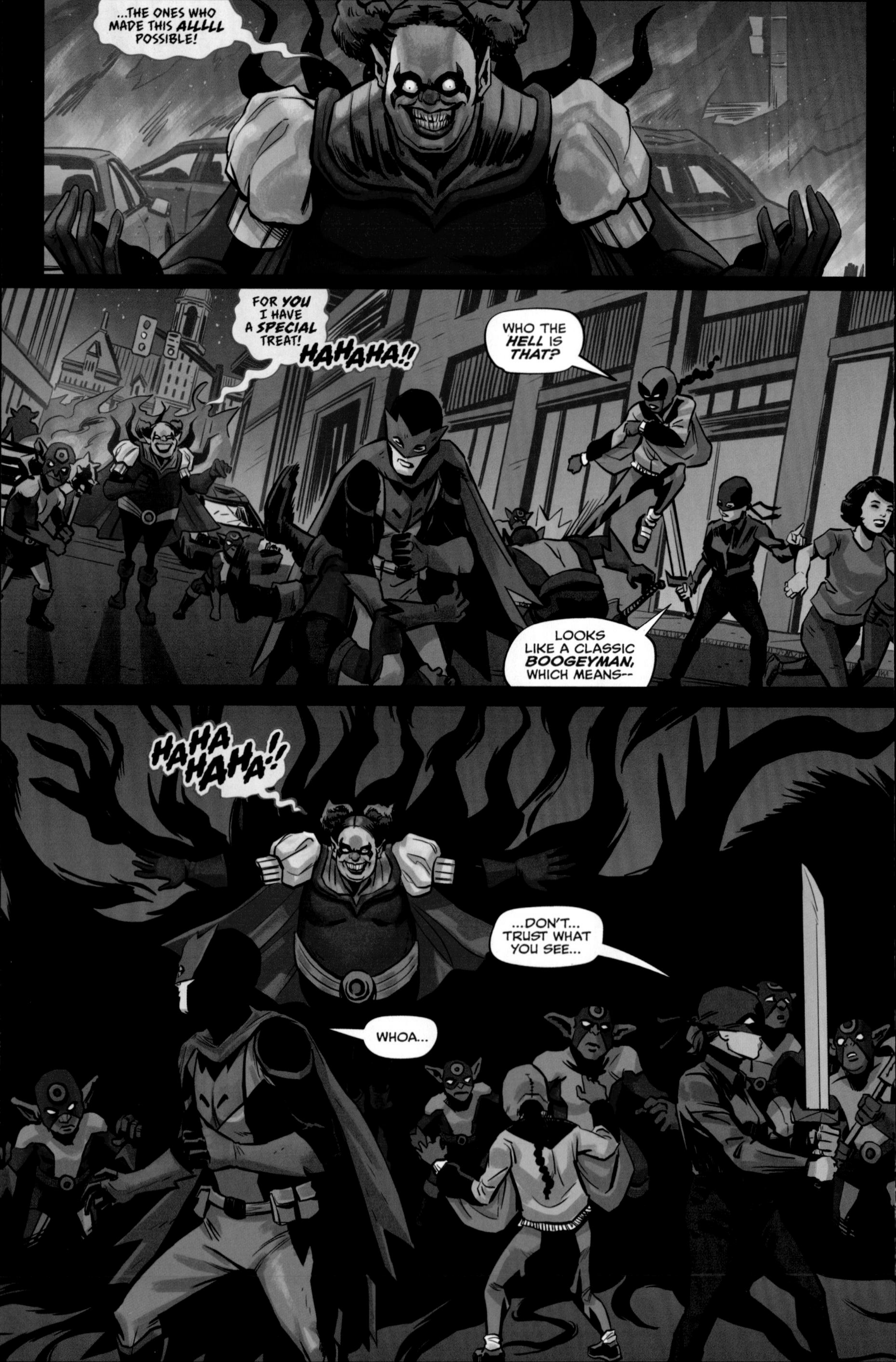
...THE ONES WHO MADE THIS ALLLLL POSSIBLE!
FOR YOU I HAVE A SPECIAL TREAT! HAHAHA!!
WHO THE HELL IS THAT?
LOOKS LIKE A CLASSIC BOOGEYMAN, WHICH MEANS--
HAHA HAHA!!
...DON'T... TRUST WHAT YOU SEE...
WHOA...

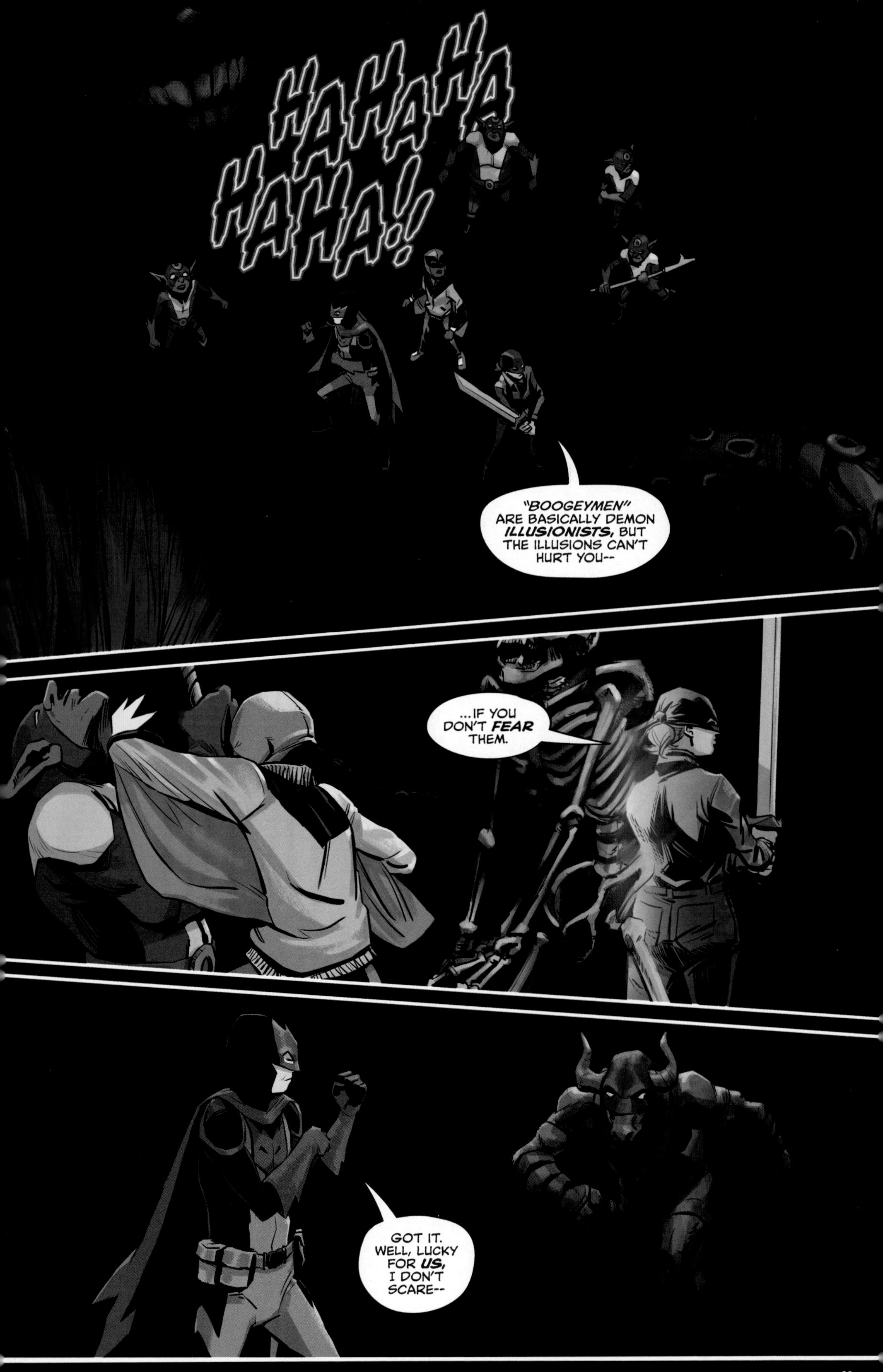
HAHAHA HAHAHA!!
"BOOGEYMEN" ARE BASICALLY DEMON ILLUSIONISTS, BUT THE ILLUSIONS CAN'T HURT YOU--
...IF YOU DON'T FEAR THEM.
GOT IT. WELL, LUCKY FOR US, I DON'T SCARE--

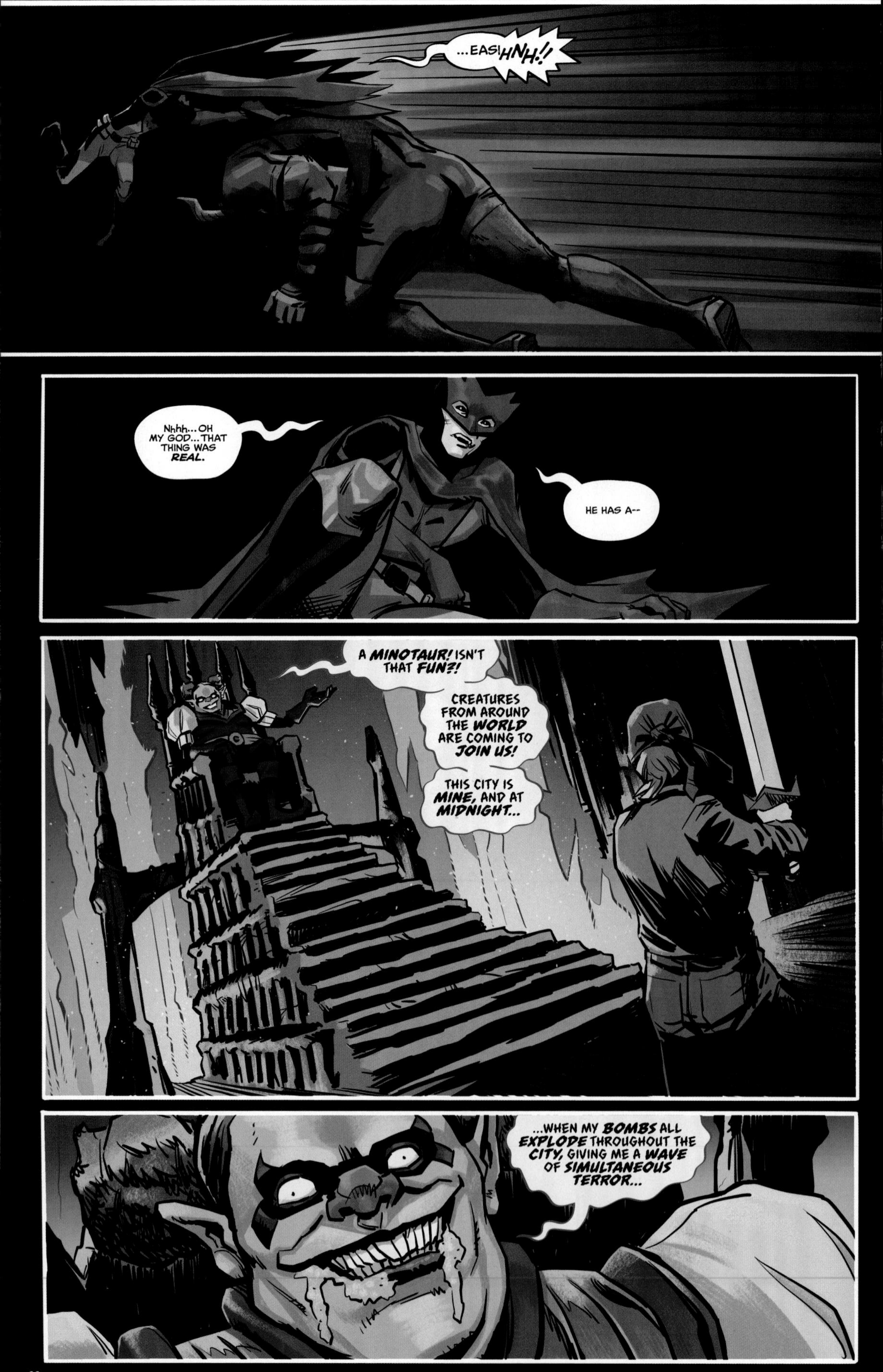
...EASIHNH!!
Nhhh... OH MY GOD... THAT THING WAS REAL.
HE HAS A--
A MINOTAUR! ISN'T THAT FUN?!
CREATURES FROM AROUND THE WORLD ARE COMING TO JOIN US!
THIS CITY IS MINE, AND AT MIDNIGHT...
...WHEN MY BOMBS ALL EXPLODE THROUGHOUT THE CITY, GIVING ME A WAVE OF SIMULTANEOUS TERROR...

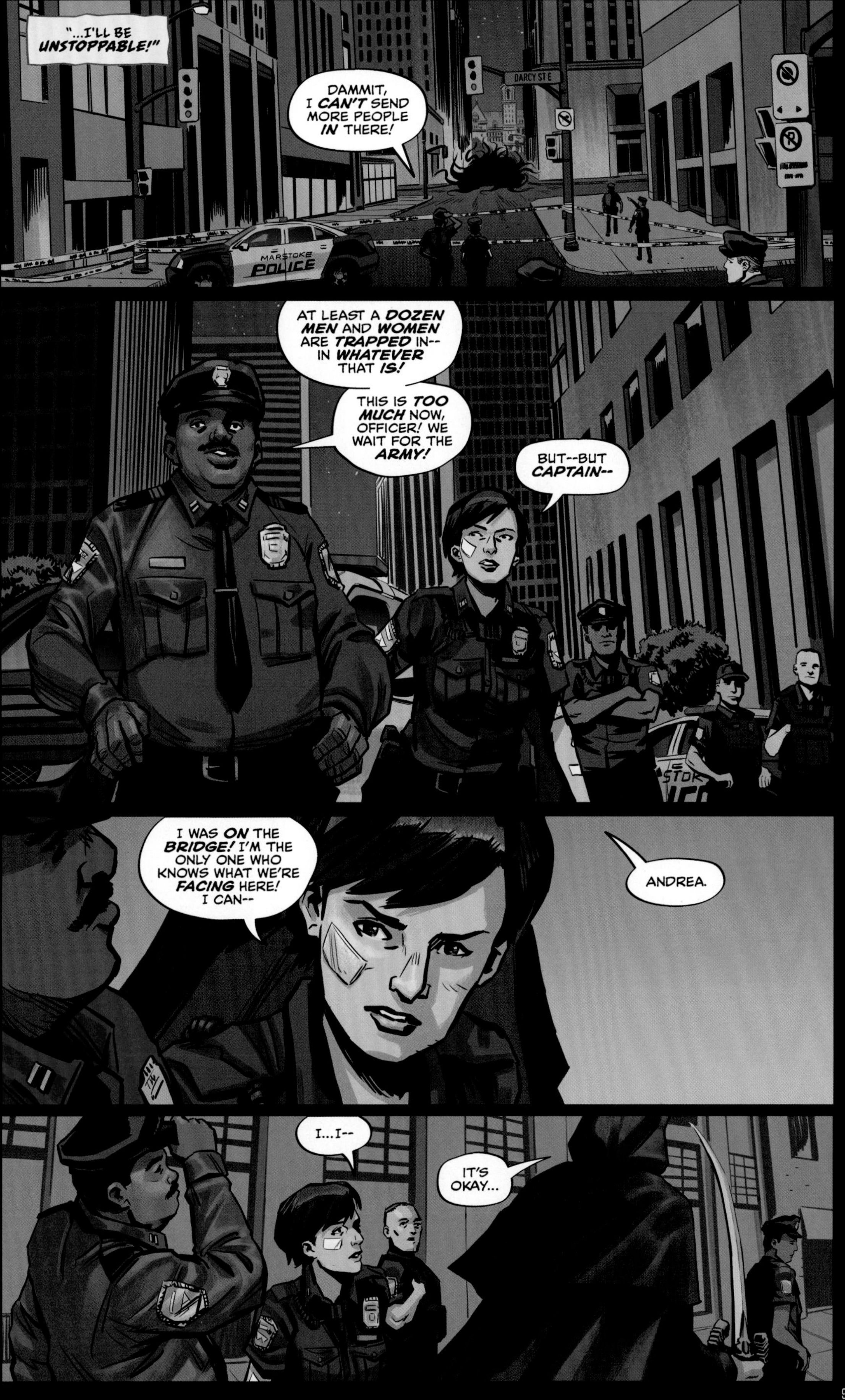
"...I'LL BE UNSTOPPABLE!"
DAMMIT, I CAN'T SEND MORE PEOPLE IN THERE!
DARCY ST E
MARSTOKE POLICE
AT LEAST A DOZEN MEN AND WOMEN ARE TRAPPED IN-- IN WHATEVER THAT IS!
THIS IS TOO MUCH NOW, OFFICER! WE WAIT FOR THE ARMY!
BUT--BUT CAPTAIN--
I WAS ON THE BRIDGE! I'M THE ONLY ONE WHO KNOWS WHAT WE'RE FACING HERE! I CAN--
ANDREA.
I...I--
IT'S OKAY...

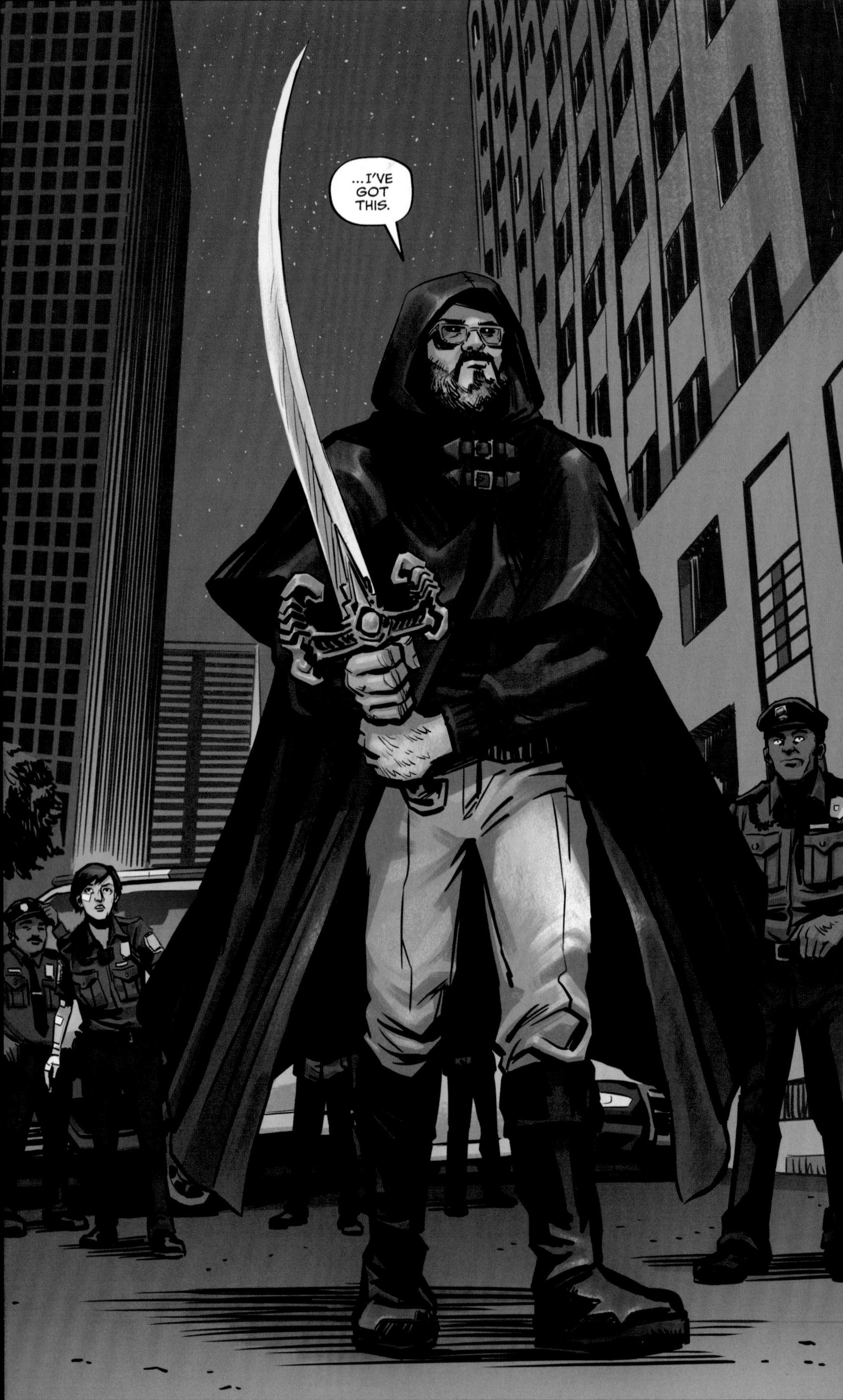
...I'VE GOT THIS.

CREEEAK

GRRRR-

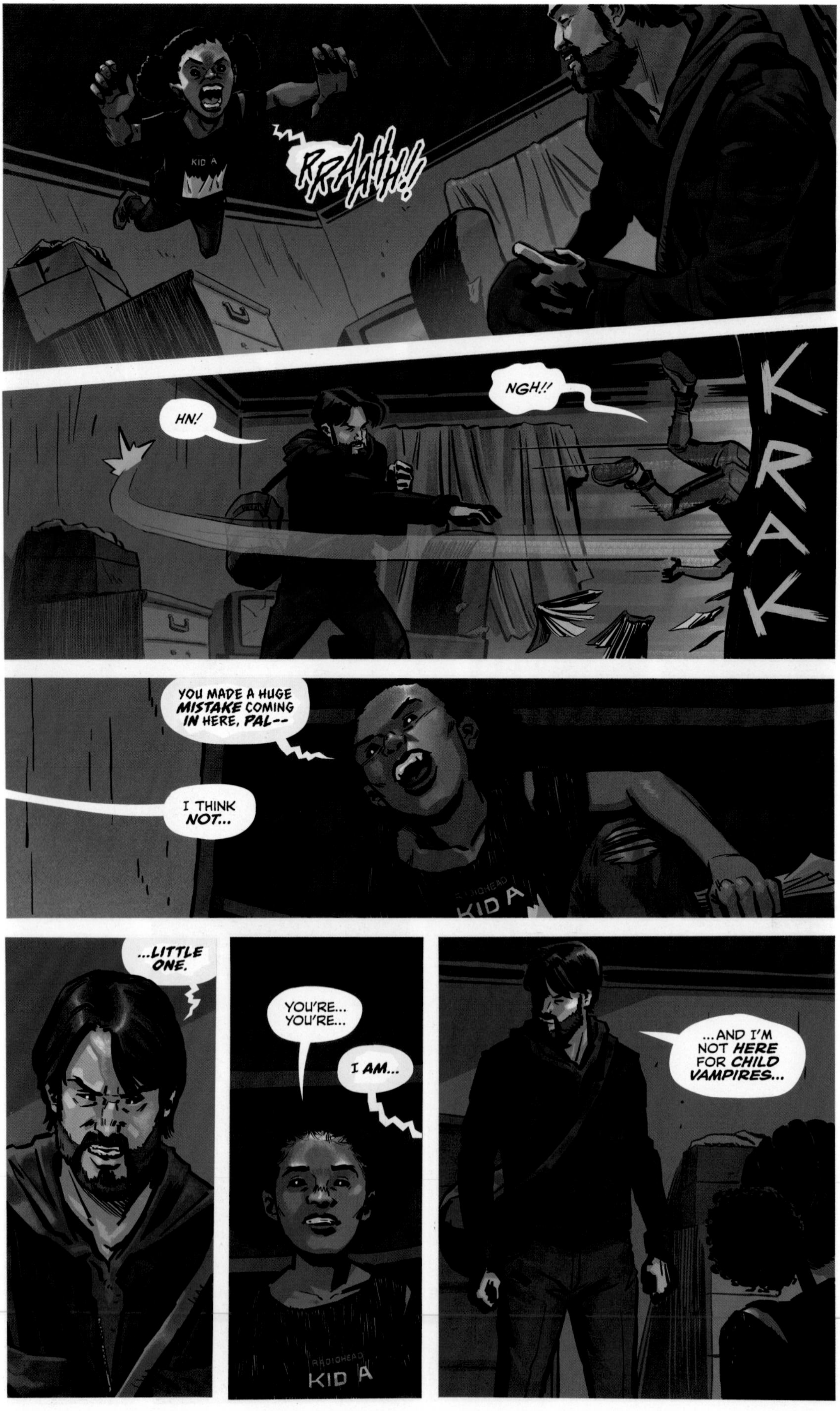
RRAAHH!!
HN!
NGH!!
KRAK
YOU MADE A HUGE MISTAKE COMING IN HERE, PAL--
I THINK NOT...
RADIOHEAD KID A
...LITTLE ONE.
YOU'RE... YOU'RE...
I AM...
RADIOHEAD KID A
...AND I'M NOT HERE FOR CHILD VAMPIRES...

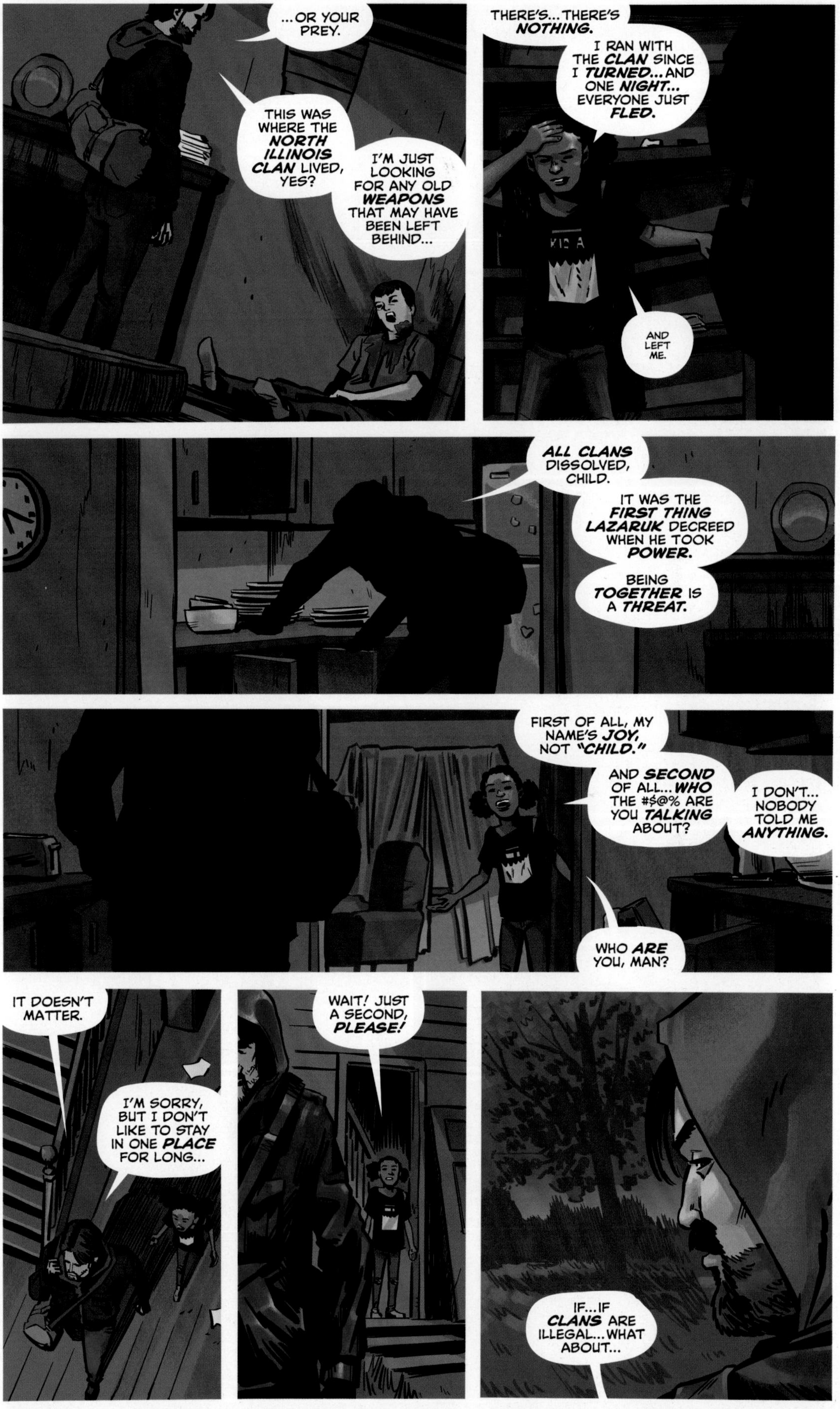
...OR YOUR PREY.
THIS WAS WHERE THE NORTH ILLINOIS CLAN LIVED, YES?
I'M JUST LOOKING FOR ANY OLD WEAPONS THAT MAY HAVE BEEN LEFT BEHIND...
THERE'S...THERE'S NOTHING.
I RAN WITH THE CLAN SINCE I TURNED...AND ONE NIGHT... EVERYONE JUST FLED.
AND LEFT ME.
ALL CLANS DISSOLVED, CHILD.
IT WAS THE FIRST THING LAZARUK DECREED WHEN HE TOOK POWER.
BEING TOGETHER IS A THREAT.
FIRST OF ALL, MY NAME'S JOY, NOT "CHILD."
AND SECOND OF ALL...WHO THE #$@% ARE YOU TALKING ABOUT?
I DON'T... NOBODY TOLD ME ANYTHING.
WHO ARE YOU, MAN?
IT DOESN'T MATTER.
I'M SORRY, BUT I DON'T LIKE TO STAY IN ONE PLACE FOR LONG...
WAIT! JUST A SECOND, PLEASE!
IF...IF CLANS ARE ILLEGAL...WHAT ABOUT...

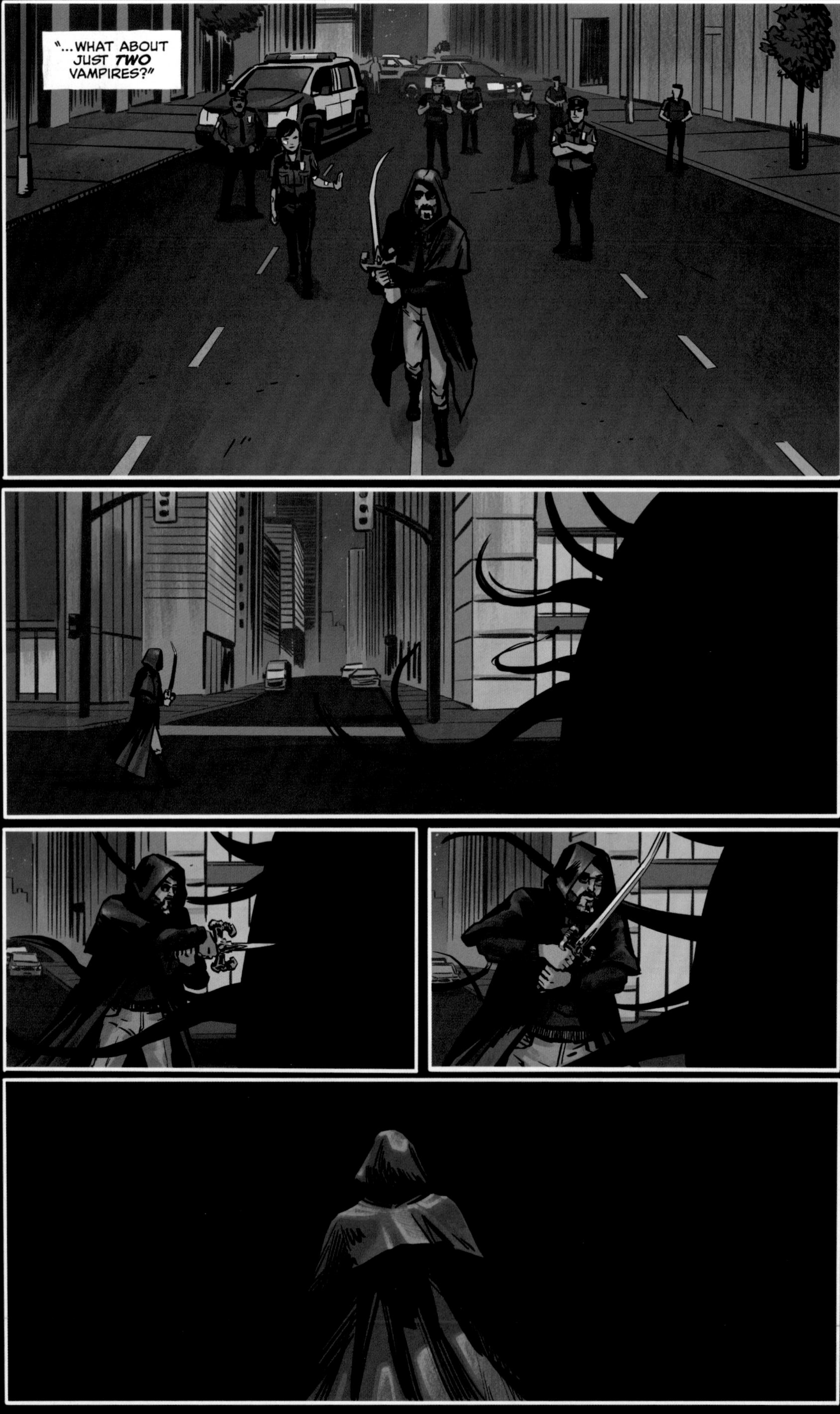
"...WHAT ABOUT JUST *TWO* VAMPIRES?"

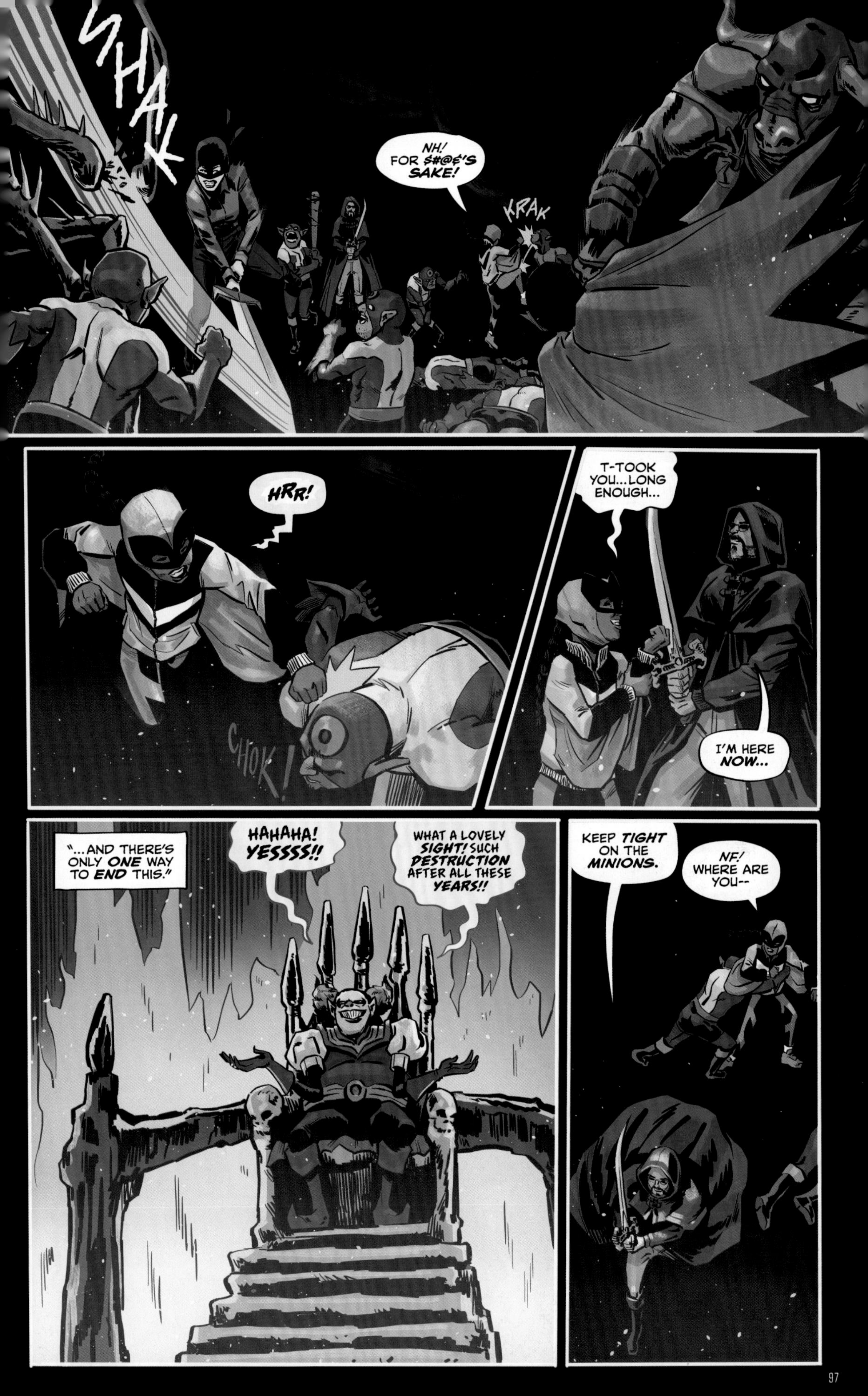
SHAK
NH! FOR $#@¢'S SAKE!
KRAK
HRR!
CHOK!
T-TOOK YOU...LONG ENOUGH...
I'M HERE NOW...
"...AND THERE'S ONLY ONE WAY TO END THIS."
HAHAHA! YESSSS!!
WHAT A LOVELY SIGHT! SUCH DESTRUCTION AFTER ALL THESE YEARS!!
KEEP TIGHT ON THE MINIONS.
NF! WHERE ARE YOU--

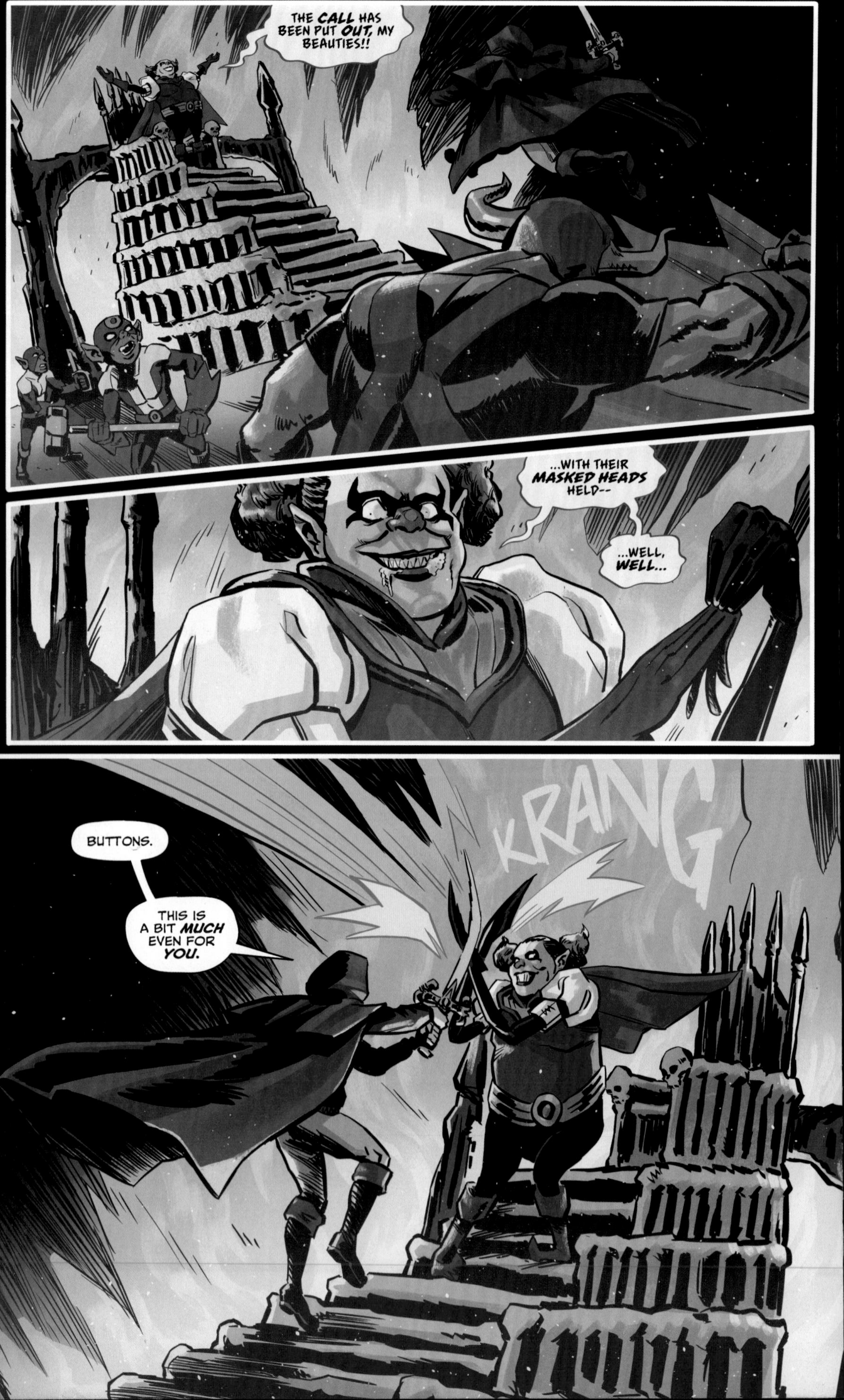
THE **CALL** HAS BEEN PUT **OUT,** MY BEAUTIES!!
...WITH THEIR **MASKED HEADS** HELD--
...WELL, **WELL...**
KRANG
BUTTONS.
THIS IS A BIT **MUCH** EVEN FOR **YOU.**

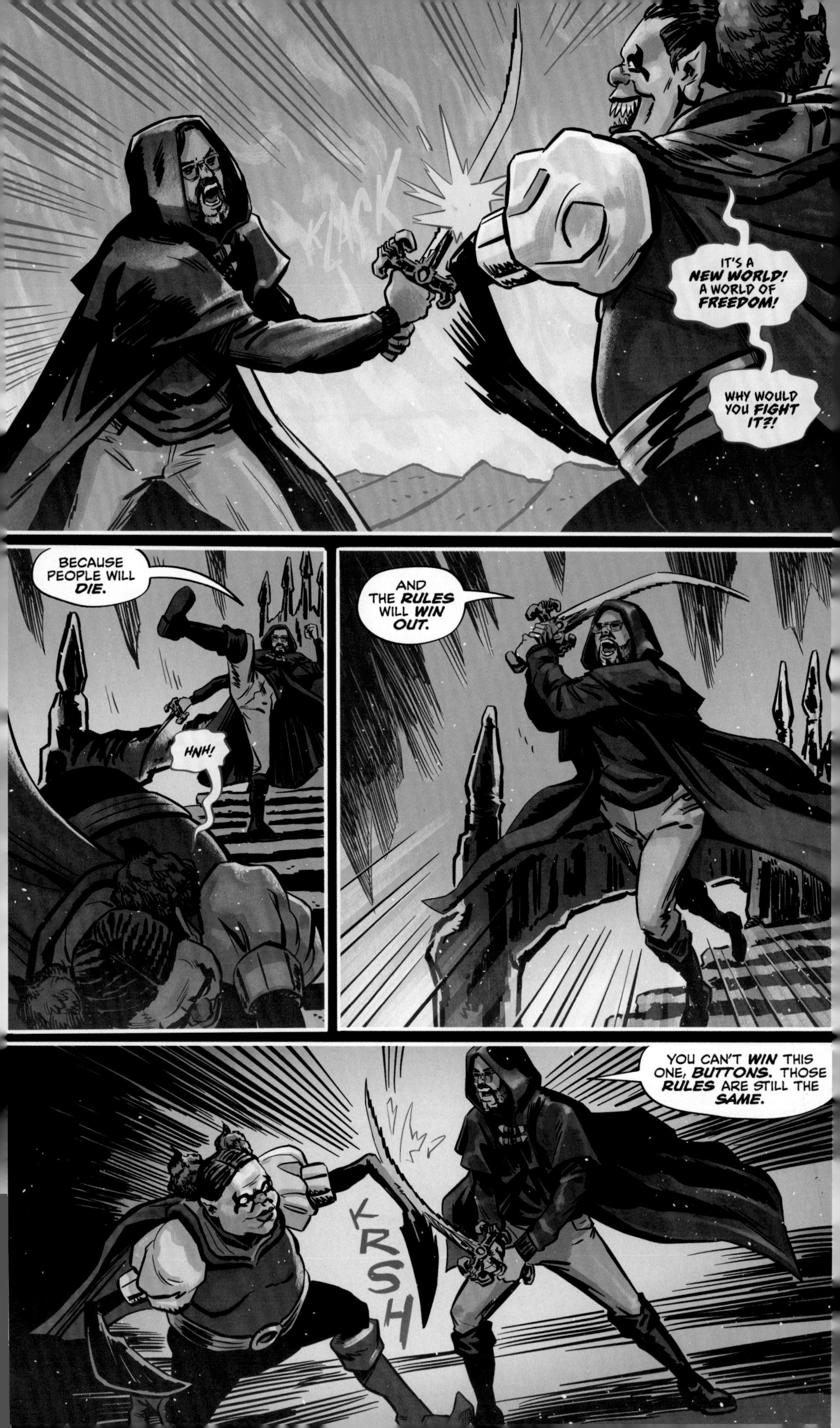
KLACK
IT'S A NEW WORLD! A WORLD OF FREEDOM!
WHY WOULD YOU FIGHT IT?!
BECAUSE PEOPLE WILL DIE.
HNH!
AND THE RULES WILL WIN OUT.
YOU CAN'T WIN THIS ONE, BUTTONS. THOSE RULES ARE STILL THE SAME.
KRSH

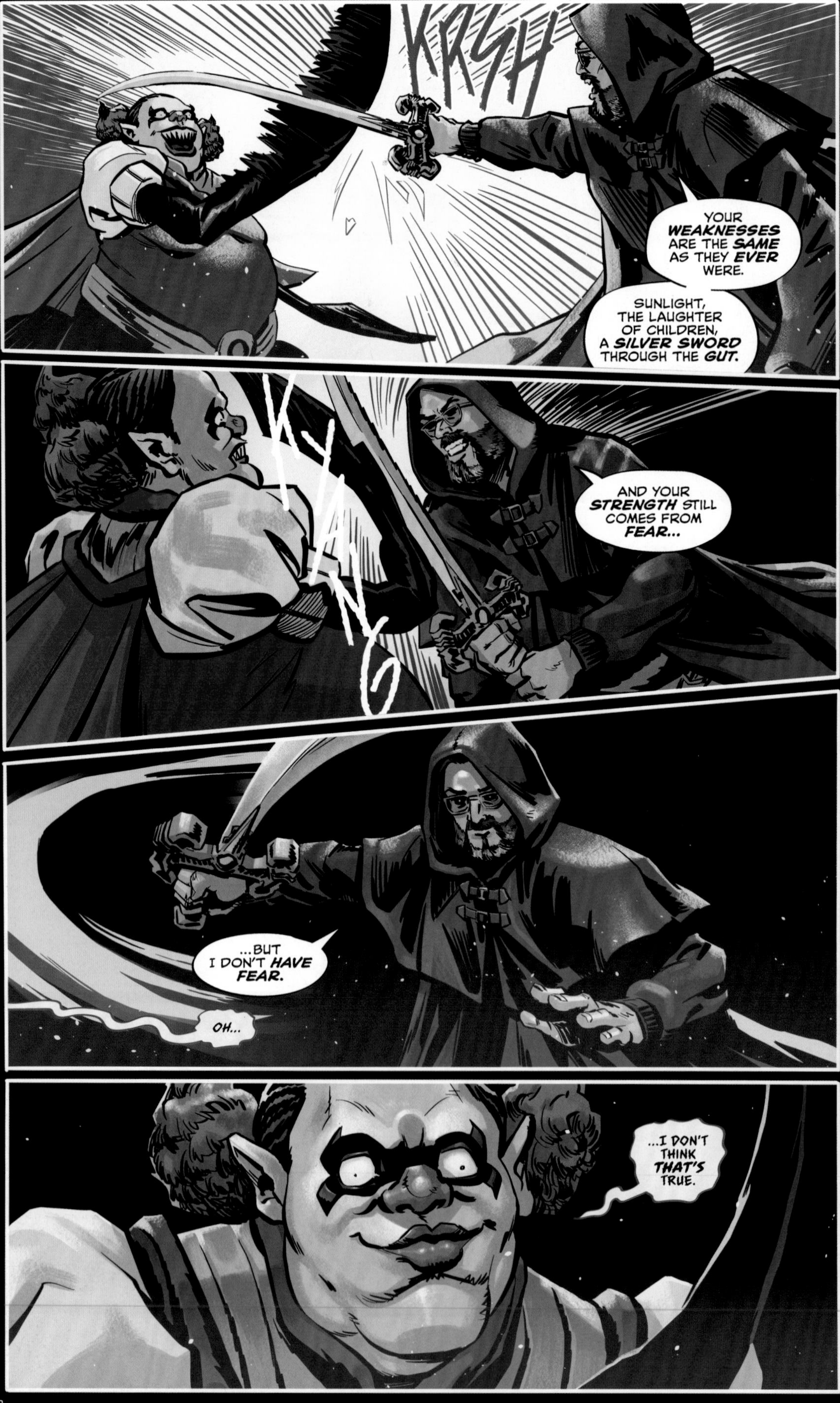
KRSH
YOUR WEAKNESSES ARE THE SAME AS THEY EVER WERE.
SUNLIGHT, THE LAUGHTER OF CHILDREN, A SILVER SWORD THROUGH THE GUT.
KYANG
AND YOUR STRENGTH STILL COMES FROM FEAR...
...BUT I DON'T HAVE FEAR.
OH...
...I DON'T THINK THAT'S TRUE.

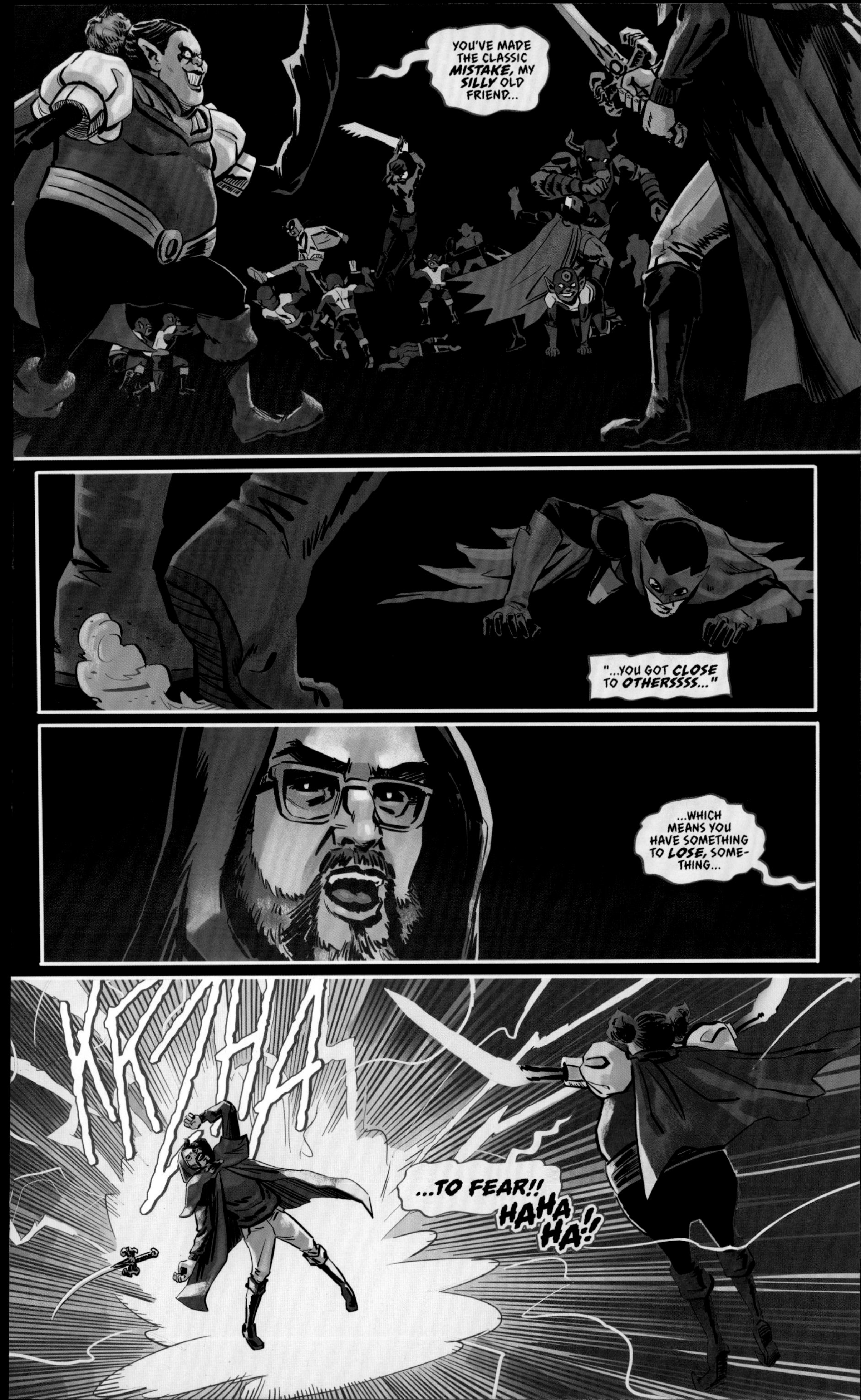
YOU'VE MADE THE CLASSIC MISTAKE, MY SILLY OLD FRIEND...
"...YOU GOT CLOSE TO OTHERSSSS..."
...WHICH MEANS YOU HAVE SOMETHING TO LOSE, SOME-THING...
KRTHA
...TO FEAR!! HAHA HA!!

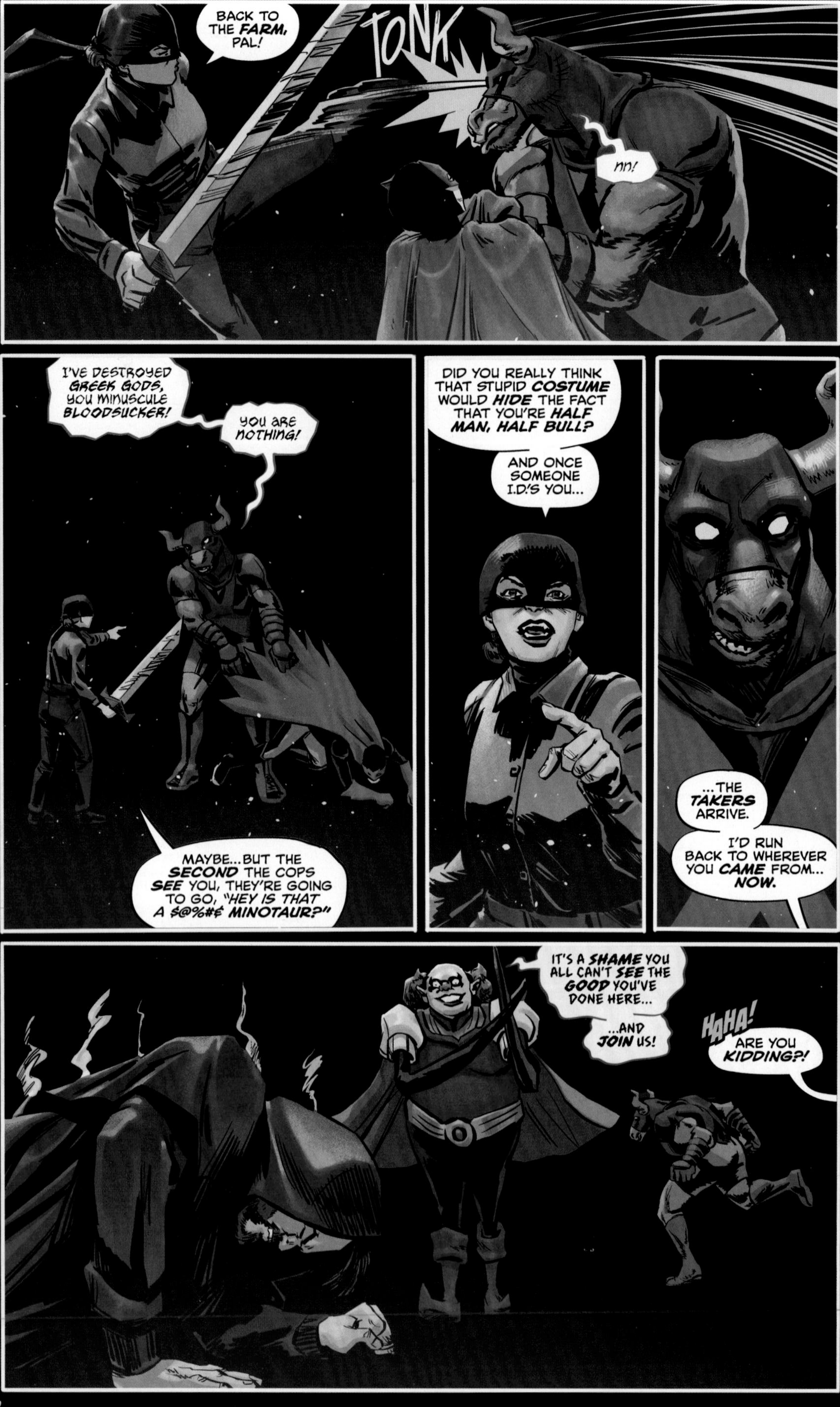
BACK TO THE FARM, PAL!
TONK
nn!
I'VE DESTROYED GREEK GODS, YOU MINUSCULE BLOODSUCKER!
YOU ARE NOTHING!
MAYBE...BUT THE SECOND THE COPS SEE YOU, THEY'RE GOING TO GO, "HEY IS THAT A $@%#€ MINOTAUR?"
DID YOU REALLY THINK THAT STUPID COSTUME WOULD HIDE THE FACT THAT YOU'RE HALF MAN, HALF BULL?
AND ONCE SOMEONE I.D.'S YOU...
...THE TAKERS ARRIVE.
I'D RUN BACK TO WHEREVER YOU CAME FROM... NOW.
IT'S A SHAME YOU ALL CAN'T SEE THE GOOD YOU'VE DONE HERE...
...AND JOIN US!
HAHA!
ARE YOU KIDDING?!

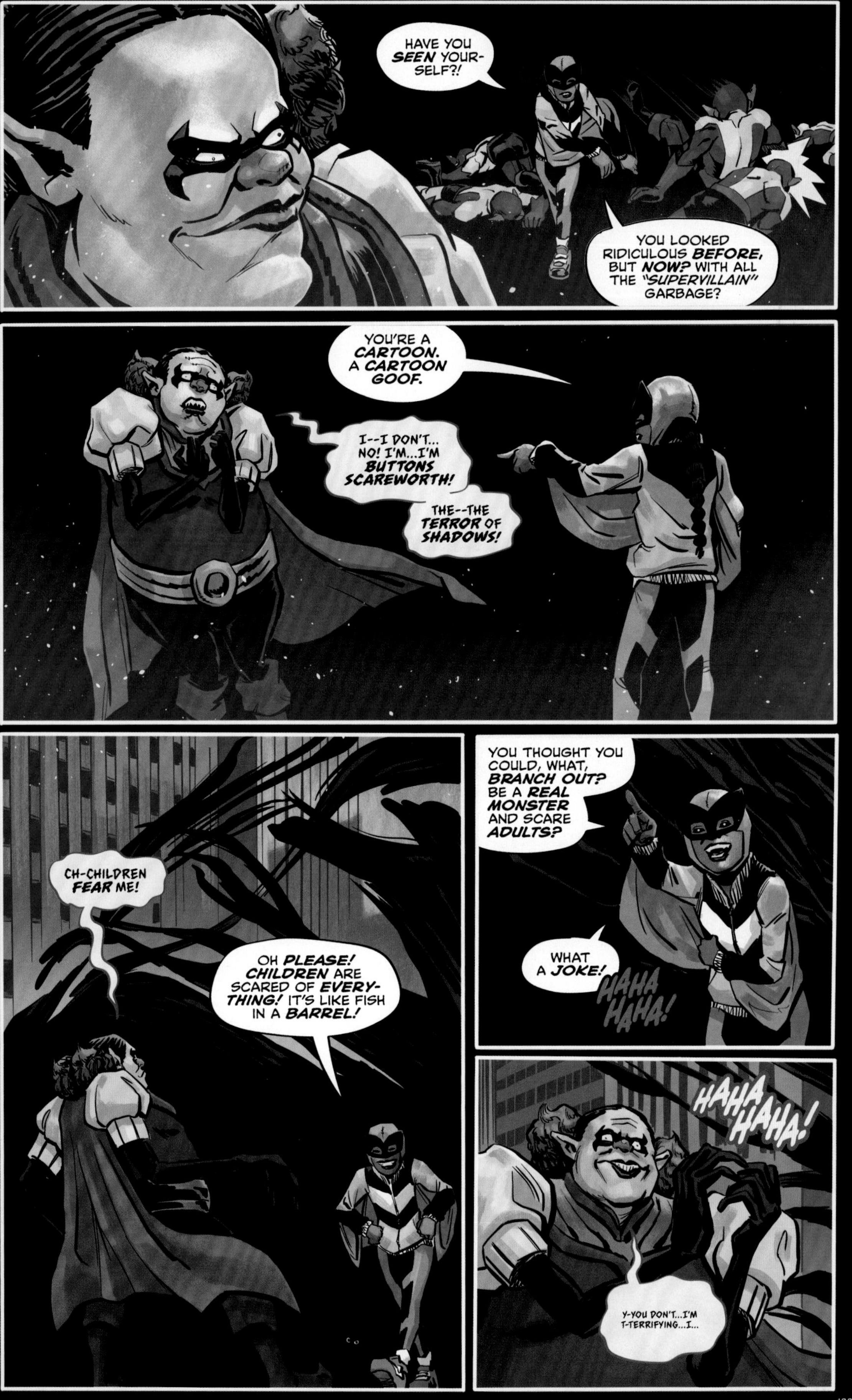
HAVE YOU SEEN YOURSELF?!
YOU LOOKED RIDICULOUS BEFORE, BUT NOW? WITH ALL THE "SUPERVILLAIN" GARBAGE?
YOU'RE A CARTOON. A CARTOON GOOF.
I--I DON'T... NO! I'M...I'M BUTTONS SCAREWORTH!
THE--THE TERROR OF SHADOWS!
CH-CHILDREN FEAR ME!
OH PLEASE! CHILDREN ARE SCARED OF EVERYTHING! IT'S LIKE FISH IN A BARREL!
YOU THOUGHT YOU COULD, WHAT, BRANCH OUT? BE A REAL MONSTER AND SCARE ADULTS?
WHAT A JOKE!
HAHA HAHA!
HAHA HAHA!
Y-YOU DON'T...I'M T-TERRIFYING...I...

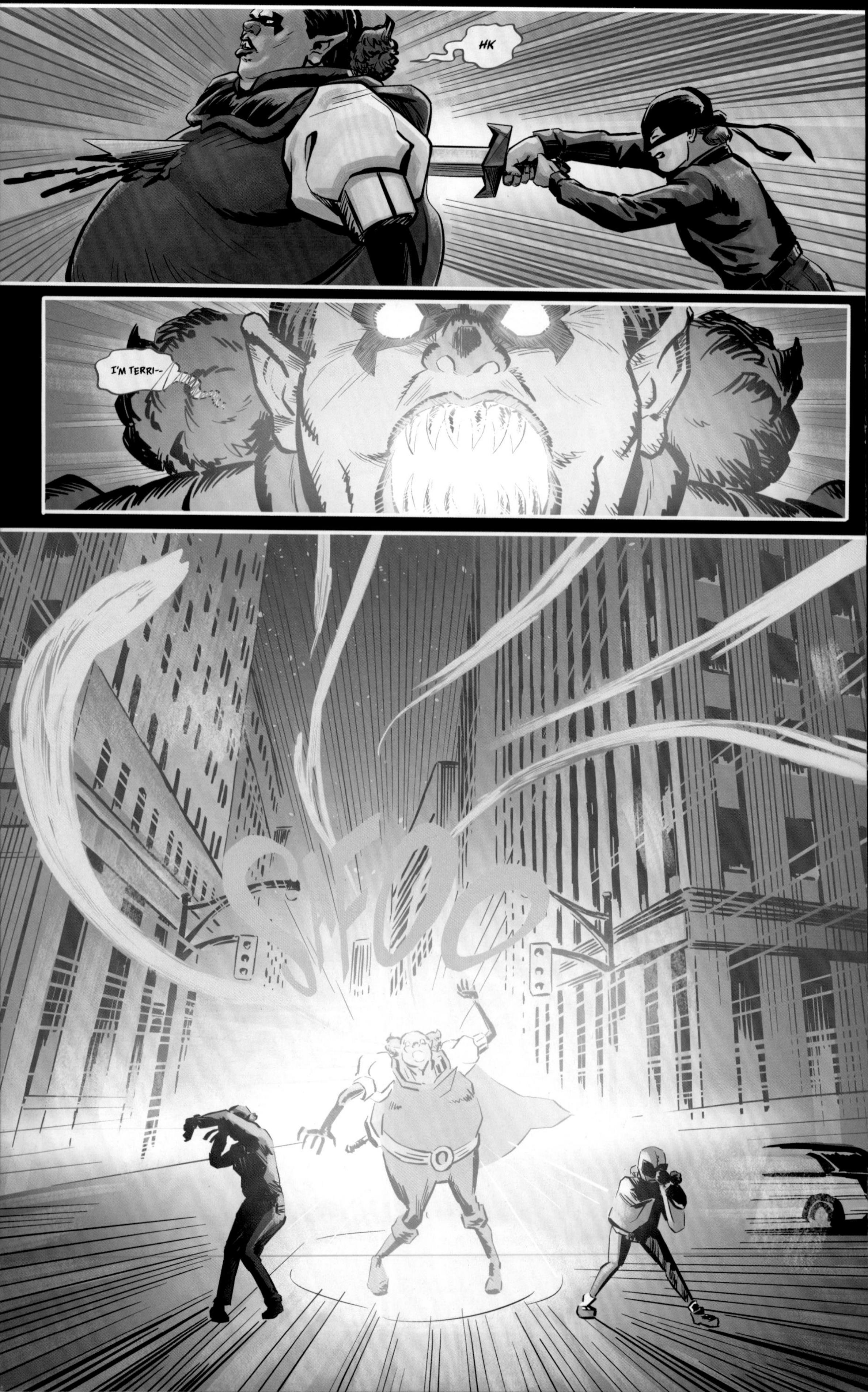
HK
I'M TERRI--
SPTOOO

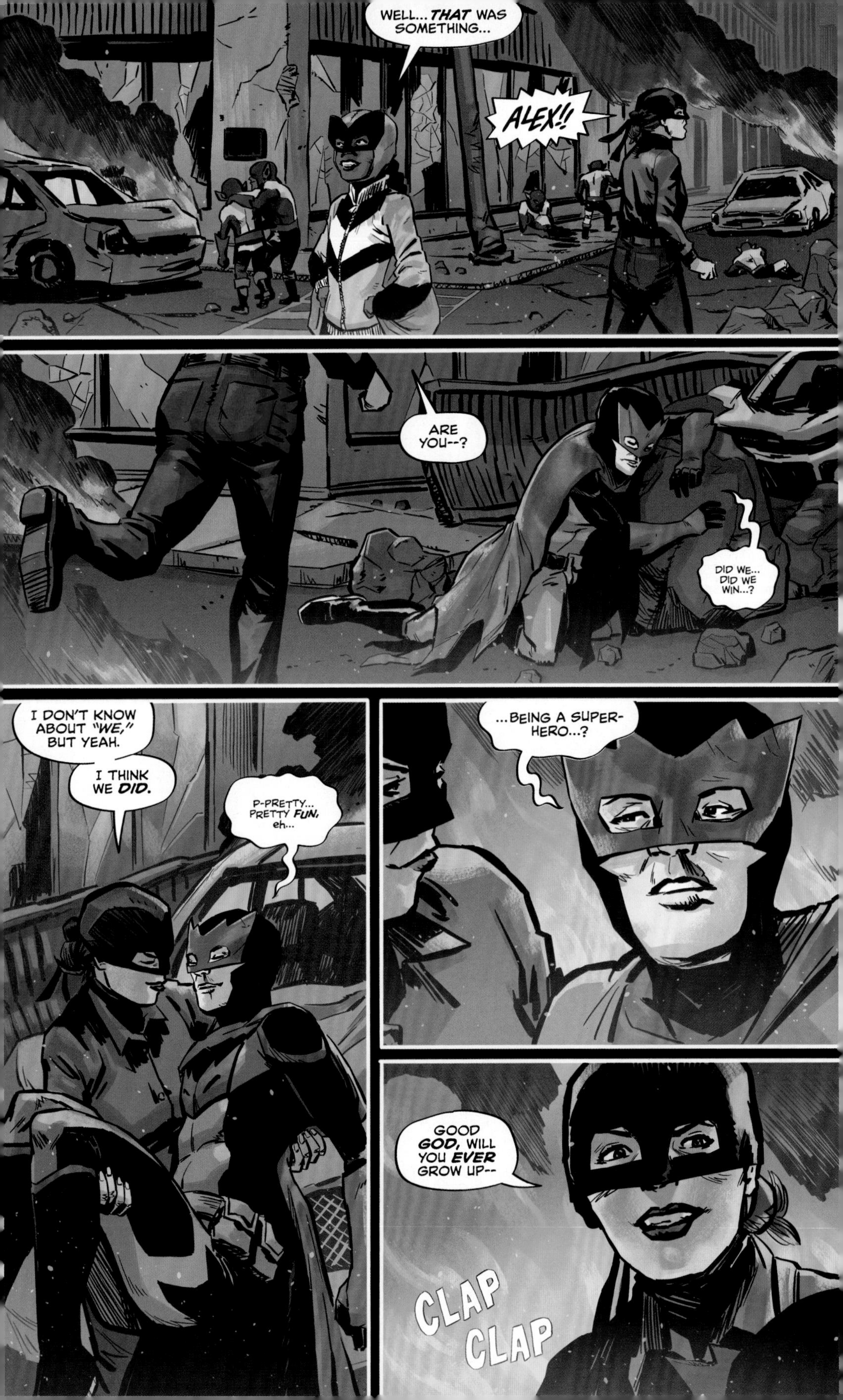
WELL... *THAT* WAS SOMETHING...
ALEX!!
ARE YOU--?
DID WE... DID WE WIN...?
I DON'T KNOW ABOUT *"WE,"* BUT YEAH.
I THINK WE *DID.*
P-PRETTY... PRETTY *FUN,* eh...
...BEING A SUPER-HERO...?
GOOD *GOD,* WILL YOU *EVER* GROW UP--
CLAP
CLAP

WoOo!

YEAH!!

CLAP CLAP CLAP CLAP CLAP CLAP CLA

CLAP CLAP CLAP CLAP CLAP CLAP CLAP

DARCY ST E

...OKAY, SURE.

THIS PART IS PRETTY FUN.

WAIT. WHERE'S...

...WHERE'S IAN?

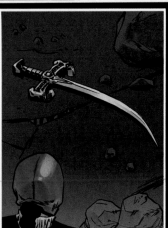

THREE WEEKS LATER:

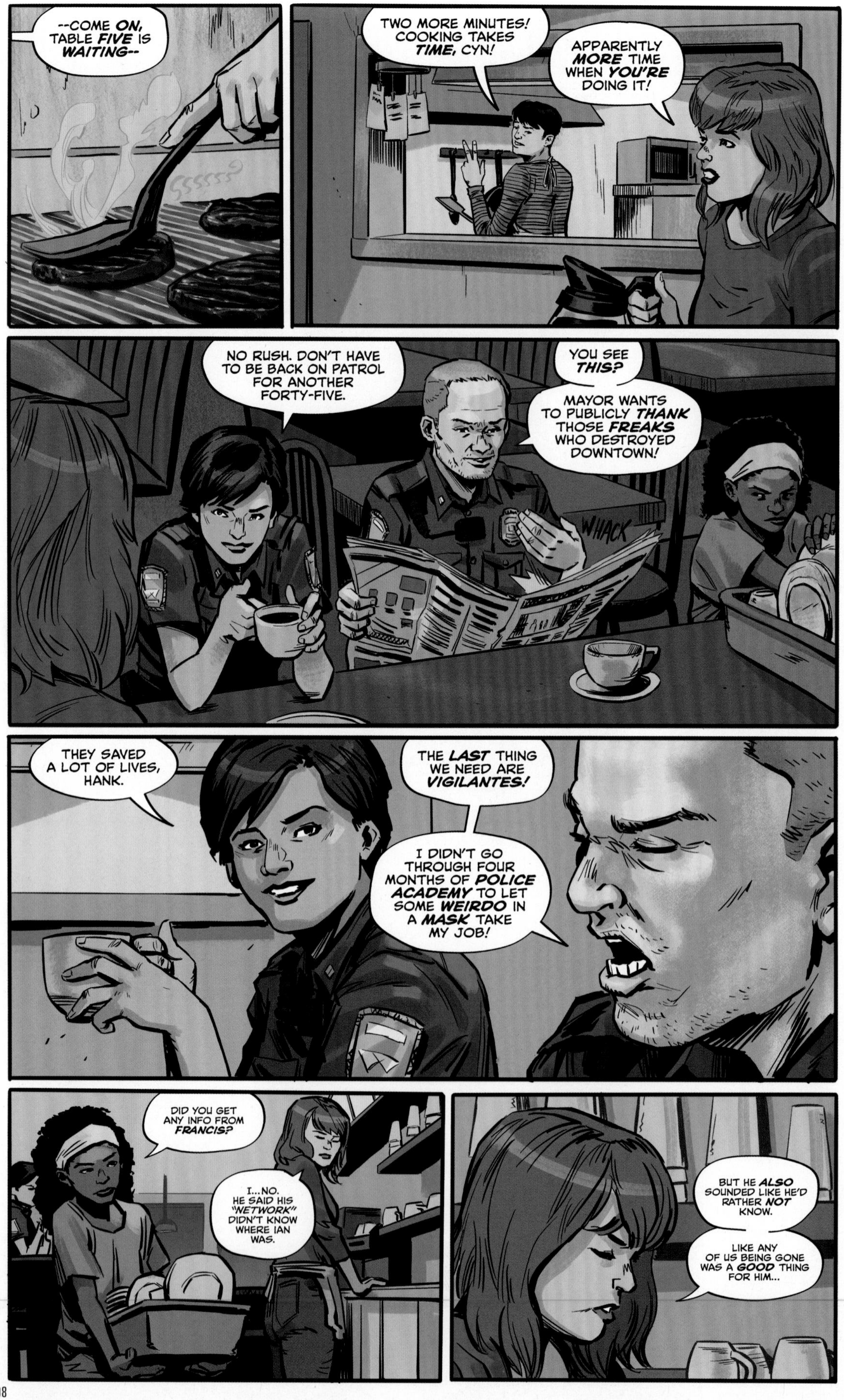
--COME ON, TABLE FIVE IS WAITING--
SSSSSS
TWO MORE MINUTES! COOKING TAKES TIME, CYN!
APPARENTLY MORE TIME WHEN YOU'RE DOING IT!
NO RUSH. DON'T HAVE TO BE BACK ON PATROL FOR ANOTHER FORTY-FIVE.
YOU SEE THIS?
MAYOR WANTS TO PUBLICLY THANK THOSE FREAKS WHO DESTROYED DOWNTOWN!
WHACK
THEY SAVED A LOT OF LIVES, HANK.
THE LAST THING WE NEED ARE VIGILANTES!
I DIDN'T GO THROUGH FOUR MONTHS OF POLICE ACADEMY TO LET SOME WEIRDO IN A MASK TAKE MY JOB!
DID YOU GET ANY INFO FROM FRANCIS?
I...NO. HE SAID HIS "NETWORK" DIDN'T KNOW WHERE IAN WAS.
BUT HE ALSO SOUNDED LIKE HE'D RATHER NOT KNOW.
LIKE ANY OF US BEING GONE WAS A GOOD THING FOR HIM...

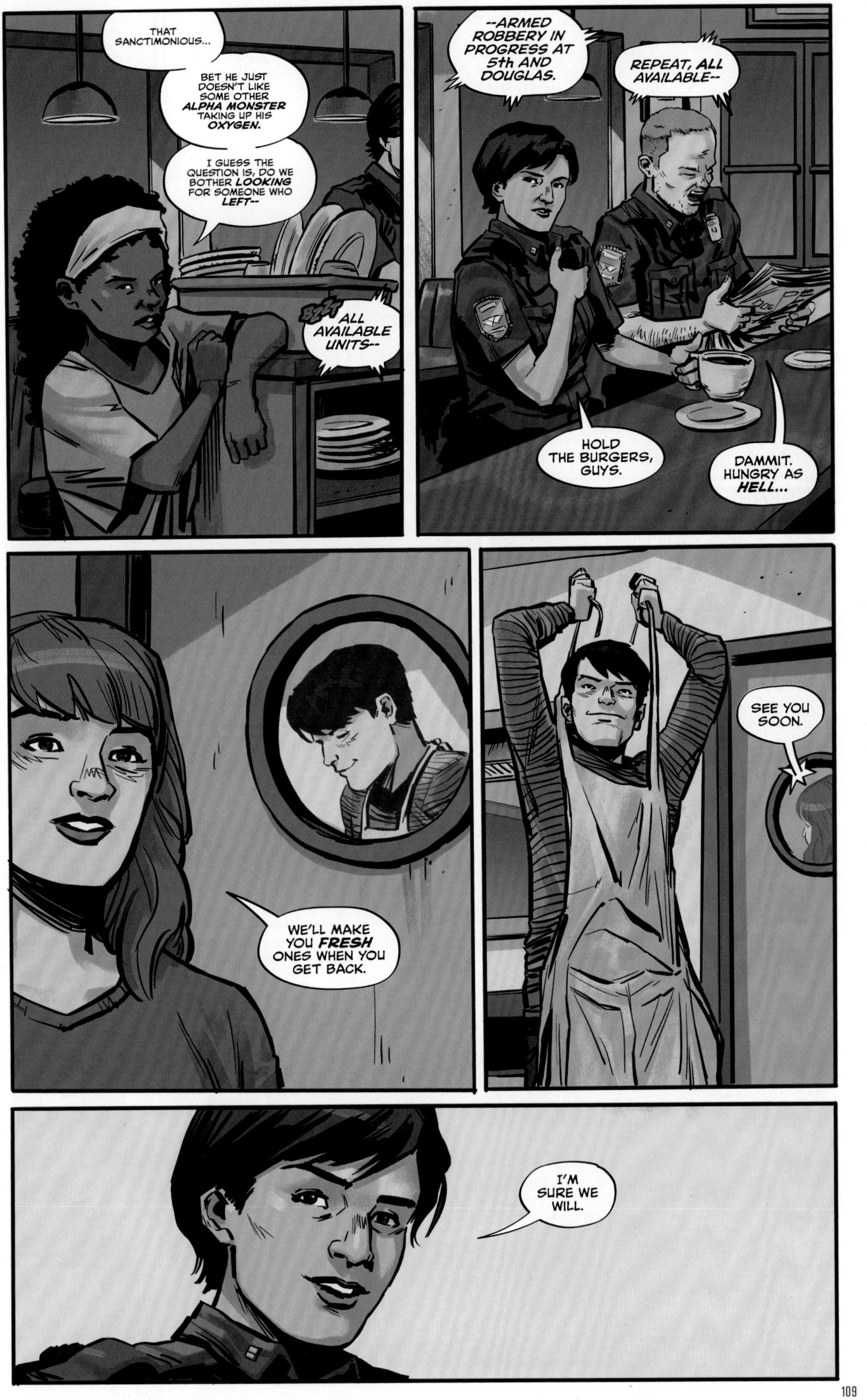

THAT SANCTIMONIOUS...
BET HE JUST DOESN'T LIKE SOME OTHER ALPHA MONSTER TAKING UP HIS OXYGEN.
I GUESS THE QUESTION IS, DO WE BOTHER LOOKING FOR SOMEONE WHO LEFT--
BZZT
ALL AVAILABLE UNITS--
--ARMED ROBBERY IN PROGRESS AT 5th AND DOUGLAS.
REPEAT, ALL AVAILABLE--
HOLD THE BURGERS, GUYS.
DAMMIT. HUNGRY AS HELL...
WE'LL MAKE YOU FRESH ONES WHEN YOU GET BACK.
SEE YOU SOON.
I'M SURE WE WILL.

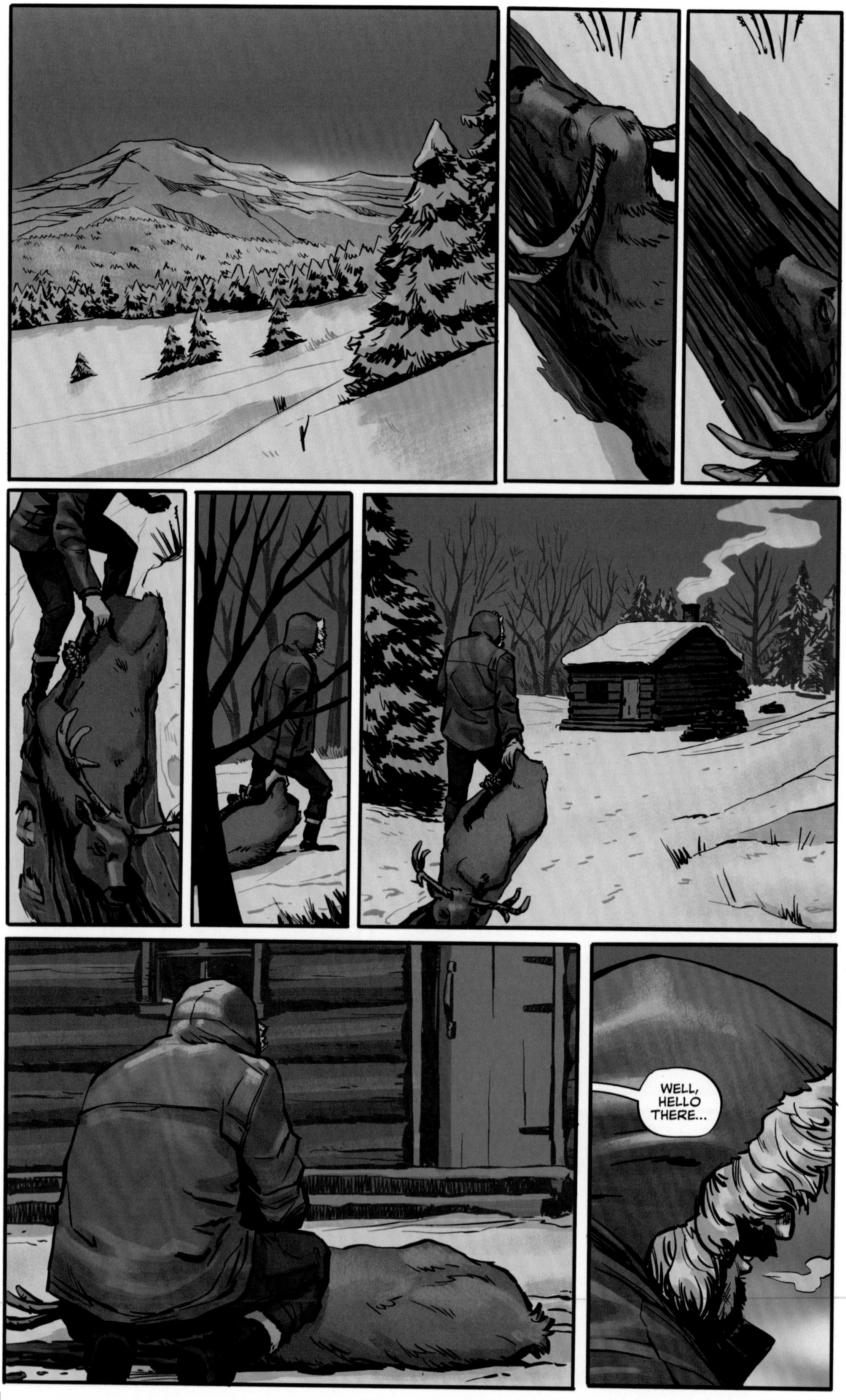
WELL, HELLO THERE...

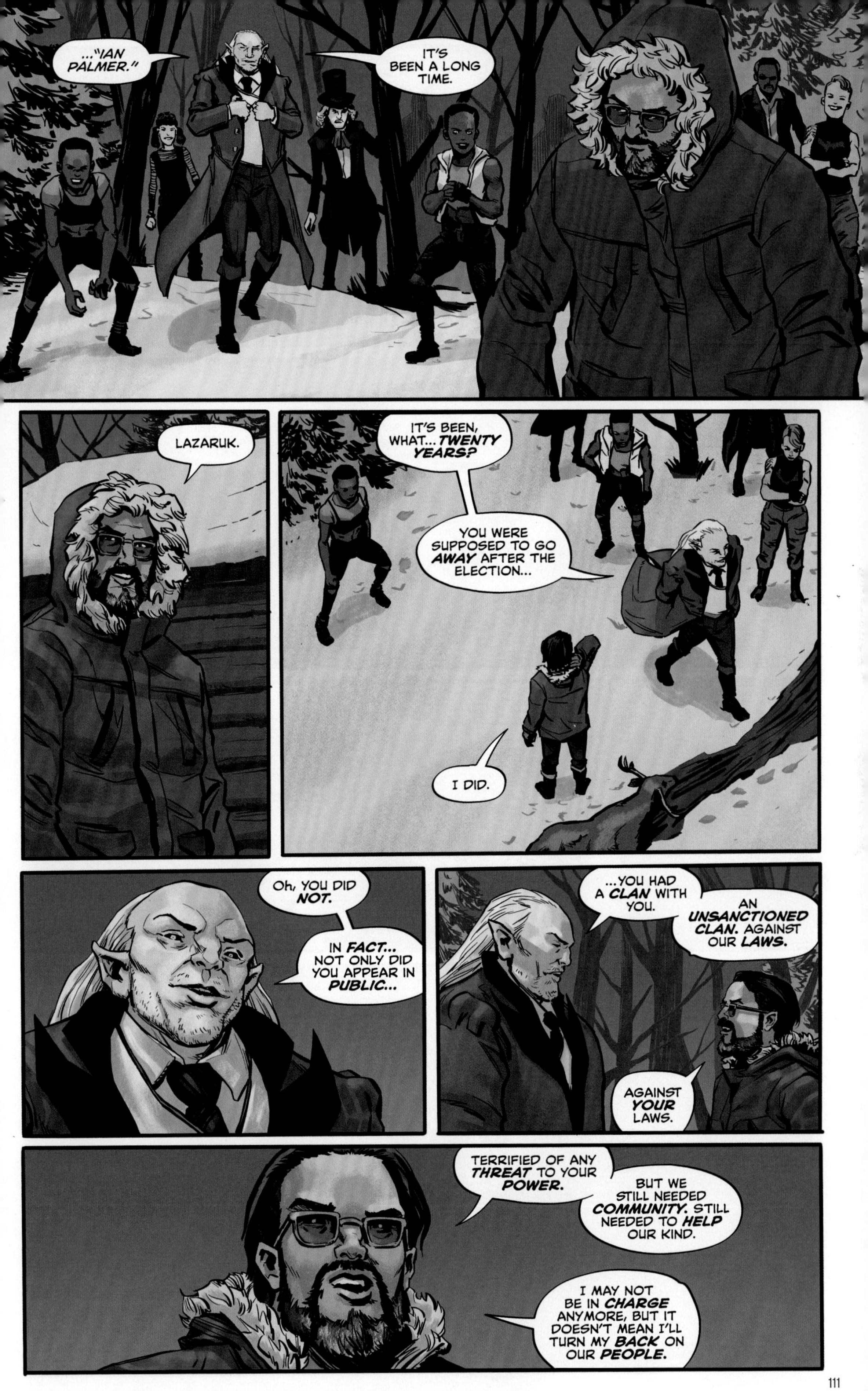
..."IAN PALMER."
IT'S BEEN A LONG TIME.
LAZARUK.
IT'S BEEN, WHAT... TWENTY YEARS?
YOU WERE SUPPOSED TO GO AWAY AFTER THE ELECTION...
I DID.
Oh, YOU DID NOT.
IN FACT... NOT ONLY DID YOU APPEAR IN PUBLIC...
...YOU HAD A CLAN WITH YOU.
AN UNSANCTIONED CLAN. AGAINST OUR LAWS.
AGAINST YOUR LAWS.
TERRIFIED OF ANY THREAT TO YOUR POWER.
BUT WE STILL NEEDED COMMUNITY. STILL NEEDED TO HELP OUR KIND.
I MAY NOT BE IN CHARGE ANYMORE, BUT IT DOESN'T MEAN I'LL TURN MY BACK ON OUR PEOPLE.

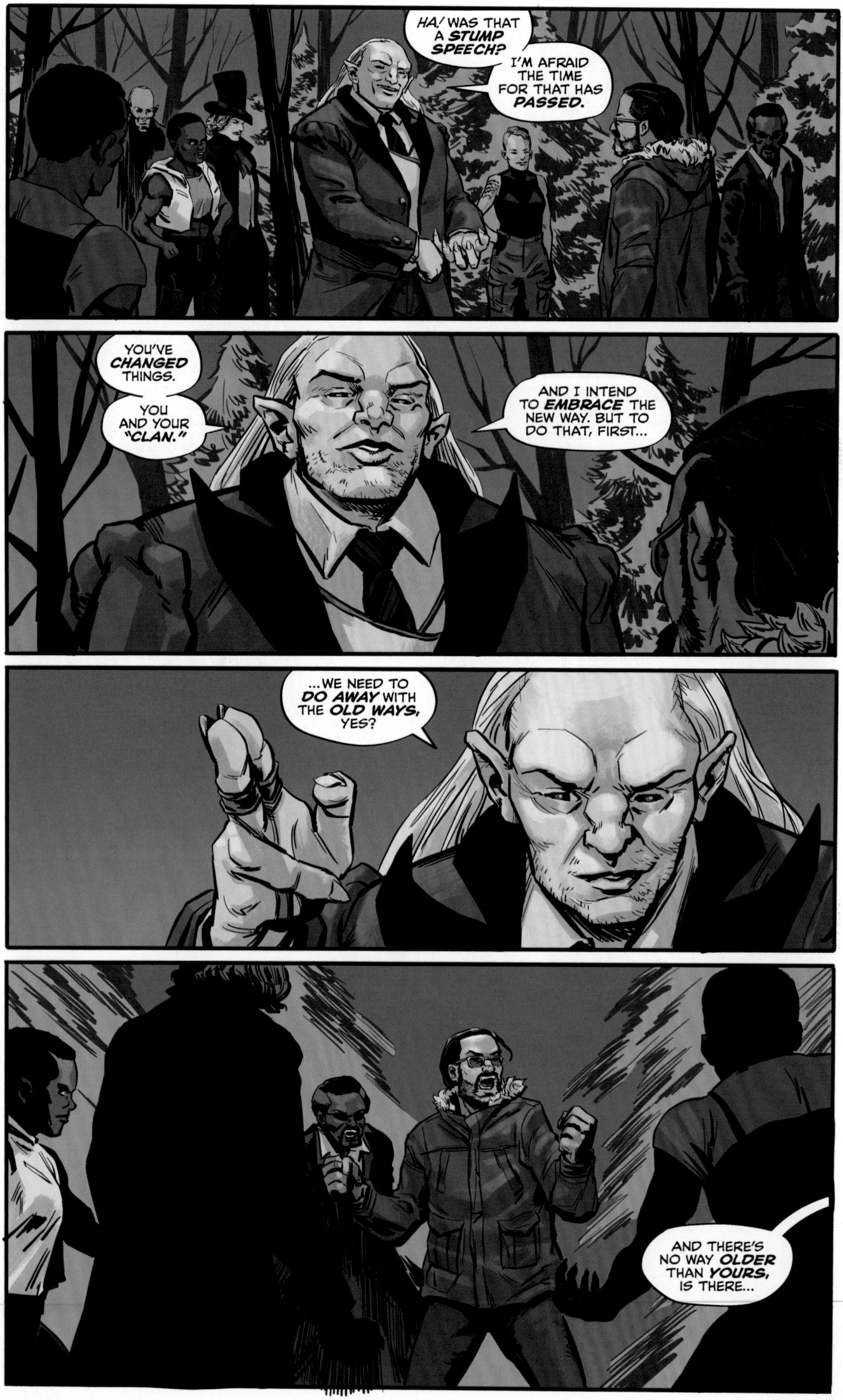
HA! WAS THAT A STUMP SPEECH?
I'M AFRAID THE TIME FOR THAT HAS PASSED.
YOU'VE CHANGED THINGS.
YOU AND YOUR "CLAN."
AND I INTEND TO EMBRACE THE NEW WAY. BUT TO DO THAT, FIRST...
...WE NEED TO DO AWAY WITH THE OLD WAYS, YES?
AND THERE'S NO WAY OLDER THAN YOURS, IS THERE...

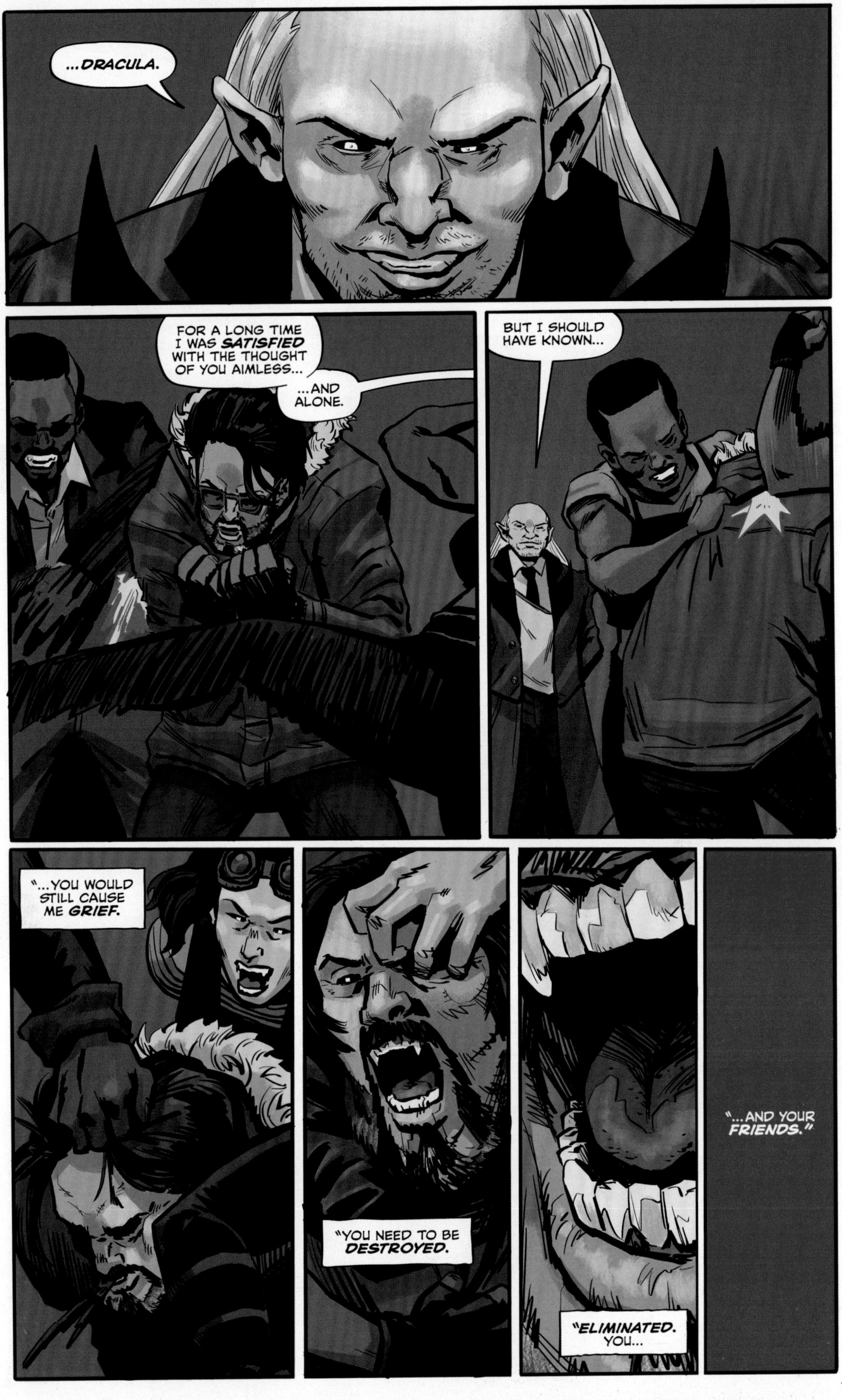
...DRACULA.
FOR A LONG TIME I WAS SATISFIED WITH THE THOUGHT OF YOU AIMLESS...
...AND ALONE.
BUT I SHOULD HAVE KNOWN...
"...YOU WOULD STILL CAUSE ME GRIEF.
"YOU NEED TO BE DESTROYED.
"ELIMINATED. YOU...
"...AND YOUR FRIENDS."

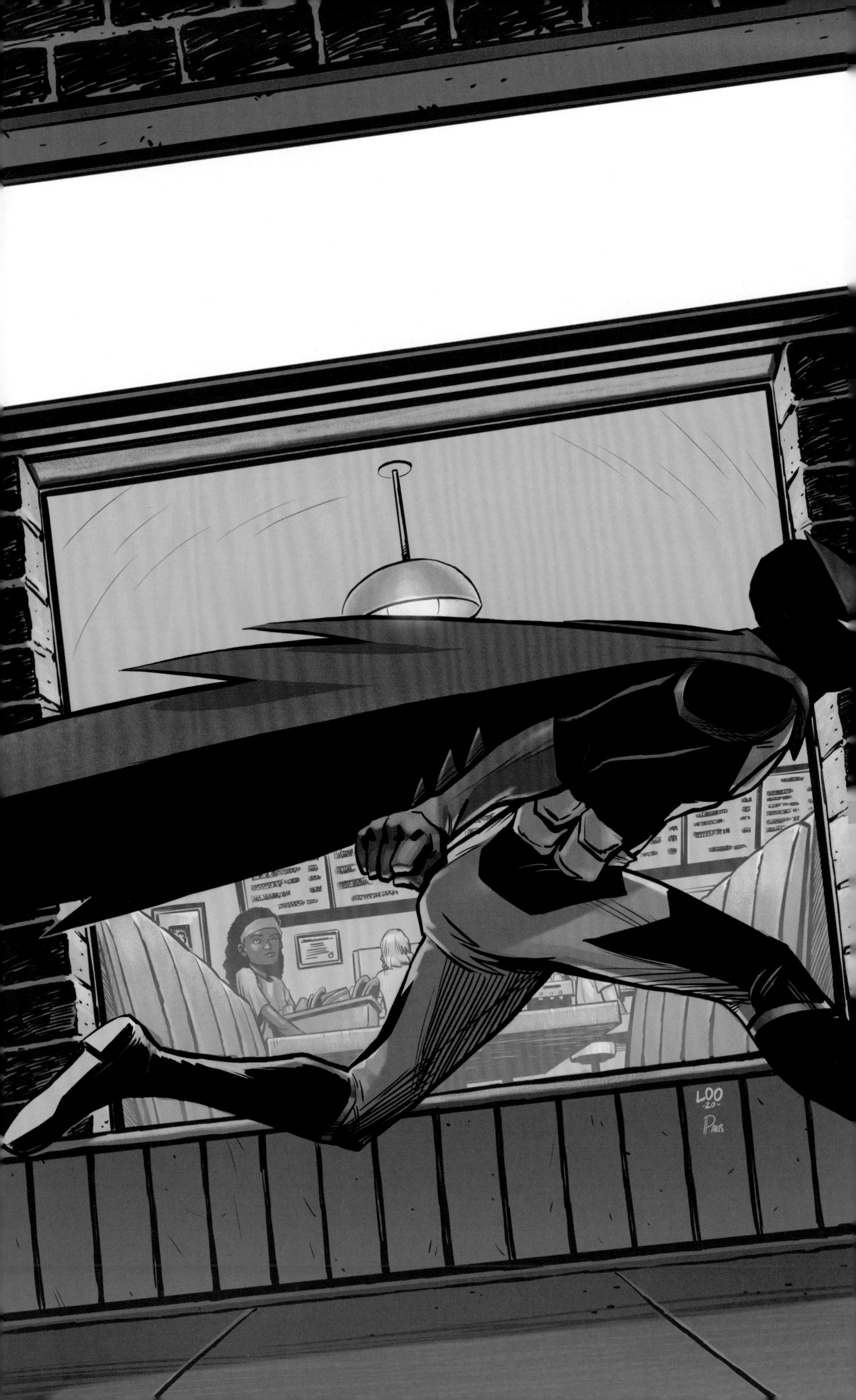
LOO
-20-
PARIS

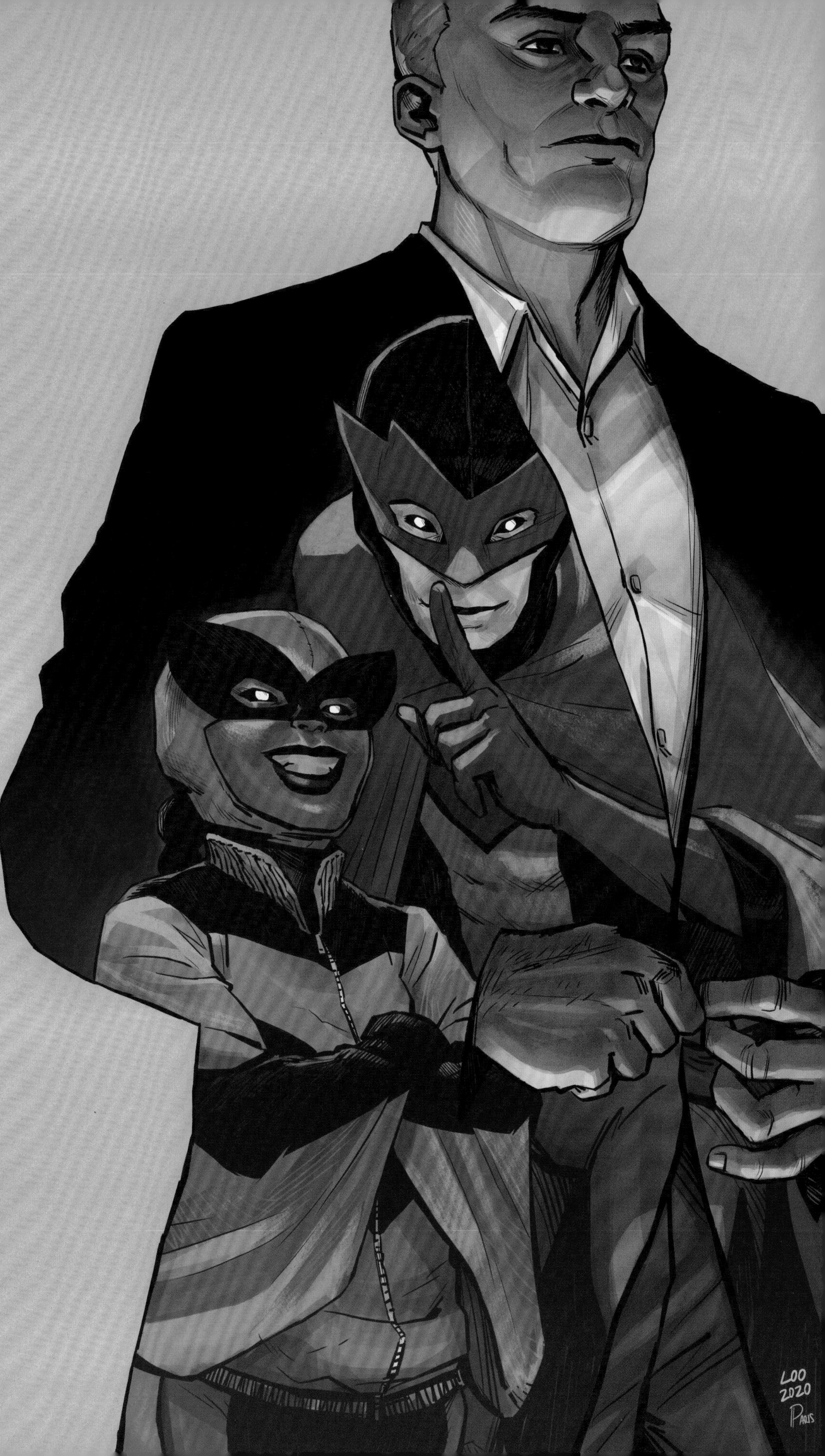
LOO
2020
PARIS

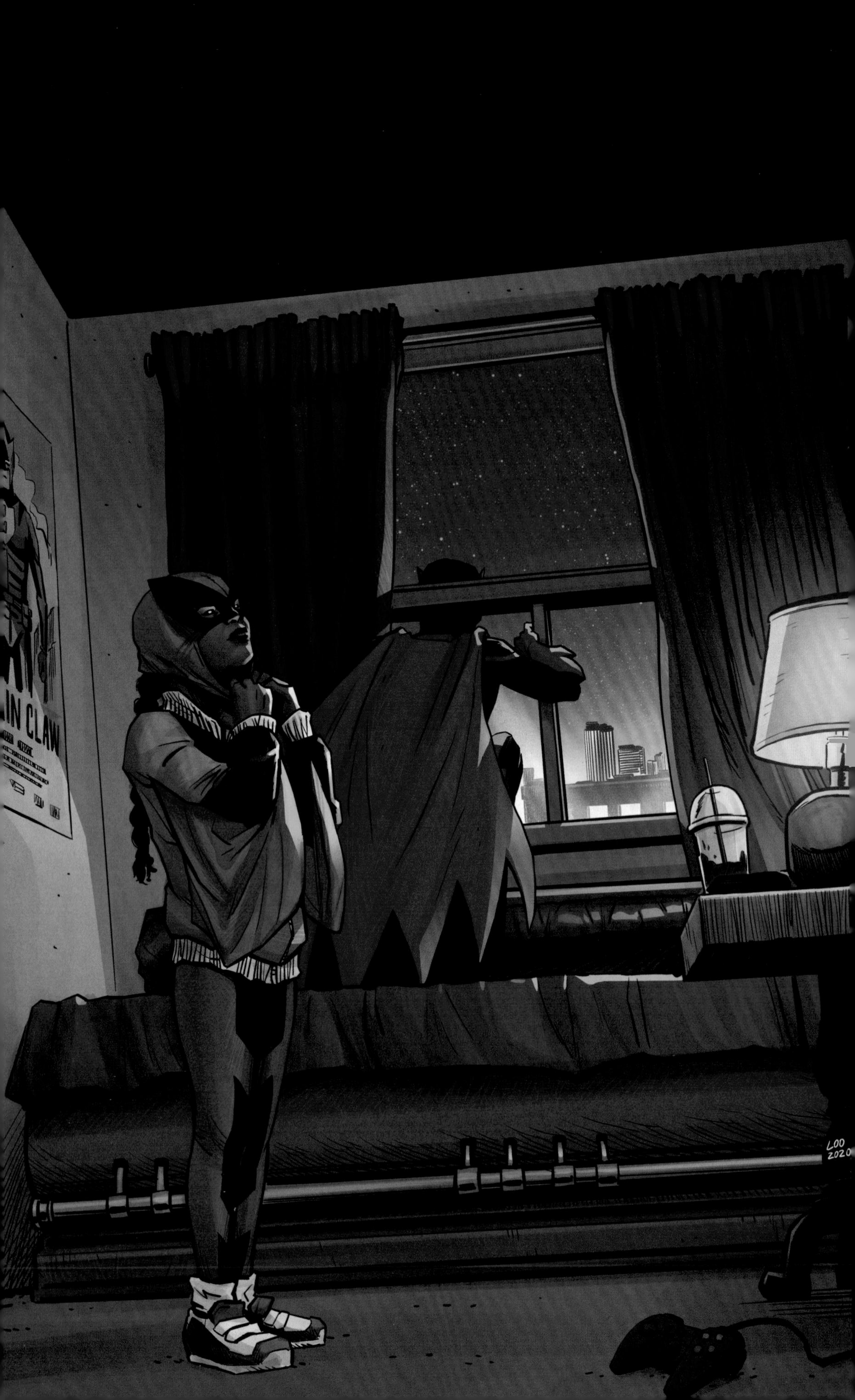
IN CLAW
LOO 2020

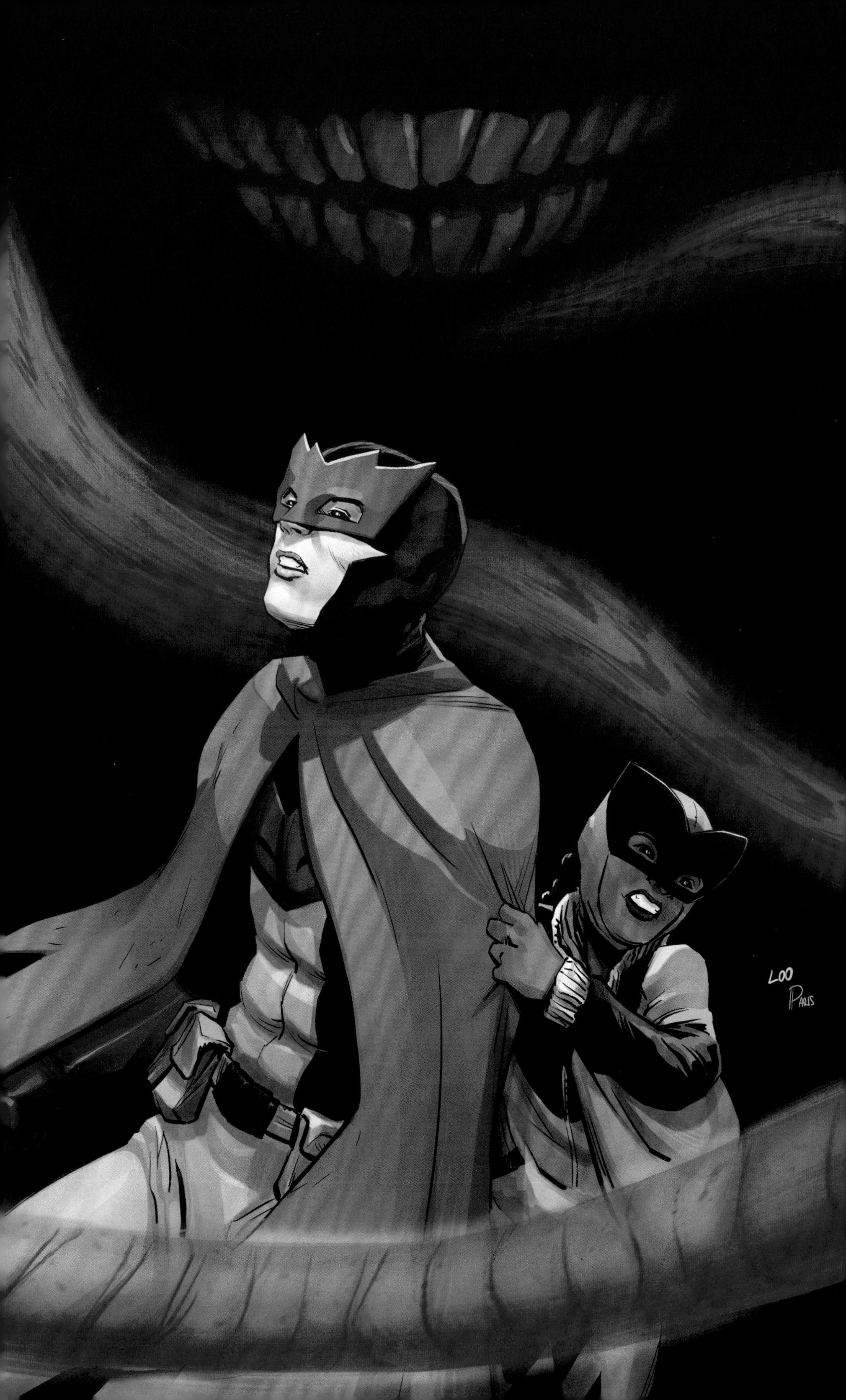
LOO
PARIS

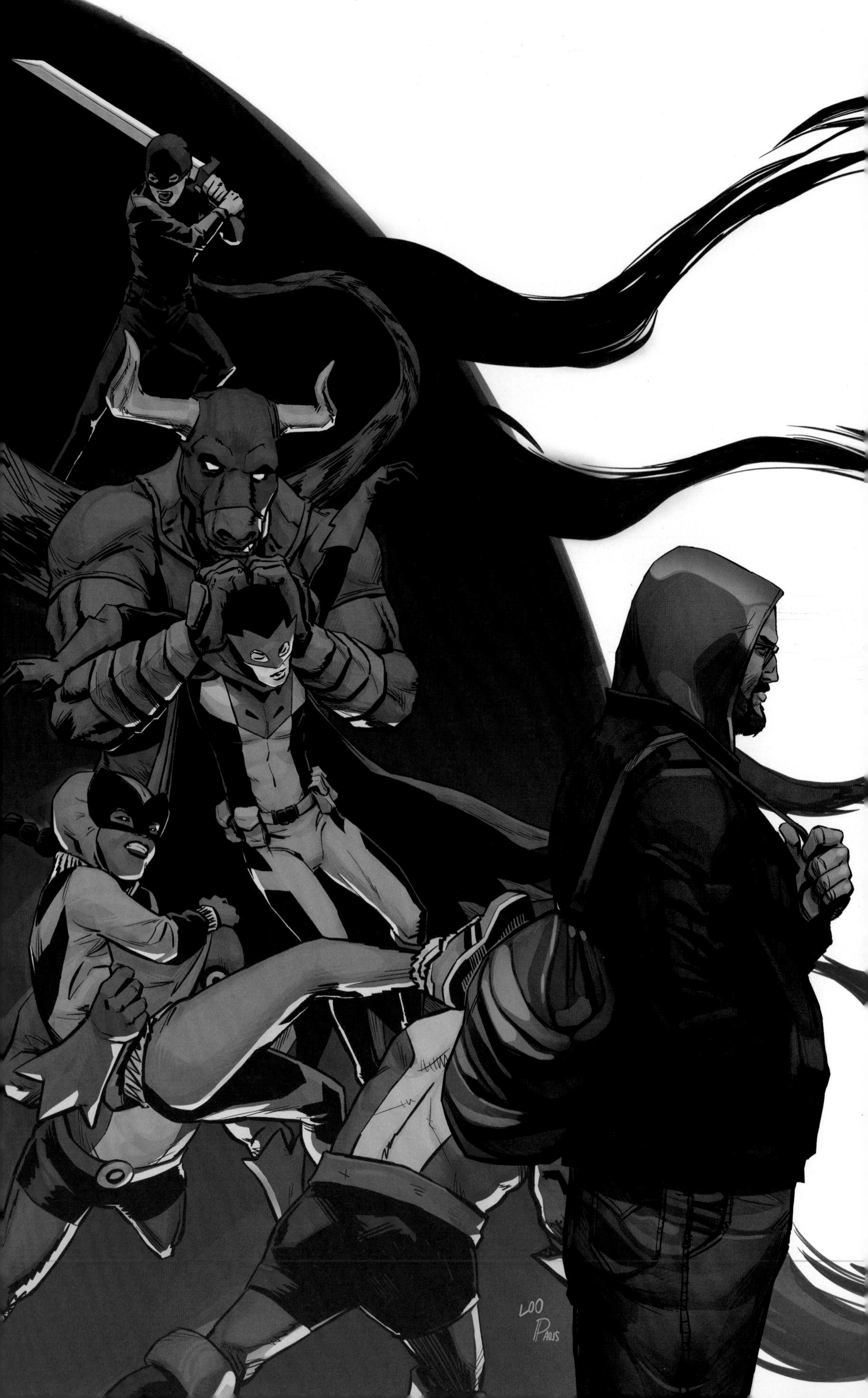

WELCOME TO THE ALL-NIGHTER!

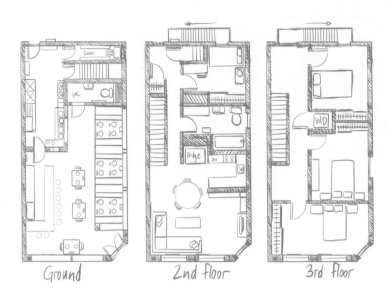

Cooler
WC
Fridge
DW
W/D
Ground
2nd floor
3rd floor

Jason: Since the diner is the central location of the series, I didn't want to just make things up on the spot. I looked at opportunities where each room or section of the diner would benefit the storytelling, especially for Alex, whose room is next to the fire escape for his superhero escapading. There's even a basement door in the cooler room which we haven't explored yet.

Ian's LATE EATS
Ian's LATE EATS
Ian's LATE EATS
Ian's LATE EATS

Ian's LATE EATS
Ian's LATE EATS

Chip: We originally called the series *Supernight*, but once we landed on the name of the diner being "The All-Nighter," it just made a world of sense to have that also be the name of the book.

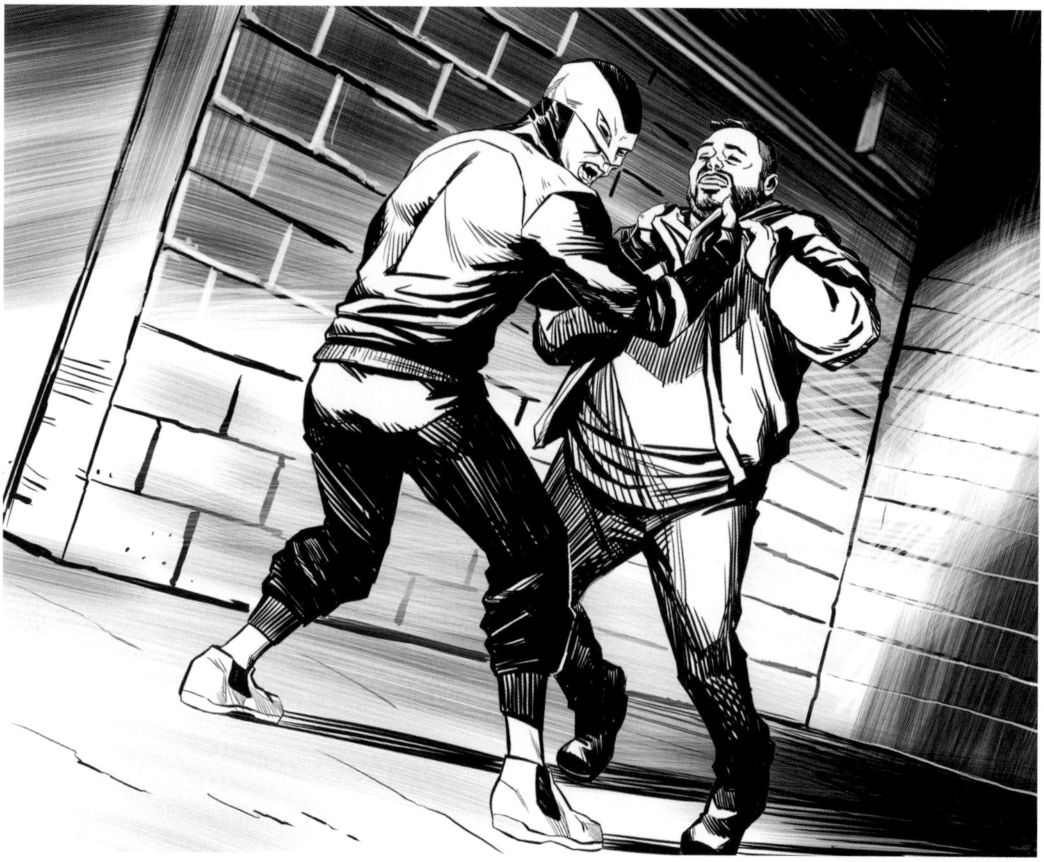

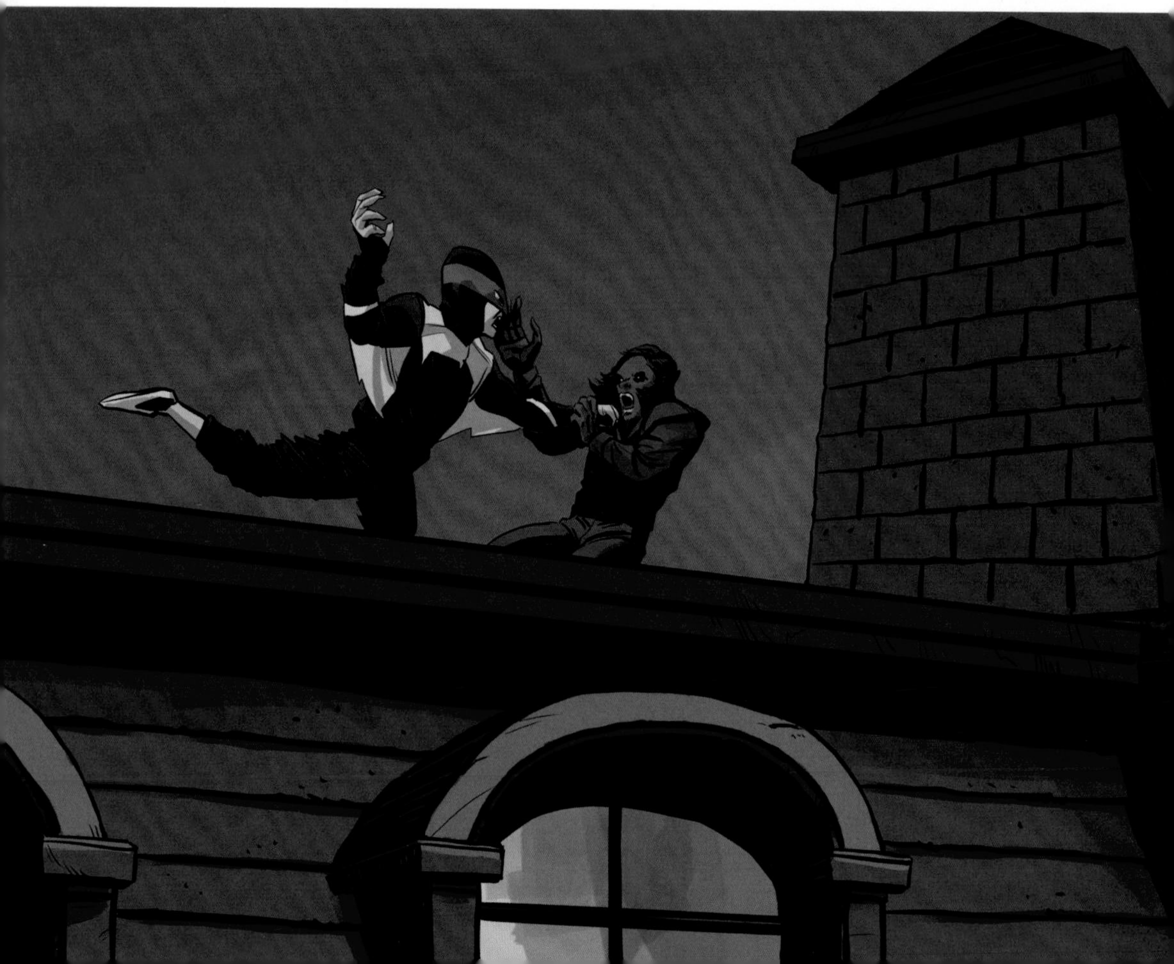

THE SERIES PITCH

Chip: Below is my initial pitch for the series, with all of my wild and unnecessary swearing removed. What can I say? I'm passionate when I pitch!

Basically a family of vampires (not technically family, but you know) run this all-night diner. It's their version of "settling down." They get to interact with people, and their meat supplier gets them animal blood. Which, you know, isn't their favourite. But it's the price to pay for ethical living. It's their version of going vegan.

One of the younger vampires hates this life. He wants to live a FULLER life. But it's too dangerous. There are RULES. A mysterious governing body over all supernatural beings that forbids them from revealing themselves to humans. If you reveal yourself to a human and DON'T kill them, you are subject to a trial, where you need to justify it. These rules have kept monsters safe for thousands of years, but the modern world could truly destroy them, so the clampdown is even more dire these days.

One night the younger vampire is out and a crime is taking place. Not knowing what to do, they put on a mask and stop it. The grateful would-be victims thank him profusely. It feels good.

And no one comes for him. Because he didn't reveal he was a vampire.

An idea forms. The modern world is obsessed with pop culture, even HE is, really. With the movies and comic books and TV shows. So . . . why not be a superhero?

Without his family's blessing, our vampire starts to go out at night as a costumed vigilante. He's the world's first real-life superhero that isn't just one of those stunted assholes in the news who put on costumes and drive around looking for crimes. It's clear he has abilities. Strength, speed, can jump far and high. The media has their first actual superhero.

It doesn't take long for the family to find out what's happened. He's confronted, but he insists he's in the clear. Nobody's come to put him on trial. He's found a loophole!

But, unfortunately, others can use this loophole.

What we start here is a new universe where all manner of supernatural beings decide to come out and play under the guise of "superheroes" and, more distressingly, "supervillains." Everything spirals out of control and, eventually, the governing body comes in to shut it all down, though too late.

Chip: Okay, so a bit of swearing. Really though, I think it's fair to call real-life superheroes "stunted assholes."

CHARACTER DESIGNS

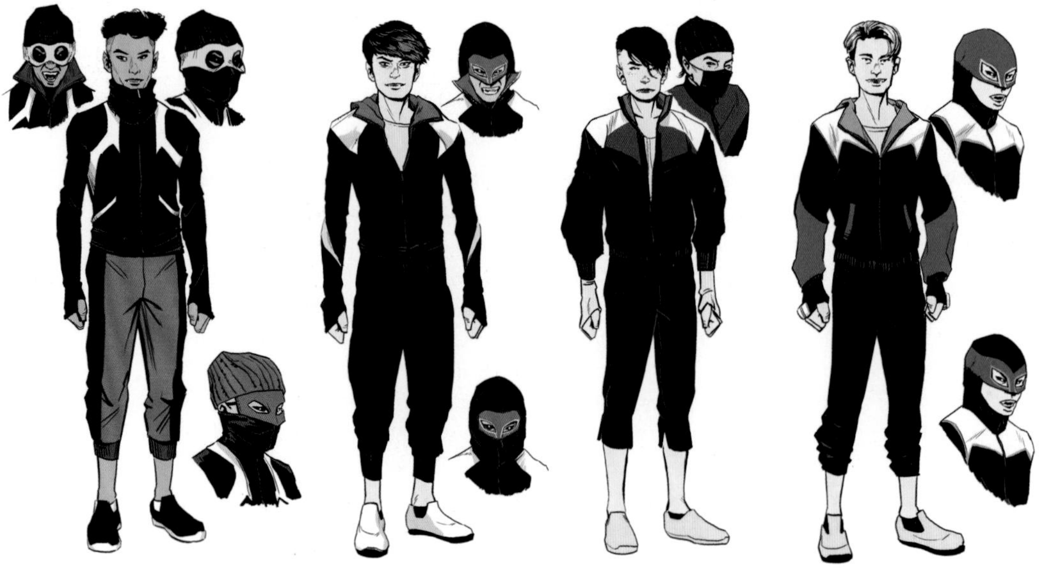

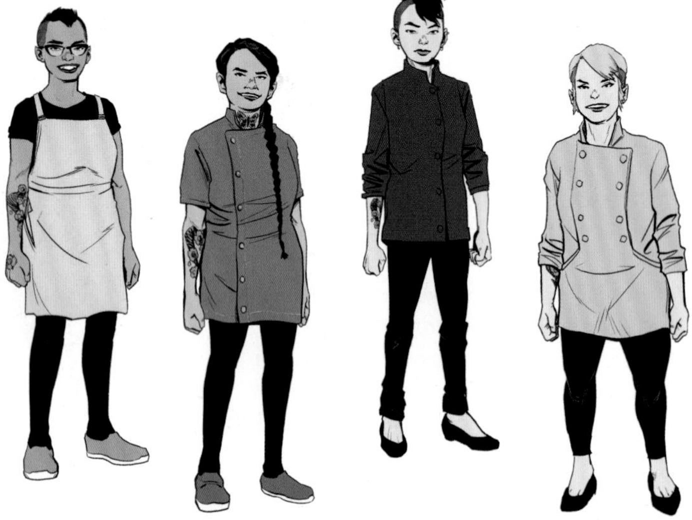

Jason: Chip and I knew we wanted a family of vampires from different backgrounds, but we were still figuring out the variables. If this was a casting call, I was looking for an Asian male in his twenties as our brash vigilante, a woman in her forties as the head chef and leader of the group, and a tween who is really older than they look.

Chip: So much of the characters stem from Jason's designs. I have loose ideas to start with, but it all really clicks when these start coming in and I can go, "Oh yeah, THAT'S the character." Jason is a master of creating fleshed-out characters from almost nothing (which is what I give him because I am a "bad writer").

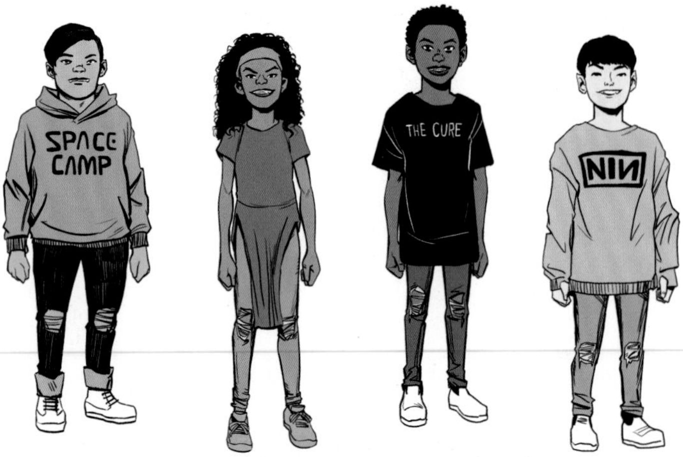
SPACE CAMP
THE CURE
NIN

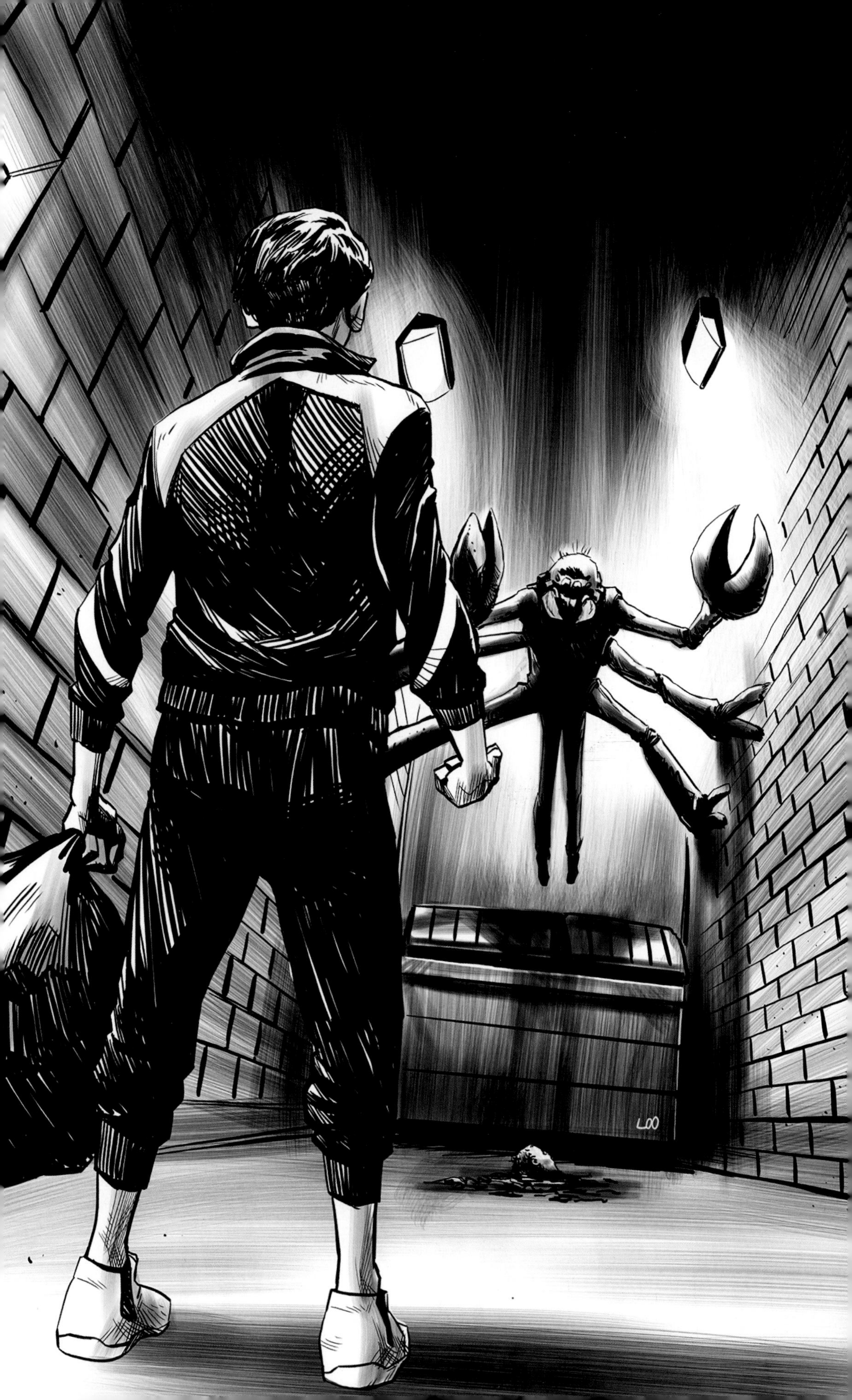

LOO

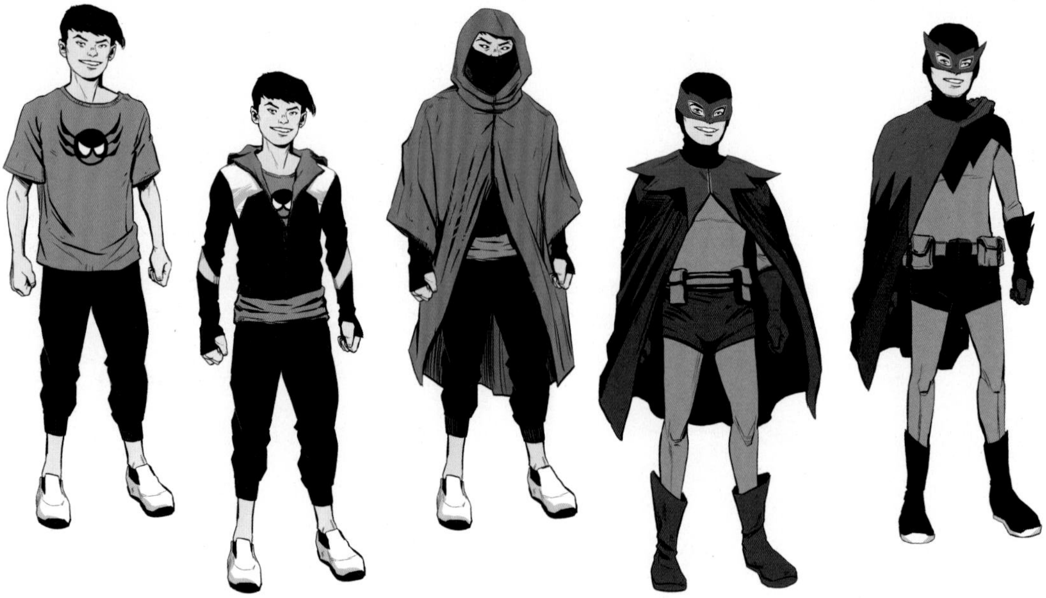

Jason: I was scratching my brain on the superhero costume design for Alex. A lot of superhero looks have been done already, so it was tough coming up with something that looked unique for our comic. I was definitely channeling David Mazzucchelli's vibes from *Batman: Year One* for Nightshock's look. I don't think we even had a name for Alex's superhero alias until after I shared the designs, and then Chip came up with "Nightshock" in the script for issue one. It works!

Chip: God, coming up with superhero names is the worst. Much like superhero designs, there aren't a lot of superhero-y names left. I was stunned that there wasn't already a Nightshock out there. I think we should also claim dibs on "Shocknight" as well.

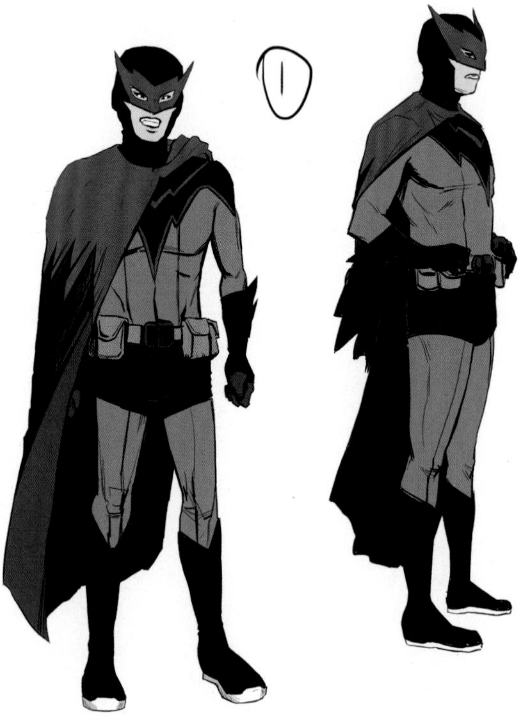
1

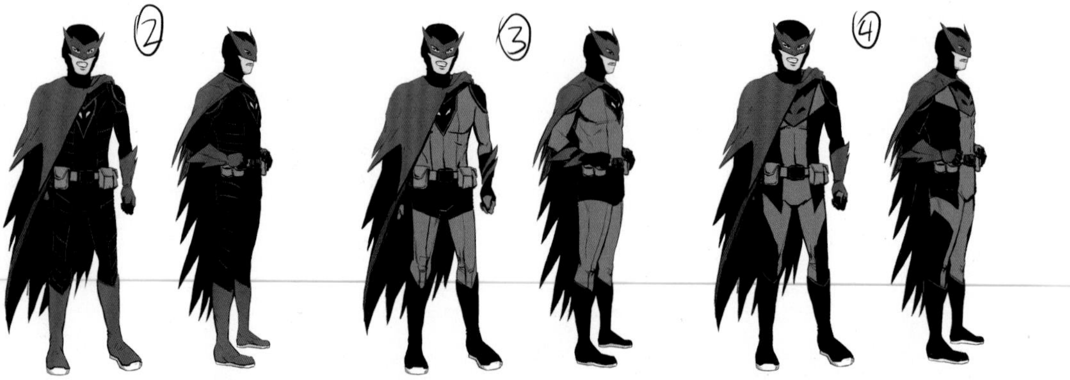
2
3
4

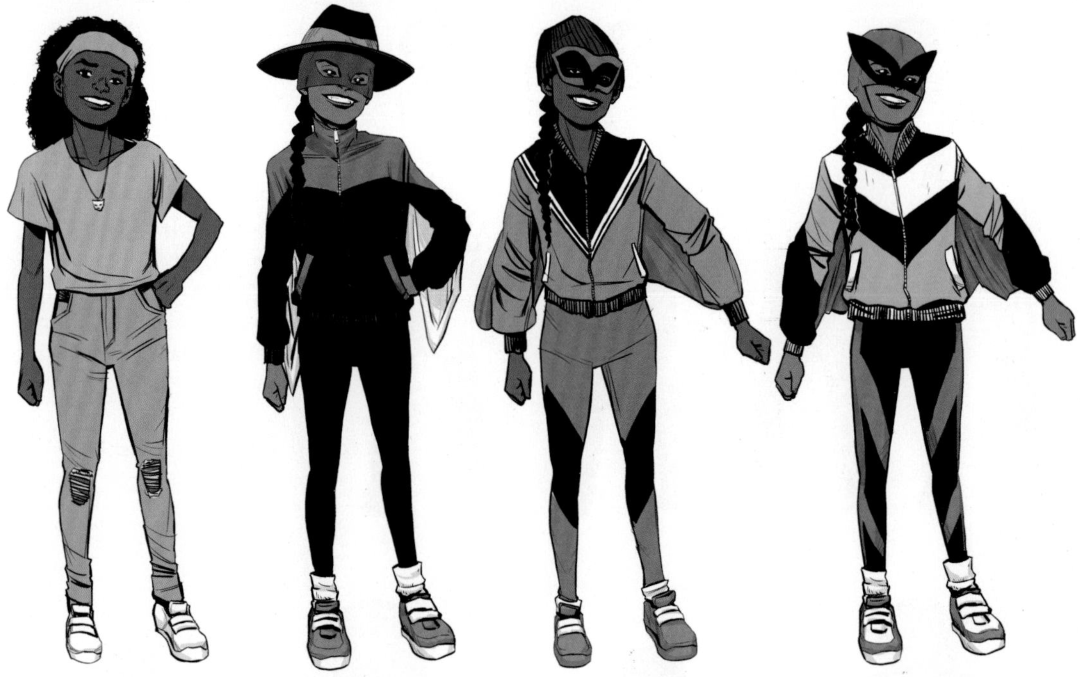

Jason: Designing Joy's costume came easy after Alex's design. She's Robin to his Batman, but using materials she could find from her closet and with slightly brighter colors.

The early designs of Cynthia have her wearing comfortable clothing mixed with an article from her previous life as a business exec. She still wears the same shoes from when she was an avid jogger.

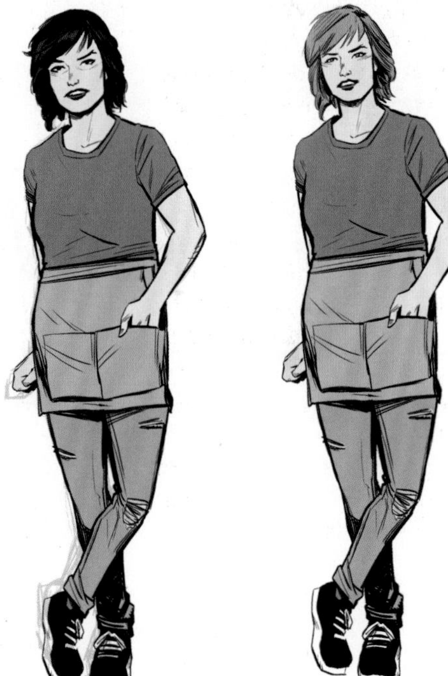

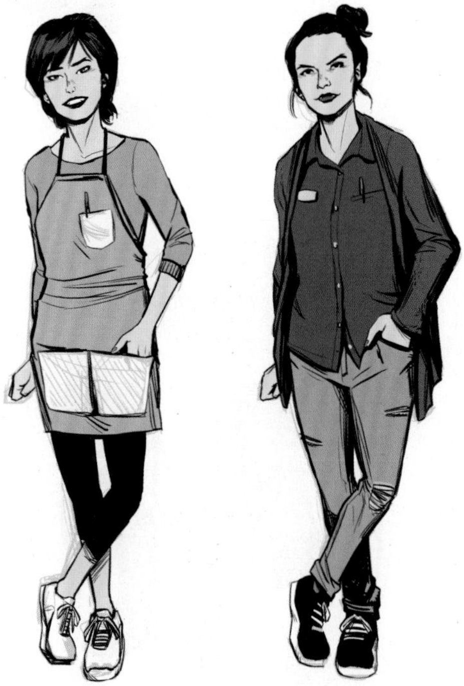

Chip: Ha! I didn't even know that about Cynthia's shoes! That's such a great character touch.

Jason and I only communicate through our lawyers, so I miss a lot of these things.

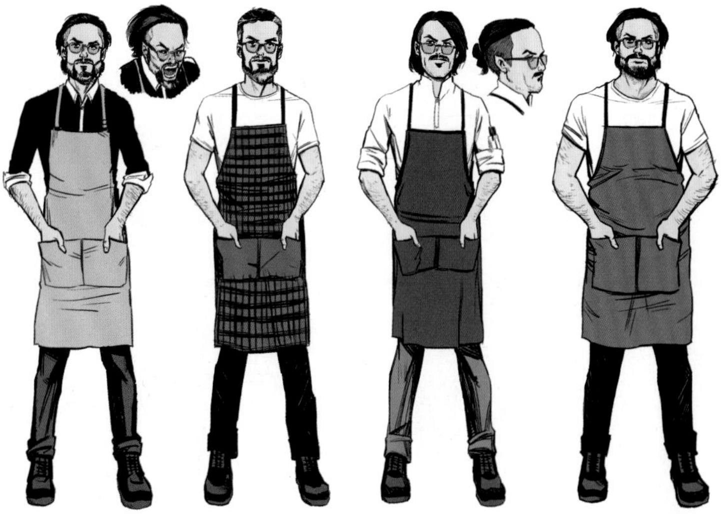

Jason: No one would guess that Ian is THE Dracula until the big reveal. I was so excited about the reveal that I designed a cover for when it happens, but Chip thought it was too on the nose.

Chip: No spoilers!!!

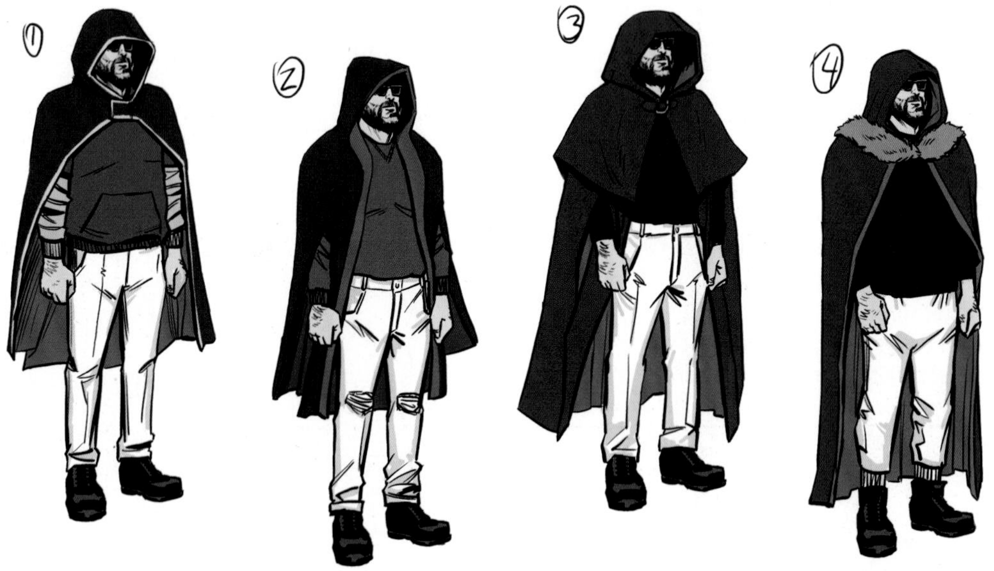
1
2
3
4

Jason: Reinventing Dracula was a lot of fun. I was thinking about how Vlad the Impaler would look if he's still around . . . and running a diner. Probably a taller, beefier Marc Maron.

I wanted Ian's badass sword to reflect his eastern European past. Something like a saber but with a decorative handle for an aristocrat like Lord Dracula.

Chip: I never want to hear the phrase "beefier Marc Maron" again.

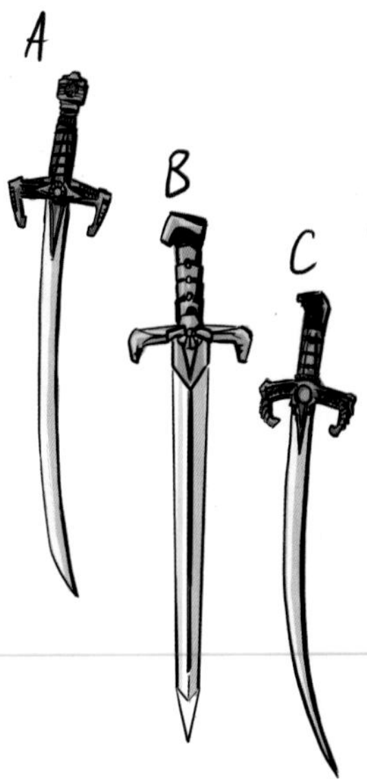
A
B
C

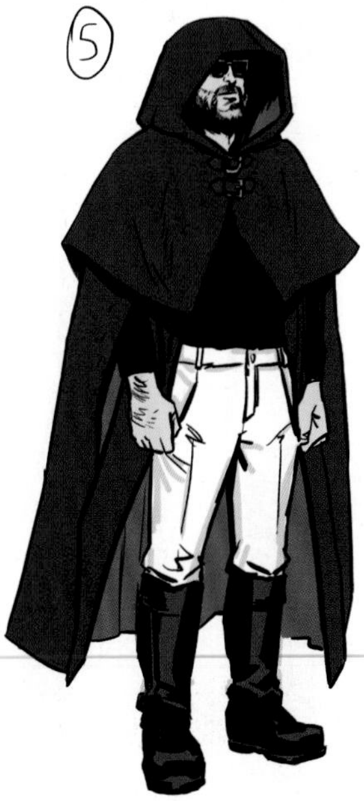
5

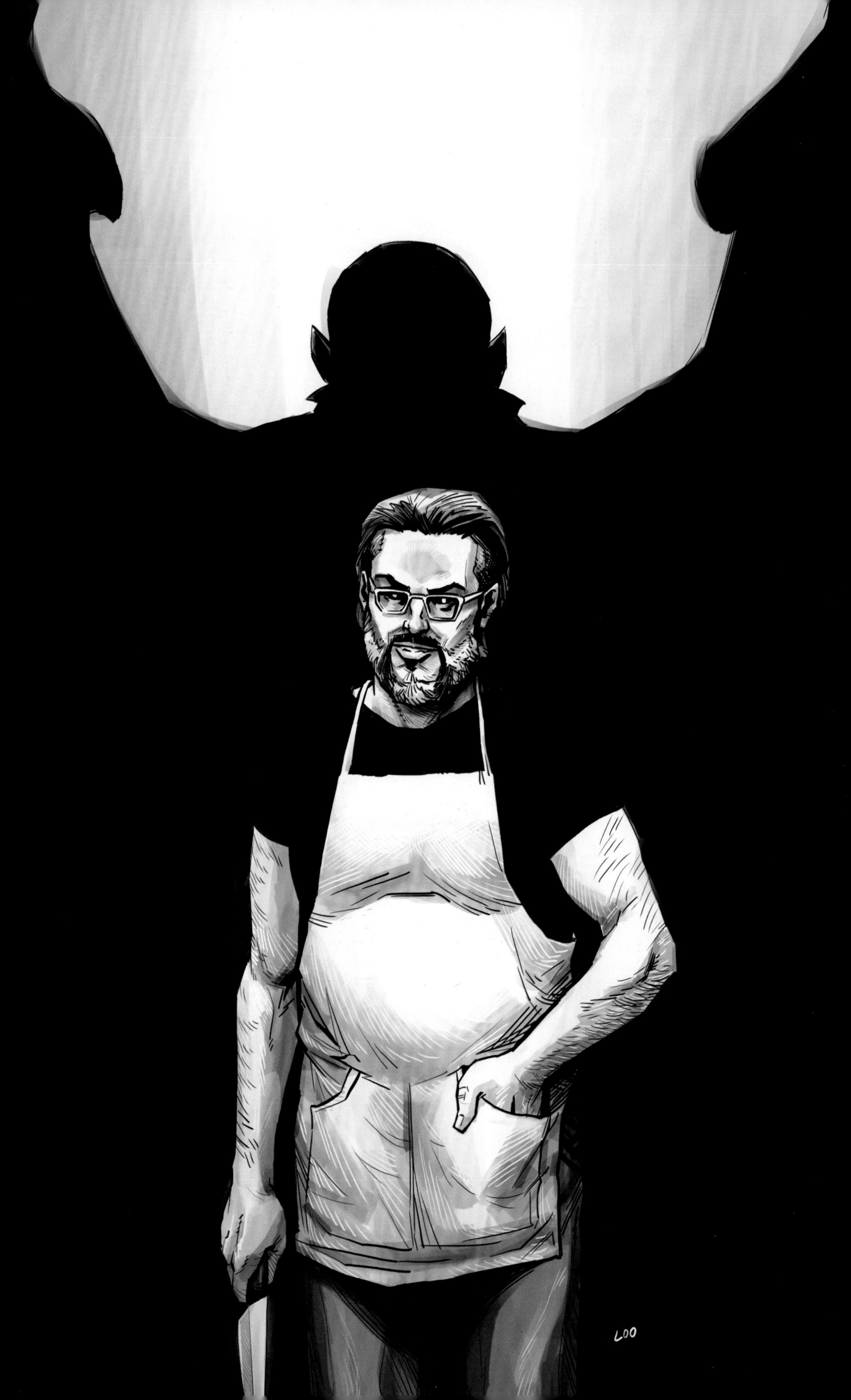
LOO

Jason: This is the most charming take on Frankenstein's monster, modernized with the help of plastic surgery to look like a Greco-Roman sculpture in an Armani suit. Only thing scary about him is how massive he is compared to everyone else.

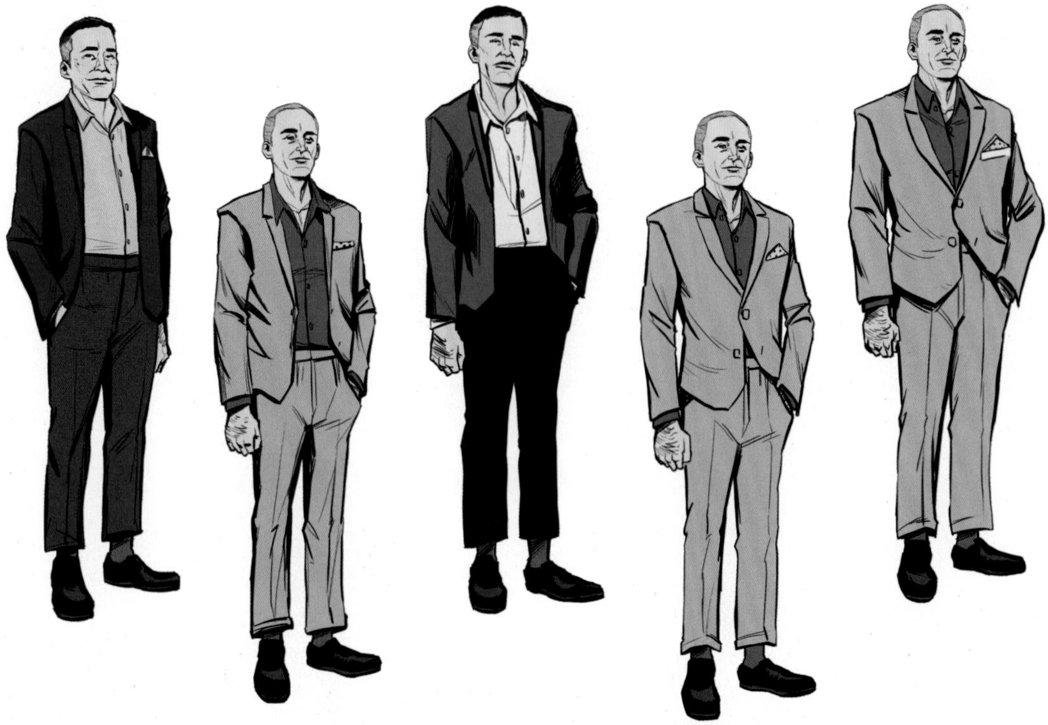

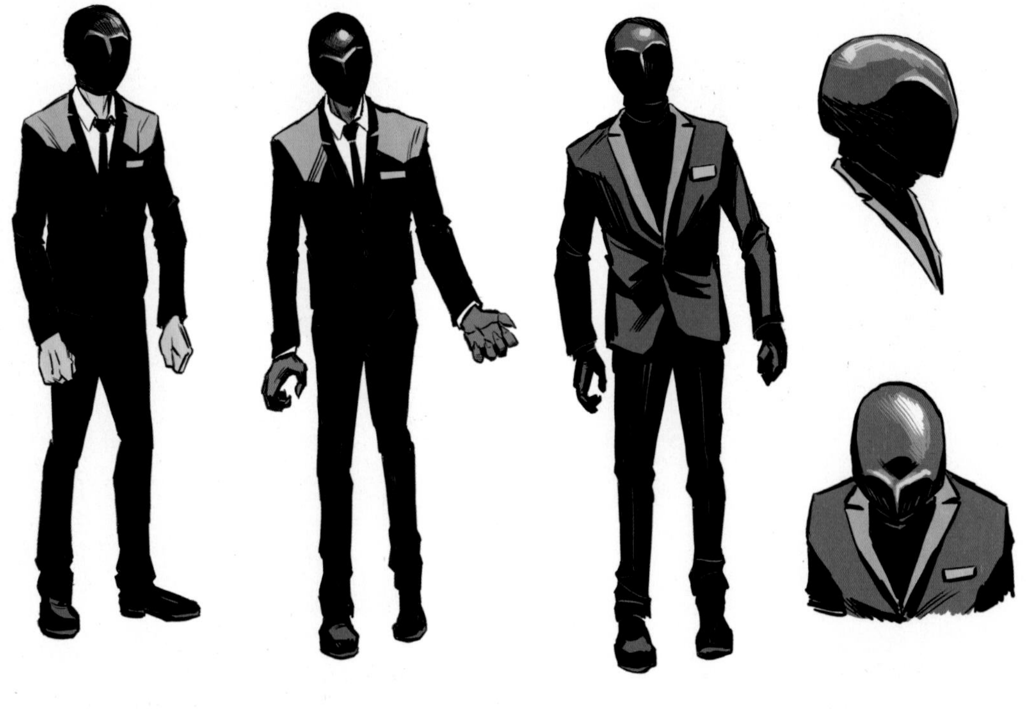

Jason: Chip (and Francis) wanted to conceal the identities of Francis's security made up of werewolves. With each one decked out in a tight suit with a shiny dark helmet, the only way I could show that primal energy was through how they fight, using grappling and takedown techniques similar to Brazilian jujitsu.

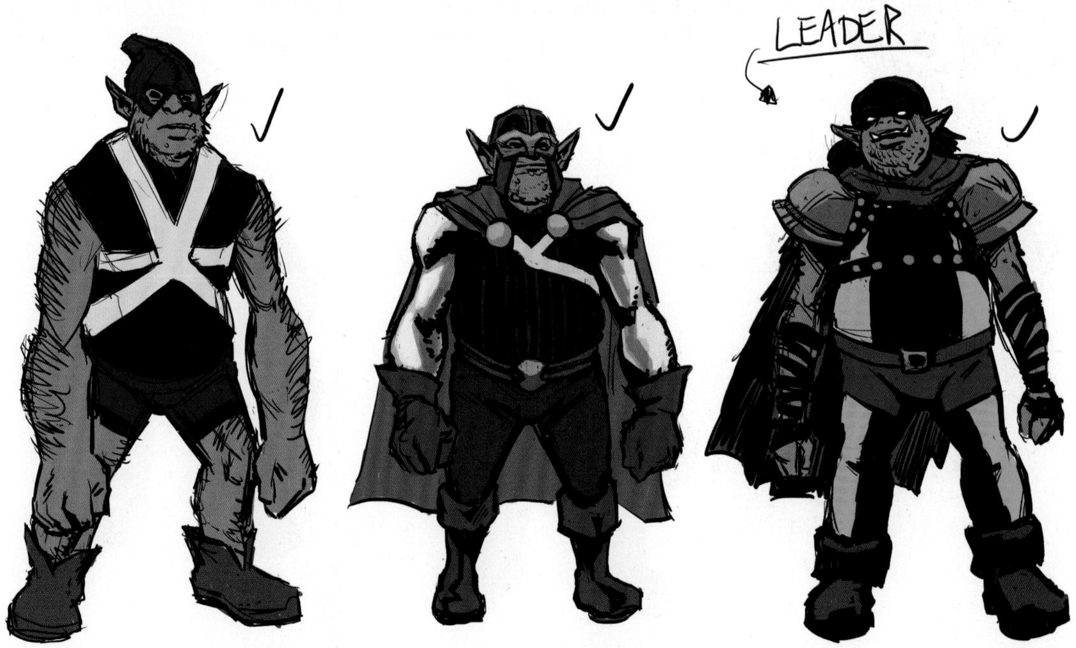
LEADER

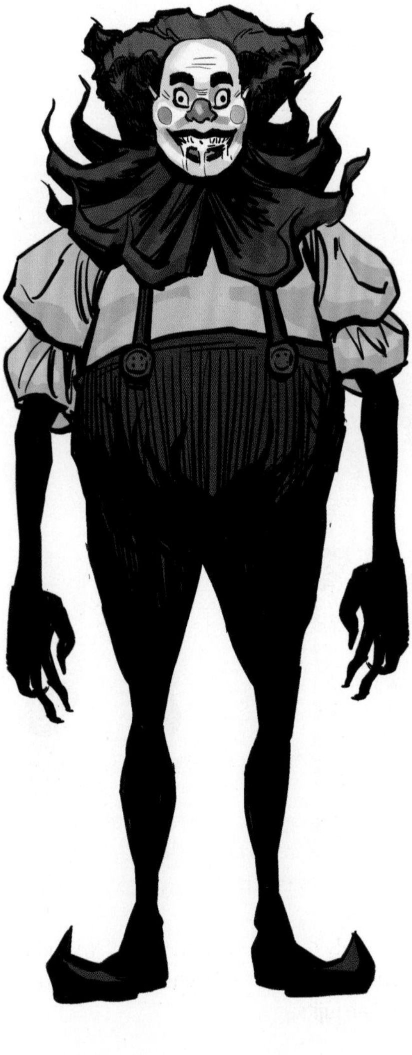

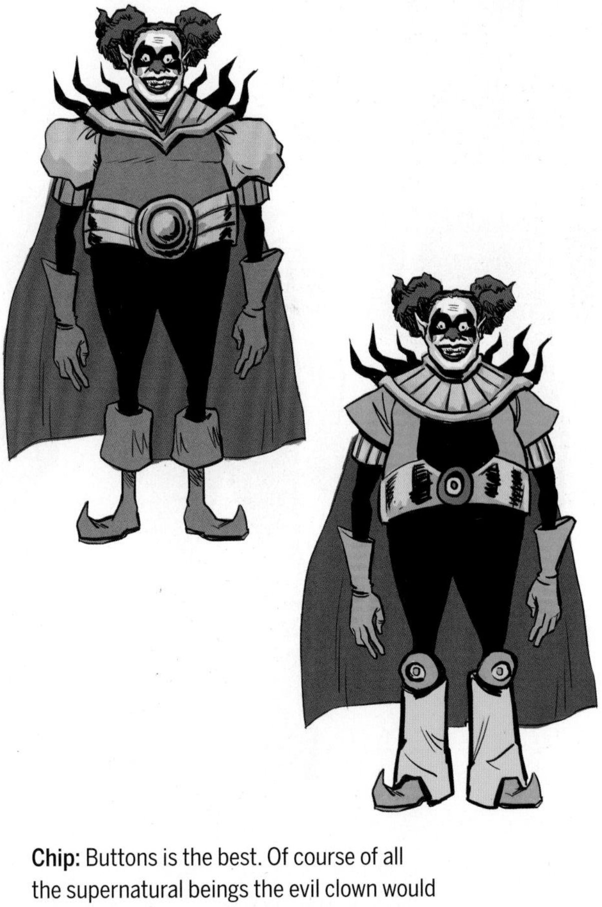

Chip: Buttons is the best. Of course of all the supernatural beings the evil clown would be the one to truly embrace being a costumed supervillain. Jason did a great job of letting Buttons be his best self.

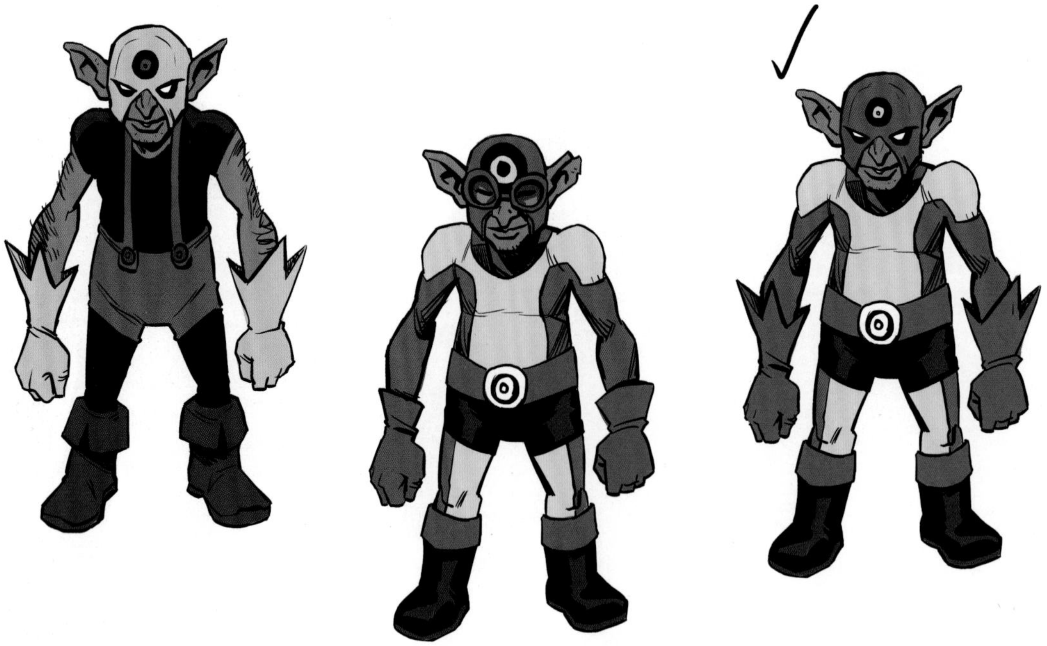

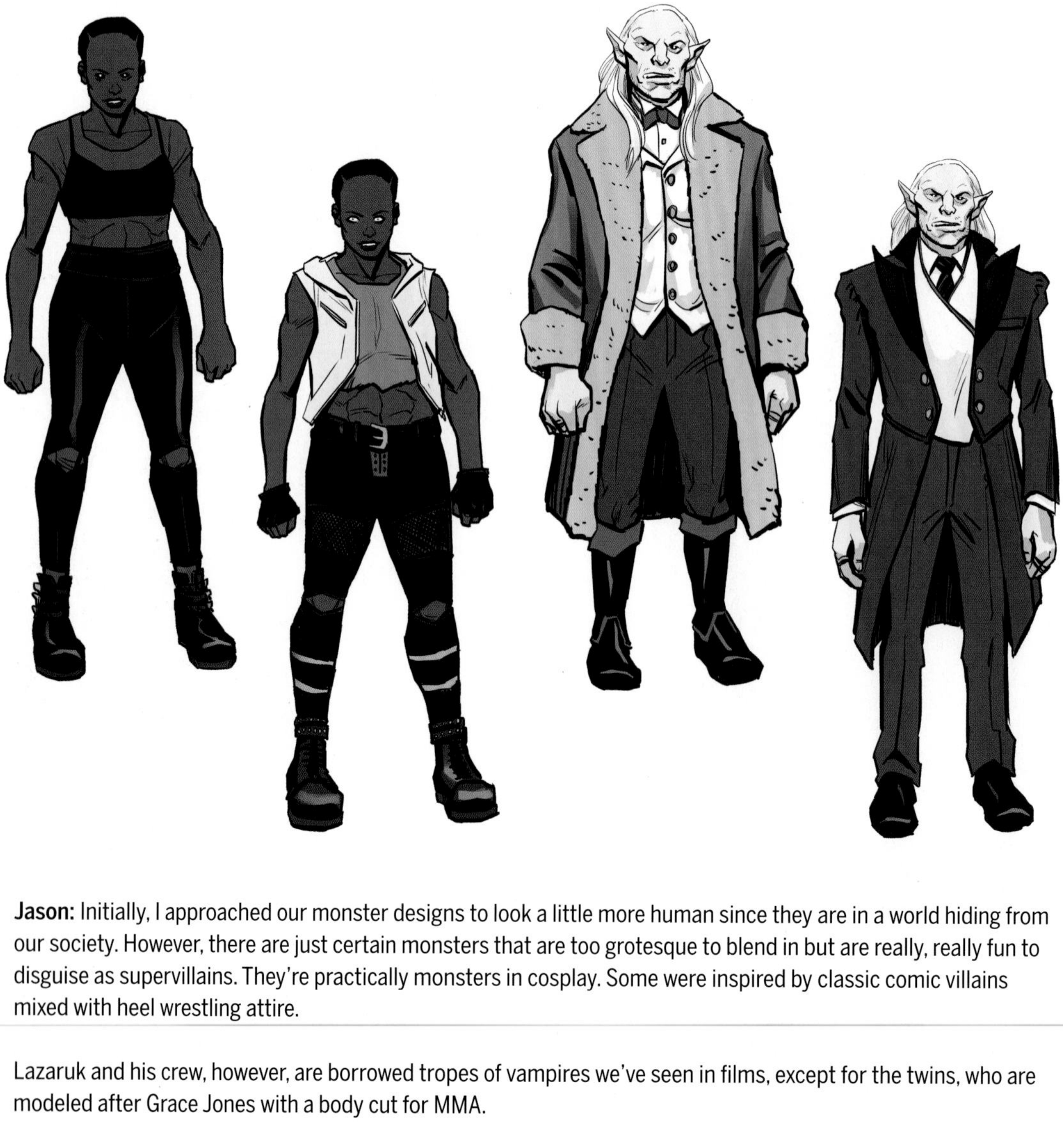

Jason: Initially, I approached our monster designs to look a little more human since they are in a world hiding from our society. However, there are just certain monsters that are too grotesque to blend in but are really, really fun to disguise as supervillains. They're practically monsters in cosplay. Some were inspired by classic comic villains mixed with heel wrestling attire.

Lazaruk and his crew, however, are borrowed tropes of vampires we've seen in films, except for the twins, who are modeled after Grace Jones with a body cut for MMA.

PAGE BREAKDOWN

Jason: *The All-Nighter* is my first comic work done digitally using Procreate. The whole process was a learning curve for me as I was getting comfortable finding the right tools. I combined the thumbnails and pencils into one preliminary stage since I'm quick that way, sketching with the technical pen tool.

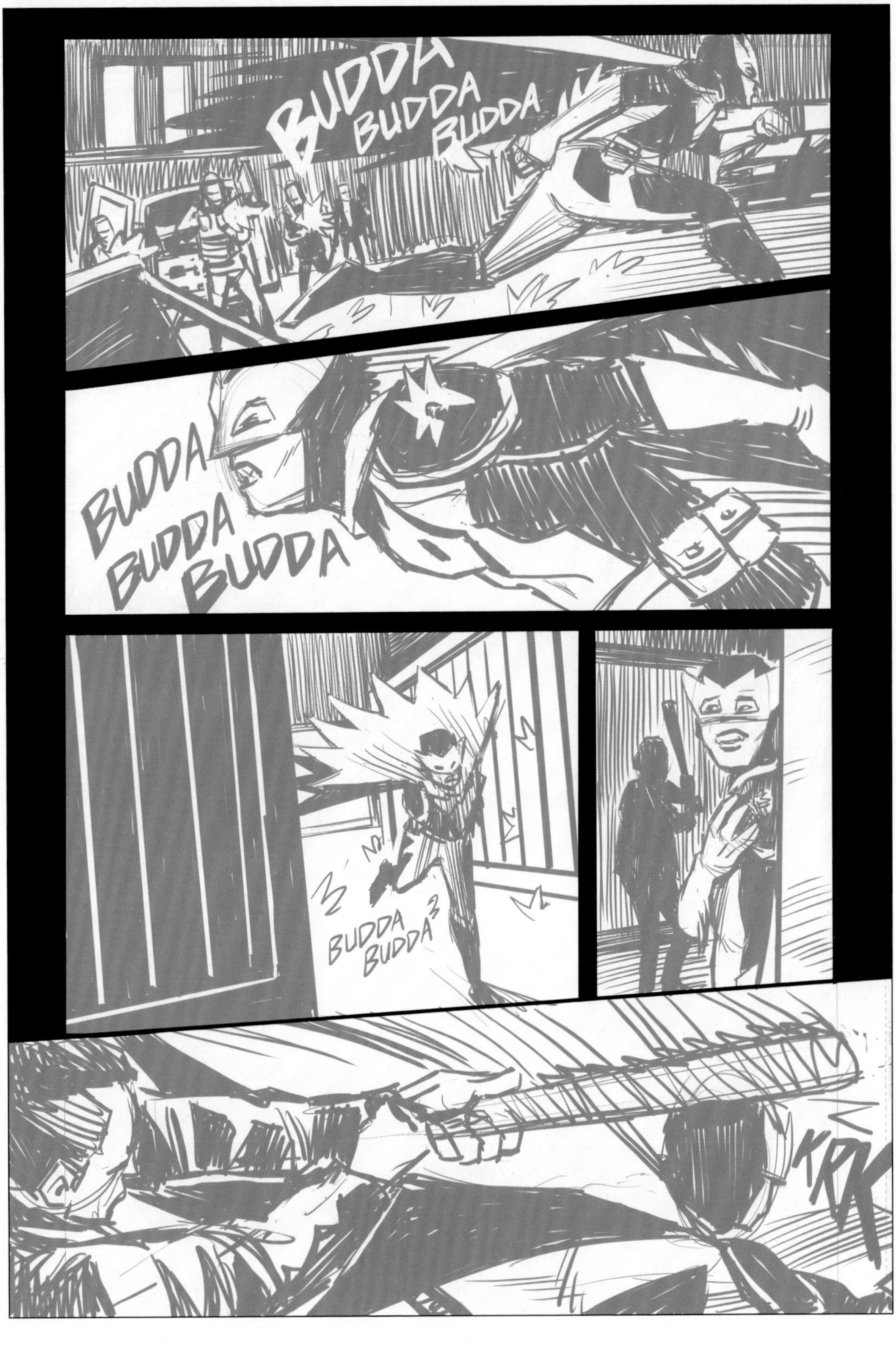

BUDDA
BUDDA
BUDDA
BUDDA
BUDDA
BUDDA
BUDDA
BUDDA
KRK

Jason: I wanted the book to look dark and moody with lots of shadows, so I used some textured gray-tone brushes during the ink process. But that was only done for the interiors in issue one, since Paris was already better at laying that level of shading in his colors.

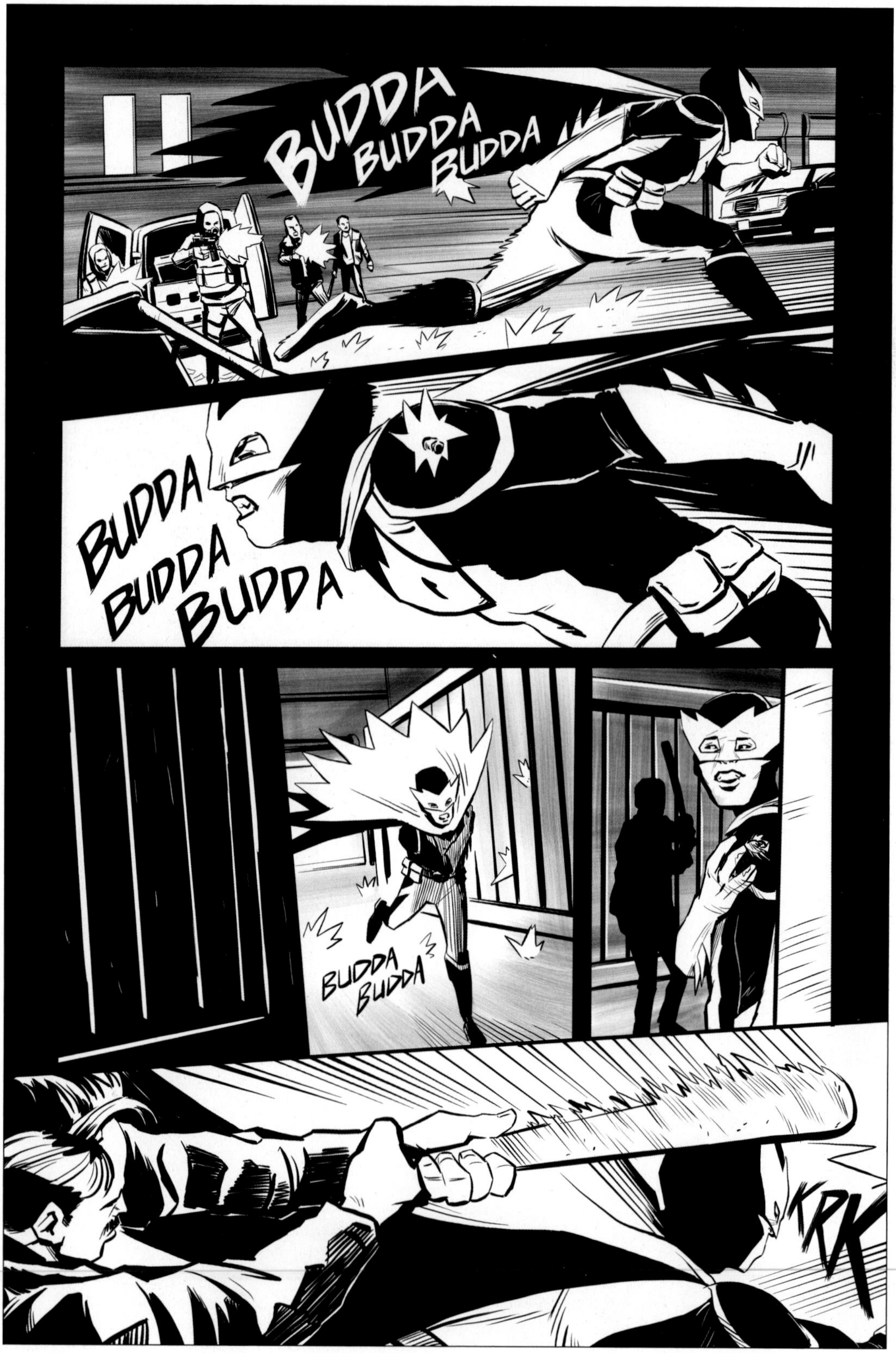
BUDDA BUDDA BUDDA
BUDDA BUDDA BUDDA
BUDDA BUDDA
KRK

Jason: I really love the bright nocturnal colors Paris chose for the style of the book. It has a pulp comic vibe that's perfect for this series.

Chip: Paris really is the secret sauce on this book (and our previous one, *Afterlift*). His color choices really make the characters pop!

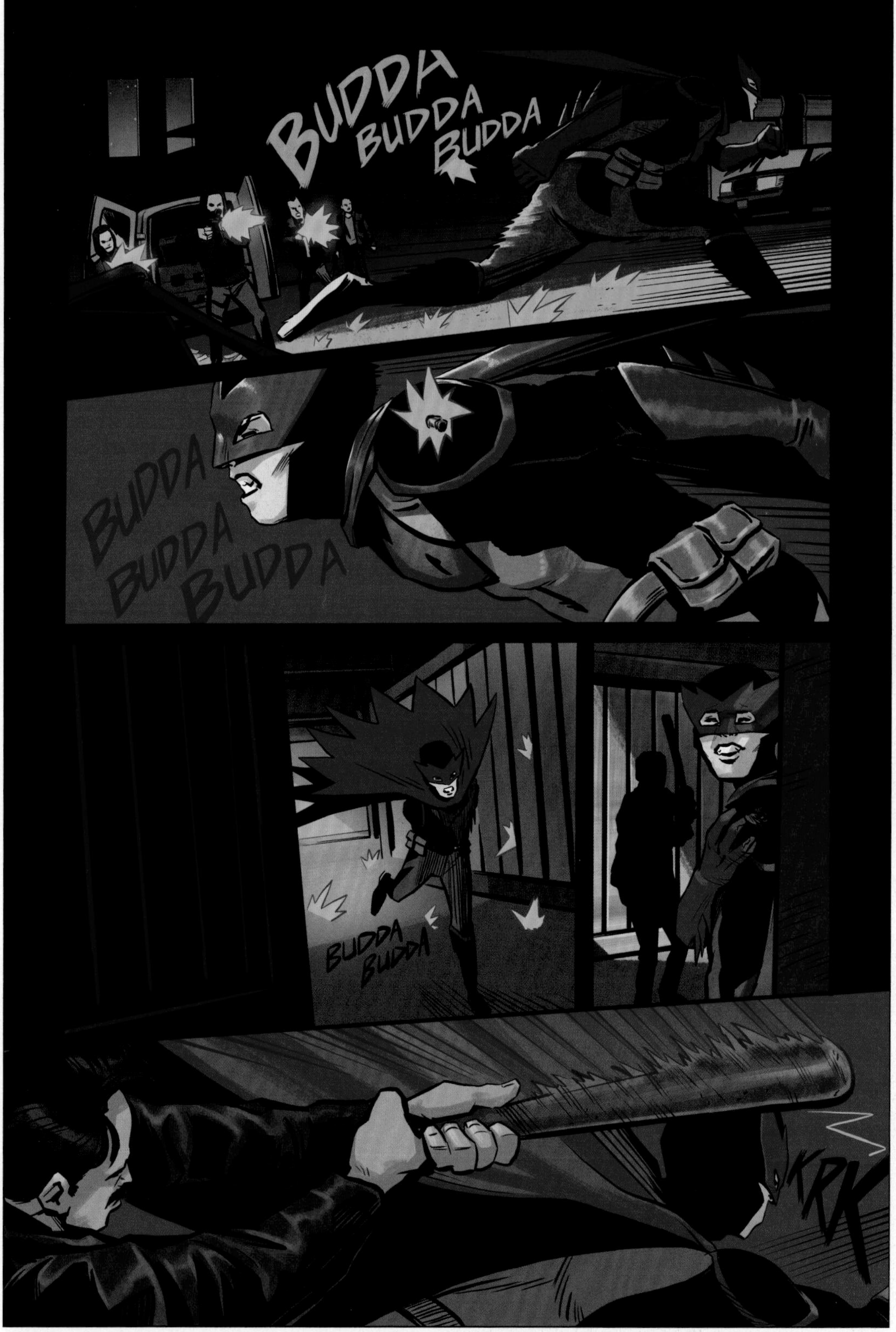
BUDDA
BUDDA
BUDDA
BUDDA
BUDDA
BUDDA
BUDDA
BUDDA
KRK

CHIP ZDARSKY

Chip Zdarsky is the award-winning writer and cocreator of *Afterlift* for ComiXology and illustrator and cocreator of *Sex Criminals* for Image Comics. He has written *Spider-Man: Life Story* and *Daredevil* for Marvel Comics, and *Jughead* for Archie Comics. He loves you very much.

instagram/twitter: @zdarsky

JASON LOO

Jason Loo is a Toronto-based cartoonist. He's the artist and cocreator of the multi-award-winning digital series *Afterlift*, earning an Eisner and a Joe Shuster Award. Jason is also the comic creator behind Toronto's own superhero the Pitiful Human-Lizard, which got him nominated for a 2018 Doug Wright Spotlight Award.

instagram/twitter: @Rebel_Loo • jasonloo.pb.online

PARIS ALLEYNE

Paris is a comic book artist and colorist from Toronto. His recent work includes the award-winning *Afterlift* from ComiXology.

instagram: @parisalleyne

ADITYA BIDIKAR

Aditya Bidikar is a comics letterer and occasional writer based in India. His recent work includes *Blue in Green*, *John Constantine: Hellblazer*, *Coffin Bound*, and *Afterlift*.

twitter: @adityab • adityab.net

ALLISON O'TOOLE

Allison O'Toole is a freelance comics editor, and a lover of monsters and dogs. She has edited a number of anthologies, including Shuster-winning *Wayward Sisters*, *Wayward Kindred*, and *Called into Being: A Celebration of Frankenstein*. Allison also edits a number of comic series, including *The Pitiful Human-Lizard*, *Afterlift*, and *Seeress*.

twitter: @AllisonMOToole • allisonotoole.com